BLOWIN' UP

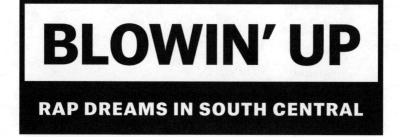

BLOWIN' UP

RAP DREAMS IN SOUTH CENTRAL

Jooyoung Lee

The University of Chicago Press

Chicago and London

Jooyoung Lee is assistant professor in the Department
of Sociology at the University of Toronto.

The University of Chicago Press, Chicago 60637
The University of Chicago Press, Ltd., London

25 24 23 22 21 20 19 18 17 16   1 2 3 4 5

ISBN-13: 978-0-226-34875-9 (cloth)
ISBN-13: 978-0-226-34889-6 (paper)
ISBN-13: 978-0-226-34892-6 (e-book)

DOI: 10.7208/chicago/9780226348926.001.0001

Library of Congress Cataloging-in-Publication Data
Names: Lee, Jooyoung, 1980– author.
Title: Blowin' up : rap dreams in South Central / Jooyoung Lee.
Description: Chicago ; London : The University of Chicago Press, 2016. |
Includes bibliographical references and index.
Identifiers: LCCN 2015029527 | ISBN 9780226348759 (cloth : alk. paper) |
ISBN 9780226348896 (pbk. : alk. paper) | ISBN 9780226348926 (e-book)
Subjects: LCSH: Rap musicians—California—Los Angeles. | Rap (Music)—
History and criticism. | African American teenage boys—California—Los
Angeles. | Music trade—California—Los Angeles.
Classification: LCC ML3531 .L44 2016 | DDC 782.42164909794/94—dc23
LC record available at http://lccn.loc.gov/2015029527

♾ This paper meets the requirements of ANSI/NISO Z39.48-1992
(Permanence of Paper).

For Flawliss

Contents

Preface

It was nighttime and I was cruising eastbound on the 10. There were a few cars here and there, but no clogged lanes—just smooth, open road. My mind roamed as I zipped to the Crenshaw exit. It only took twenty minutes, which wasn't bad from the Westside of LA.

At Crenshaw, I exited and continued southbound, driving past beige-colored apartments, minimalls, gas stations, Yum Yum Donuts, and the Liquor Bank. As I got closer to Leimert Park Village, I passed the Magic Johnson Theatre, a three-story Walmart, and the West Angeles Church, which looked like a flying saucer.

At a red light, a silver Mustang pulled up alongside me. The driver was leaning back, with one hand resting on the wheel. He bobbed his head. Our car windows were open, so I turned down the volume on my music and listened. He was bumping "How We Do" by the Game, a Compton rapper. I bobbed my head a little, and the passenger seemed to smile—or was it smirk? Who was I kidding? The light turned green, and we drove off.

Minutes later, I approached Forty-Third Place, home of Leimert Park Village. The storefronts here were colorful. There were jazz cafés, barbershops, soul-food restaurants, African jewelry and art stores, and a bunch of other places celebrating Black art and culture. I'd never seen—much less heard about—this side of South Central.[1] It was very different from its depiction in gangsta rap and movies like *Boyz n the Hood*.

Over the next five years, I would spend most of my Thursday nights and early Friday mornings at Project Blowed, a weekly hip hop open mic in Leimert Park. The open mic was held at KAOS Network, a community center started by Ben Caldwell. A Vietnam-veteran-turned-filmmaker, Caldwell started KAOS Network to promote the arts in South Central, an area facing massive cutbacks in public arts funding. He believed that the arts could empower youth who were growing up amid gang violence and police surveillance. In addition to Project Blowed, a world-renowned underground hip hop open mic, KAOS Network hosted workshops in multimedia, filmmaking, dancing, and other creative activities.[2] It continues to be an important community space for the arts in South Central.

For the first couple of years, I thought my project would focus exclusively on Project Blowed. It was an important scene for rappers, who came back every Thursday night to freestyle, battle, and workshop new songs with one another. It was where they learned how to rhyme and where they created friendships with other rappers. For many, it was a creative sanctuary away from gangs, a neutral zone where youth from different neighborhoods could get together around their shared love of hip hop. This was no small feat in South Central. In many neighborhoods across the city, young people are asked by gang members and police alike whether they are gang affiliated. "Who you claim?" "Where you from?" and "What 'hood you bang?" are common questions that young people face when navigating the streets.[3] But things were different at Project Blowed. People were not interested in where you were *from*. They wanted to know if you could rhyme—if you had "bars."

As time went on, I realized my project was moving outside Project Blowed. As some rappers got older and more experienced, they became interested in "blowin' up," or becoming successful recording artists. I began to see what sociologists call a "career," or a moving perspective on people's lives.[4] At first, Project Blowed nurtured the creative lives of young men who wanted to become rappers. Later, rap would become an aspiration, a career path, a way up in the world.

While they spent their time at Project Blowed learning how to rhyme and trying to impress their peers, many of these men would shift their energies toward getting discovered. They wanted to get signed, and they hoped to record albums, tour, and make a living from their music.

Some also wanted to become famous—or at least well known and respected in the music industry. This took me into late-night recording sessions, performances at new venues, and the networking and hustle involved in trying to "blow up." It also changed the course of this book.

I came to see the importance of following the same people over time. If I'd kept my eyes on my original interests—community life at Project Blowed—I would have missed out on the unexpected twists and turns that eventually shaped this book. In academia, there is a lot of pressure to publish or perish, not unlike the hurry for rappers to blow up. But our rush to gather data and publish quickly can blind us to the unexpected ways people change over time.[5] Spending extended time with the same people enriches our thinking and our writing.

The book you are now reading is the result of nearly five years of uninterrupted fieldwork. I started this research in January 2005 and concluded regular data collection in the fall of 2009. During this time, I collected thousands of pages of fieldnotes, most of which I wrote in the early morning hours, after returning from Project Blowed, concerts, or late-night recording sessions. I also interviewed thirty of the rappers I met in this scene, most multiple times. Interviews allowed me to compare my observations with how rappers described their own lives and experiences. They also helped me understand people's pasts and how that past shaped their pursuits.

I also used videos. After a few months in the scene, I started bringing a small, handheld video camera to Project Blowed. Some rappers were recording themselves to promote their music on YouTube. Others wanted to get in on that action but didn't have a camera or someone willing to record them. I was happy to help. If anything, recording gave me a way to just be around. But what started as a small way to give back became something much bigger. I would eventually collect ninety hours of videotapes, many of which have enriched my analysis. This process helped me see the value of using videos in ethnographic fieldwork (more on this in the methodological appendix).

I continued occasional data collection until spring 2015, when I was putting the final touches on this book. I mostly connected with people whenever I'd visit Los Angeles during holidays and breaks from teaching. These visits were brief but they gave me a chance to check in with people. I also kept in touch with people through social media: Facebook, Twitter, SoundCloud, and Instagram. In some cases, I used Facebook chat to reinterview people whose stories are featured here.

While finishing this book, I also reconnected with people and asked if they still wished to be in the book. I did this because consent should be an evolving process. People's lives change over time. They should have the option to consent or withdraw their participation throughout the life of a project. Some people asked to read the book first. For personal reasons, one person asked to be taken out of the book. But everyone else said that they still wished for their stories to be here.

I also gave people a choice over how they would be identified. Names that first appear in quotation marks are of those people who asked me to use a pseudonym. In a couple cases, I have created composite characters to further conceal the identities of people who wanted their stories in the book, but for various reasons did not wish to be identified. All others are actual stage names used by these men. I have used stage names to honor people's requests and as a way to increase transparency.[6] Of course, there are situations when ethnographers cannot reveal their fieldsite and people in it. But when possible, ethnographers should follow the lead of journalists and documentarians, whose work documents real people and real communities. This ensures that future researchers can use our work as a historical reference point. It also ensures that people can revisit our fieldsites and judge our descriptions and analyses for themselves. For clarity and flow, I've eliminated conversational utterances like "um" or "ya know" in some places.

In the end, the stories here provide a lens onto the lives of young Black men who are growing up in the shadows of gang violence and Los Angeles's glittering entertainment industry. Their stories reveal the existential dilemmas that youth encounter when navigating contrasting worlds and transitioning into adulthood. These men were drawn as teenagers to hip hop as a "creative alternative" to gangs. Becoming skilled rappers provided them with a masculine identity that was respected on the streets. As they got older, hip hop became a creative activity that facilitated friendships and collaboration with people from other neighborhoods. These relationships didn't just emerge out of thin air. They were anchored at Project Blowed, an open mic workshop that shielded young people from gangs in the area. And as they entered their twenties, hip hop came to represent a path to upward mobility and validation, pillars of the American dream. Like middle- and upper-class young adults, these men were trying to figure out what they would do for the rest of their lives. They wanted to avoid menial jobs and hoped they could get paid to do something they loved. Hip hop was a way up in the world.

But these men also faced challenges specific to their social world. Unlike their more privileged counterparts, they didn't have safety nets and couldn't foresee many fallback options. Gang violence, in particular, dampened their outlook on the future. Although very few had personal experiences in gangs, most had grown up knowing friends whose lives were derailed by violence. These experiences extinguished their youthful sense of invincibility. As a result, they didn't know if they had time to waste. Their lives were marked by *existential urgency*, my concept for heightened time sensitivity around life and career goals. This theme runs throughout this book, highlighting the particular, sometimes daunting experience of growing up around gang violence.

One final note: although there were a few regular "femcees" when I did my fieldwork, the vast majority were young men. Also, I was immediately drawn to the freestyle and battle scenes, which were dominated by men. These initial relationships became the anchor of this book. As ethnographers, we are at the mercy of those who let us come around, but we are also drawn to certain people and activities. In the end, I have tried my best to offer a balanced perspective of this social world, but my perspective is necessarily partial. For the sake of a coherent and balanced narrative, I've decided to focus here on the people I know best—the young men at Project Blowed.[7]

Introduction

"It's hot as fuck in there." Flawliss stepped out of the recording booth $\quad$ 1
and was fanning his armpits. He flopped down next to "Corey," a sound
engineer who was already tweaking the recording.

After cooling down, Flawliss pulled a nugget of "stress" from his
pocket. He broke the cheap weed into grainy pulps and sprinkled it into
a scented blunt. While licking and sealing the cigar paper, he said:

> Everybody thinks they're going to be that guy. Even me. That's what
> keeps it good, because without that real one hundred percent drive in
> your heart and in your mind, it's going to make everything wack. If I
> came in here and I was like, "I don't even think I can do this," I would
> probably slow the fuck down! I could just work two jobs. I don't need to
> hustle, run around, try to make DVDs, CDs, and shit. I could just work
> two jobs and get paid more.

Flawliss slid his chair over to a computer and surfed the Internet. He
talked about how social media was saturated with aspiring rappers:

> All those motherfuckers believe that they're the next one! You *got* to keep
> that alive! If people actually start realizing that only one person out of
> two billion rappers is going to blow up, who would keep going?

I was shocked: I'd never heard Flawliss doubt his dreams. The Flawliss
I knew oozed confidence. We had met years before at Project Blowed.
On one of my first nights in the scene, Flawliss was hard to miss. Six

feet tall and weighing more than three hundred pounds, Flawliss stood out physically, but his skills were the real draw. He was a gifted battle rapper who was always making people laugh. And he never seemed rattled. He'd just "flip the script" on opponents who tried to make fun of him.[1] His peers would talk about him as someone who had a *real* shot at blowin' up.

But on this night in the recording studio, Flawliss revealed a different side of himself. He was twenty-six, unsigned, and grappling with the prospects of *not* making it. Although Jay-Z had rhymed "30's the new 20," Flawliss knew that his time to blow up wouldn't last forever.[2] He knew that success could be elusive in the music industry:

> Even if I'm super talented and I've got all these angles [into the industry], it still might not happen! It's still a very slim chance of that happening! Now *that's* the fucked-up thing! I could be the most talented cat and have one of the best flows in LA. You know what I mean? I could be one of the best cats in the United States and still not blow up because I'm slackin' in my connections department or my physical attributes aren't attractive to the label. Anything could just pause my whole fucking career.

Flawliss was expressing some of the larger uncertainties of young Black men who want to blow up. Blowin' up is hard to do. There are no data on the percentage of aspiring rappers who are later signed by labels, but there are data showing how hard it is for signed artists to turn a profit. Even if they don't know these figures offhand, aspiring rappers like Flawliss know that very few people blow up. And they know that their window of opportunity to do so is slim.

Going gold or platinum (selling five hundred thousand or a million units, respectively) is typically the watershed moment when an artist starts seeing big returns in royalties. For new artists, though, the chances of achieving this are bad: in 1998, there were 477 hip hop records released; twelve went platinum and fourteen others went gold—that's roughly 5 percent. In 2012, just two hip hop albums went platinum and three went gold. In 2013, three went platinum, and three others gold.[3]

The data on online sales aren't much better. Artists typically make less than 10 percent of online album and single sales, or about $0.94 for every album and $.09 for every single downloaded from iTunes and other retailers. In more practical terms, an artist would need to sell 1,229 albums, or 12,400 singles, *every month* to earn the equivalent of US minimum wage from music sales alone.[4]

Given these odds, why would anyone even pursue a rap career? What drives young Black men like Flawliss toward rap dreams? How do their lives change along the way?

To answer these questions, we need to move beyond what Tricia Rose calls the "hip hop wars."[5] In the past twenty years, hip hop has become an increasingly contentious topic. Critics argue that rap is a cultural problem in Black communities. They argue that young people consume and emulate music that too often glorifies violence, contains misogynistic themes, and encourages an adversarial stance toward school, the police, and other social institutions.

For example, the linguist John McWhorter is one of hip hop's fiercest critics.[6] He has argued that hip hop teaches Black youth a culture of victimization and has betrayed the goals of the civil rights generation:

> The attitude and style expressed in the hip-hop "identity" keeps blacks down. Almost all hip-hop, gangsta or not, is delivered with a cocky, confrontational cadence. . . . The problem with such speech and mannerisms is that they make potential employers wary of young black men and can impede a young black's ability to interact comfortably with co-workers and customers. The black community has gone through too much to sacrifice upward mobility to the passing kick of an adversarial hip-hop "identity."[7]

One of the problems is that McWhorter provides little empirical evidence about how consuming, identifying with, and ultimately producing hip hop damages, let alone shapes, young people's lives. This is a great irony: critics like McWhorter write about Black youth and hip hop, but they don't engage with them at sites of cultural production or consumption.[8] Moreover, critics rarely give young people a chance to narrate their experiences from *within* the culture. As a result, the same critics make problematic inferences about how lyrics and images translate into behaviors, dispositions, and aspirations.

Meanwhile, hip hop supporters argue that it is a "hidden transcript," a voice of political resistance among marginalized youth.[9] Young people across the globe use hip hop to critique social, economic, and political inequalities in their backyards and worldwide.[10] Supporters also argue that critics scapegoat hip hop instead of looking at the structural factors that constrain the lives of working-class Black Americans. Music about gangs, violence, and police brutality are a window into the harsh daily realities of life in racially segregated, low-income neighborhoods.[11]

I sympathize with these latter accounts and appreciate that they place hip hop in a larger social, economic, and political context. But they too quickly reduce hip hop into a political instrument. Hip hop *has* helped mobilize a generation of hip hop heads, but it's a mistake to ignore the other ways youth are drawn to and participate in hip hop.[12] At the end of the day, hip hop is a fun and deeply rewarding creative outlet.[13] It's a collaborative art form that brings together youth from different neighborhoods and walks of life. This is especially important in areas like South Central LA, where young people grow up in neighborhoods that constrain the scope of their peer groups. The specter of gang violence and restrictive gang injunctions makes it difficult for young people to move freely and make friends across neighborhoods. And so in these areas, hip hop facilitates friendships and collaborations among youth who might not otherwise have these opportunities.

What's more, the meanings of hip hop aren't fixed or static. They change over a person's life course. Mos Def (now Yasiin Bey), a rapper and actor, perhaps says it best in his song "Fear Not of Man":

> People talk about Hip-Hop like it's some giant livin' in the hillside
> comin' down to visit the townspeople
> We are Hip-Hop
> Me, you, everybody, we are Hip-Hop
> So Hip-Hop is going where we going

So the next time you ask yourself where Hip-Hop is going
Ask yourself: where am I going? How am I doing?

Mos Def's perspective points us in the right direction. As a person's circumstances change, so too does that person's relationship to hip hop.

In *Blowin' Up*, I examine the changing meanings of hip hop in the lives of young Black men from South Central and other working-class LA neighborhoods. In the first section, "Becoming Rappers," I show how young men grew up seeing hip hop as a "creative alternative" to gangs. Through hip hop, they could become locally known for their creativity and talent. Hip hop offered them a cultural space to cultivate different kinds of masculinity. From there, I analyze how these men developed their skills at Project Blowed. At Project Blowed, young people hung out and created music away from the daily stresses of their neighborhoods. But more than that, Project Blowed was a powerful alternative to Los Angeles's gang injunctions and other punitive approaches to "the youth problem." While the city enforced gang injunctions across South Central, Ben Caldwell created a space at Project Blowed that encouraged creativity and collaboration among youth. KAOS Network provided youth with a neutral zone away from the streets and violence in their neighborhoods.

I also draw from Marcyliena Morgan's work conducted at Project Blowed in the mid-1990s.[14] A linguistic anthropologist and race scholar, Morgan wrote about the early days of Project Blowed (and the Good Life, its predecessor). She wrote about how rappers competed for recognition and respect in the scene. And she drew attention to the collective efforts of various community activists in creating a local culture of mentoring and intervention in Leimert Park. Her work is an important historical foundation for my book and raises important questions that I expand on here.

But while Project Blowed was an important part of my fieldwork, the men I write about also experienced a major turning point in their *careers* as rappers. With dreams of "blowin' up," some would change how they spent their time, branching out of Project Blowed. By the time I entered the scene, these rappers had already seen a generation of "veterans" (senior rappers) make names for themselves in underground hip hop. They had learned how to rhyme from underground legends like Aceyalone, Medusa, Ellay Khule, Myka 9, and other artists who had started out at the Good Life. Although they idolized these veterans, they had also seen the limits of their path in underground hip hop. They knew that being an underground rapper was rarely lucrative. And they grew up with access to social media. While a previous generation of Project Blowed rappers fought for respect in underground hip hop circles, this new generation was seeking fans on Facebook, YouTube, SoundCloud, Myspace, and other websites. Social media changed how these men — and aspiring musicians more generally — thought about their careers. It was now possible to go viral. The Internet made blowin' up feel more attainable.

These patterns set up the second half of the book, "Trying to Blow Up," which zooms in on how these men organized their lives around blowin' up. Although there is no formal definition, rappers use the phrase "blowin' up" when talking about their future goals and aspirations. It's shorthand for achieving upward mobility and respect as a recording artist. It usually implies getting signed to a label, making enough money to move out of the 'hood, and achieving a level of recognition — if not fame — in the music industry.

At the same time, when people talk about blowin' up, they are referencing much more than just imagined or even specific career outcomes. The idea of blowin' up is a lens onto how some young Black men envision their opportunities in the world. Rather than making a gradual ascent, they feel that their best shot at achieving upward mobility is a meteoric rise in the music industry.

Existential Urgency

Although I sometimes describe their teenage years, I spent most of my time with these men as they navigated early adulthood in their twenties. At first glance, their lives are "typical" for early adults in this transitional time. The story goes something like this: In their twenties people are full of uncertainty. Young people have graduated from high school and college and don't know what they want to do with their lives. Many meander through this period, experimenting with jobs, relationships, and identities.[15] Others use this time to pursue their passions: writing, acting, traveling, and other things they can't easily do once they marry, settle down, and have children.

Although this time is stressful, people from middle- and upper-class worlds have safety nets that reduce their anxiety. Many feel a vague sense of security knowing that things have worked out for others around them. Some can live with their families until they figure it all out.[16] And others go to graduate and professional schools, which have become costly fallback options for young adults who are confused and unsure about what to do in the future.

Flawliss and other young men were grappling with similar existential questions, but they did not have the same safety nets or fallback options. They were not graduating from college. They did not have families who could put them up while they figured things out. Some of them already had children and were hoping that achieving their rap dreams would provide a better life for their families. Adding to this, they had grown up in social worlds that forecasted a precarious adulthood. This made their twenties feel especially urgent. They felt what I call *existential urgency*.

Existential urgency is a heightened sensitivity to time. It is motivated by experiences that foreground a person's diminishing time to achieve life and career goals.[17] Different experiences make a person feel this urgency, that there is no time to waste. For example, people who find out that they have a terminal illness are often inspired to do things on their "bucket list." People might feel existential urgency around career decisions. Some have midlife crises and leave a job to take a more meaningful path. They fear that they may waste the rest of their working lives at an unfulfilling job and miss out on opportunities to achieve their life goals. And in some careers, there is a small window of opportunity for someone to "make it." In these and many other cases, perceptions of diminishing time refocus people's commitments onto meaningful pursuits. Of course, structural factors shape the nature and tenor of these experiences. But in different ways, the sense of waning time inspires people to pursue meaningful goals, activities, and relationships over others that feel extraneous.[18]

Violence and Existential Urgency

Violence, perhaps more than anything else, sows the seeds of existential urgency among working-class young Black men in South Central. From an early age, they have learned about the fragility of life. Witnessing, hearing about, and experiencing firsthand violence signals to them that their tomorrow is not guaranteed. Even those not immediately connected with gangs hear about and witness violence that derails the lives of family and friends who were simply in the wrong place at the wrong time.[19]

In 2010, the Centers for Disease Control and Prevention released troubling data on homicide rates: young men were six times more likely to die by homicide than young women (12.7 versus 2.1 per 100,000), and the numbers were worse for Black and other minority youth. The homicide rate for Black males between the ages of ten and twenty-four was nearly three times that for homicide among American Indian males, four times that for Hispanic males, and nearly eighteen times that for non-Hispanic White males and non-Hispanic Asian males (51.5 versus 17.6, 13.5, 2.9, and 2.8 per 100,000, respectively).[20]

Assaults, of course, happen far more commonly than homicides. These include nonfatal gunshot injuries, which are the most costly nonfatal wounds to treat and the most devastating to a young person's health.[21] Again, Black males are the most at-risk group. The nonfatal gunshot injury rate for young Black men in the 2010 report was nearly three times that for Hispanic men, seven times that for "other" Non-Hispanic males, and twelve times that for Non-Hispanic White males (224.3 versus 76.6, 32.7, and 18.6 per 100,000, respectively).

Similar patterns emerge in Los Angeles. In 2012, the homicide rate among Black men was more than four times that for Hispanic men and more than fourteen times that for White men (46.2 versus 11.2 and 3.2 per 100,000, respectively). Similar patterns emerged in nonfatal shootings. Black men were nearly six times more likely to be injured in firearm-related shootings than Hispanic men and nearly nineteen times more likely to get shot than White men (85 versus 15.6 and 4.5 per 100,000, respectively).[22]

These statistics provide a big picture, but they don't capture lived experiences. To get at this, we need to go into the everyday lives of young Black men who grow up in South Central. By the time all of the men in this book had reached their twenties, they had witnessed or personally experienced different forms of gang violence. Not only did they grow up in a world in which becoming a gang member was seen as a rite of passage; they had seen friends and family get critically wounded and killed. Many also had their own near brushes with violence. These experiences became tragic reminders that the future wasn't always guaranteed, that they didn't have time to waste.[23]

Elijah Anderson illuminates the culture and social worlds of young Black men growing up around violence.[24] In many working-class neighborhoods, young people become socialized into the "code of the street." This informal set of rules shapes public interactions and violence. Street-oriented youth, he argues, come to see violence as a key resource in their campaign for respect. But even when young people aren't affiliated with the "street" life, they still have to know its rules so they can protect themselves. This hypervigilance has its consequences. Young people become nihilistic and live "fast and large" because they do not expect to see old age.

The men in this book faced similar conditions growing up in Los Angeles, which journalists have labeled the "gang capital of the United States."[25] This phrase captures the dense concentration of gangs in and around LA. In 2011, the Los Angeles Police Department estimated that there were 450 active gangs and forty-five thousand active gang members in Los Angeles proper. At the county level, these numbers balloon to 1,000 gangs and seventy thousand members.

In addition to the stress of growing up around gang violence,[26] neighborhood gang injunctions,[27] and police surveillance, the young men in this book also came of age as Black and Brown gang violence was escalating across Los Angeles. Racialized gang violence exerts a special kind of social psychological pressure on young people who aren't affiliated with gangs. Unlike other gang "beefs" (rivalries) that nonaffiliated youth could avoid through "ranking out,"[28] young men felt especially unsafe when civilian targets were shot and killed because of their perceived race. They worried that they, too, could become random targets of racialized gang violence. These fears came to a head when Flawliss was shot, which I return to at the end of the book.

But instead of instilling in them a nihilistic view of the future, exposures to violence inspired these men to invest in their creative talents. When the future appears uncertain, people are moved not only to despair or to immediate gratification. They also channel their energies into identities and careers that feel meaningful.[29] They feel existential urgency and focus on paths that are personally gratifying and hold the promise of a better life. As these men entered their twenties, they worked hard to blow up as recording artists. Compared to the unattractive options in front of them—as gang members or in the low-wage labor market—rapping and pursuing their creative talents seemed like a better way to spend their time.

Sustaining Existential Urgency

Existential urgency is also sustained by experiences that inspire hope. Not just abstract or wishful thinking, hope springs from events people interpret as "momentous interactions" or steps toward a desired future—positive signs that they are moving closer to their goals. These need not be rational calculations: people read what they want into interactions, even if they appear crazy, irrational, or uninformed to outsiders. Instead, it's enough that people see certain interactions as symbols that they are on the right track, inching closer to their dreams.

Here, I draw from Randall Collins's theory of interaction rituals.[30] Collins writes about interactions that leave people feeling happy, excited, and enthralled. People enter different rituals feeling depleted and emerge from them charged up. For example, birthday parties, concerts, graduations, and other social gatherings fill people up with positive emotional energy that sustains them in their everyday lives.

But Collins's theory is not only useful for understanding the general allure of interaction rituals; it also helps us see how interactions can leave people feeling excited and hopeful about the future. Interactions with people who are believed to be gatekeepers into a desired world feel tantalizing. They make future goals feel attainable. And they demystify the prospect of success, which can often feel mysterious and unattainable to aspirants. These forces combine to propel people deeper into their own identities and chosen courses of action.

As I show in this book, the men here were trying to blow up in a social ecology ripe for these kinds of interactions. Los Angeles, Hollywood, and Southern California are home to the world's largest entertainment industries. The region is home to the filming of television shows like *American Idol*, *The Voice*, *X Factor*, *So You Think You Can Dance?*, and *America's Got Talent*, all of which play on the idea that ordinary people can get discovered and become overnight success stories.

LA is also a place where seemingly anyone can rub shoulders with people in the entertainment world. While crowds go to Hollywood film premiers and ritzy areas to spot the stars, trips to the grocery store, restaurants, retail districts, sporting events, coffeehouses, parks, the Department of Motor Vehicles, and other routine settings hold out the prospect of a brush with the rich and famous.[31] Hopefuls can also access a world of "support personnel" in LA.[32] Studio engineers, producers, photographers, managers, promoters, and many others working behind-the-scenes live and work in LA in even greater numbers than the stars; any one of them could have connections needed to help an aspiring artist get noticed—or signed.

Even though these interactions rarely changed the lives of the men in this book or advanced their careers, they still left an impression and made blowin' up feel attainable. The men imagined that, with a little luck, one of these interactions would catapult them closer to their goals. They felt that they were a chance meeting and a demo away from getting signed and realizing some of their dreams. So their existential urgency came from knowing not just that they didn't have time to waste, but also that the big break could happen at any moment.

Down in the Underground

When people hear about my work, they usually wonder two things. The first is, "Did you ever rap?" Nope. I flirted with the idea once or twice, but I never tried to rock the mic. My high school attempts at poetry taught me that I wasn't a wordsmith. Some critics bemoan the dumbing down of commercial hip hop, but underground hip hop—particularly at Project Blowed—is a completely different animal.[33] As I show later, it is a competitive training ground where rappers are serious about their craft. Nobody would have thought less of me if I tried, but instead I found other ways to hang out in the scene.

The second question is, "How did *you* do this study?" These people are trying to gently point out the obvious: I am not a young Black man from South Central. They're also trying to figure out how "Blowedians" (what locals in the scene call one another) responded to a second-generation Korean American guy. Although the 1992 Rodney King riots occurred more than a decade before I began this study, people usually want to know how I, affectionately nicknamed "Bruce Lee" and "Jackie Chan" by Project Blowed regulars, gained access to the world of underground hip hop.

These questions point to a longer history of strained relations between Koreans and the Black community in South Central.[34] And more broadly, they point to thorny questions about race, ethnicity, and reflexivity in ethnography. Although I often felt like an insider and was even referred to as a Blowedian, I was also sensitive to my privilege as a Korean American at a research university.[35] I felt this privilege whenever I visited the men in this book. In nearly five years of fieldwork, I was never stopped by police or gang members and asked if I was gang affiliated. But that was not the case for the young men in this book. Even if they weren't gang affiliated, they lived in places where constraints imposed by gangs and police interventions restricted their mobility.

Thus, instead of talking about being an insider or outsider, I like to think about how I showed cultural competency—how I was *down*. Being down means being knowledgeable of a culture. People who are down can be accepted into a culture and are often afforded a provisional status based on their shared knowledge and interests. Sometimes, people can be down if they are sympathetic to a culture, even if they're not necessarily knowledgeable about it; but there's generally an expectation that they will try to learn the inner workings of that culture.

In addition to being a fan of hip hop music, I came into the scene as a hip hop practitioner: a DJ. This helped ease my entrée. As an undergraduate, I DJed for fun and got a weekly gig at a pub in Berkeley. Sometimes I told people that the job helped me pay my way through college. Depending on the situation, I sometimes omitted that promoters eventually stopped paying me money and started paying me in pizza and beer. I wasn't very good at DJing. But through practice, I learned how to mix beats and scratch, foundational techniques for turntablists.[36] And when I came to Project Blowed, I referenced this past, which helped rappers and producers see me as a practitioner of hip hop culture.

More important, I was (and still am) an active hip hop dancer. I first learned how to "pop" in 2000 from a street performer named Tron in Berkeley.[37] Popping was originally a funk style of dance, popularized by Michael Jackson in the 1980s. Most people associate popping with the robot and moonwalking (a move that is part of a larger style called floating). But popping includes an array of dance styles: waving, tutting or King Tutting, strutting, and electric boogaloo, to name just a few. Each style has regional roots, and "poppers" typically learn from mentors.[38] When I started hanging out at Project Blowed, Tick-a-Lott, a popper from Compton, could tell right away that I had learned to pop in the Bay Area. He was very critical of my style and would make fun of me: "That's just tricks, man! You need to hit the beat!" Over time, he took me under his wing and showed me a style that he and others had pioneered.

My popping past and Tick-a-Lott's mentoring came in handy one early morning, when I helped battle krump dancers who showed up to the street corner outside Project Blowed.[39] Little did I know that this dance battle would change my relationship with regulars in the scene. It let me show that I was down.

Defending the Block

It was about two in the morning and a caravan of cars rolled up to the corner. Nobody knew who they were. One by one, the cars parked across the street. Doors swung open and the muffled sounds of 808 drumbeats spilled out of their car stereos.[40] Krump dancers jumped out onto the middle of Forty-Third Place, a small side street that connects Crenshaw Boulevard and Leimert Boulevard to the west and east. This caused quite a scene. Some of the Blowedians ran over to see what was happening.

I was mesmerized, but Tick-a-Lott wasn't impressed. He was rarely impressed. "That ain't nothin'!" he said while unzipping a duffle bag containing his costume and other street performance props. After digging around, he pulled out a pair of white cotton gloves and a rubber ghost mask, like the one in the teen slasher film *Scream*. He put them on and waited.

At first he hung back, letting the krump dancers have center stage. A few of them went out into the circle and started busting moves. Tick-a-Lott continued waiting until a break in the action—and then he sprung. His body flexed tightly, synchronizing with the beat. This got the krumpers excited. One yelled, "Oh! He wants to battle. He wants to get served!" The battle was on.

Tick-a-Lott held his own and some would say even dominated the first four or five exchanges. But battling a crew is hard, and he eventually got tired. After one exchange, Tick-a-Lott pulled off his mask. His bald head glistened with sweat and little clouds of steam rose from his skin.

"Ay, J," he said, winded.

"Yeah?"

"You gotta get my back, young student."

A couple of the krumpers glanced over, trying to size me up. I shook my head at Tick-a-Lott, but before I could resist, he nudged me into the middle of the dance circle. The krumpers and rappers looked surprised.

A couple seconds passed—and nothing. All eyes were on me, and I froze. I scanned the crowd. Everyone stared back, expecting me to make my move. I clumsily threw together a few moves. Instead of feeling the beat, I tried to bust out all of my best moves, one after another. I started floating (a style that makes it appear as if one were sliding and floating across the ground) into the middle, and then did some waving (an undulating style that makes the body appear fluid). But the crowd wasn't feeling it. "This isn't going well," I thought. I tried to string together a few more tricks but couldn't find the beat. I was being called on to help defend the block, and I was failing miserably.

Just as I felt my confidence slip, I slowed down and started flexing my body *on* the beat. I could feel my body spasms locking into the beat and my confidence grew. The crowd of Blowedians started cheering.

The krumpers seemed shocked. Some scooted closer to the action, dissecting my moves. I was immediately followed by "Mayo," a White guy in their dance crew. His entrance sent his side into "Ohs!" and "Ahs!" A few krumpers ran around yelling, "It's over! It's over! We got a secret weapon!" None of this impressed the Blowedians. After he exited the battle, "Dru" yelled, "Yeah, we got a White boy, too! 'cept he *Asian!*" Our crew laughed and cheered.

We battled for another twenty minutes. Tick and I proved a formidable duo as we traded rounds with the krumpers. We felt that we had won. I'm pretty sure that the krumpers felt they had won, too. As with many close battles, both sides went their separate ways with stories they'd tell for weeks.

My role in this street battle helped solidify my place in Project Blowed and in the lives of the young men who had watched that night. I was greeted warmly the following Thursday. Some talked about how we had "defended the block" against intruders. Others reenacted parts of the battle. I recorded the scene in my fieldnotes:

As I get closer to the block, E.M.S. spots me in the distance and begins doing the robot like the guy on *Chapelle's Show*. He begins chopping the air with his arms at his side and looks up into the sky like a possessed robot zombie. After doing this for a bit more, he breaks character and greets me with daps [a half-handshake, half-hug greeting common among men in hip hop culture]. A few of the other guys standing around him look puzzled, almost as if they are wondering, "Who the hell is E.M.S. talking to?" E.M.S. then tells the other guys, "You guys shoulda been here last week. Tick was all like this [he pretends to pop]. And, this man [pointing to me] got *down!*"

Later that night, a guy I didn't know approached me with his hand out, "Wassup, fam?" We gave each other daps and he told me, "I saw you last week. You was killin' it!" One of his friends came over: "Yo, is this the guy who was out there doing this [pretends to pop]?"

When I look back at my time at Project Blowed, I point to this battle as a turning point. Although I had been dancing and learning from Tick-a-Lott, many of the regulars didn't know I was a popper. After the battle, Project Blowed regulars began to open up to me. In the weeks, months, and years after the battle, Blowedians would seek my help shooting music videos or performing. E.Crimsin invited me to his apartment for a cameo—popping in a house-party scene—in a music video he was shooting for "Fill Your Cup," a song he had recorded with

Figure 1. Tick-a-Lott and the author practicing a popping routine

Trenseta and Big Flossy. I was asked to dance at some Project Blowed concerts and appeared in snippets of videos about the events. I became known as "Joo the Popper."

My role as a popper made me feel accepted. At times, I imagined I had crossed some magical threshold and had become an "insider." Rappers treated me accordingly, calling me a Blowedian, referring to me as "fam" (short for *family*), and so forth. And during this time, my relationships with rappers evolved. Some would become confidants and friends, like when one of my college friends died. And I talked to many about my fears of the job market and my feelings when my dog was gravely ill. In these moments, I felt a kinship with the guys in this book that's not easily captured by words like *participants* or *research subjects*. For these and many other reasons, I don't refer to them with these terms. Although I met them in the course of doing research, the bonds I feel with them are authentic.

Still, there were moments that reminded me of the limits in my identity as a researcher. These moments were humbling, and they forced me to confront the privilege I sometimes took for granted. For instance, one day I got a call from Tick-a-Lott. He was adamant that I visit him while he worked a security shift for a Korean-owned liquor store near Leimert Park. When I showed up, he slung his arm around me and marched into the store. He announced to his boss, "See, I got Korean friends, too. I'm down with your people!" His boss, a first-generation Korean immigrant, stared at us. Tick-a-Lott later explained that his boss had threatened to fire him because he had shown up to work late. He figured having a Korean friend would bolster his job security. Such moments made salient aspects of my identity that were less important when I was popping, hanging out, and talking with people about hip hop.

For these reasons, I have chosen to talk about my work as a process of showing that I was "down" instead of getting "in." Language that identifies someone as an insider glosses racial-ethnic, class, and gender differences (among other factors) that prevent ethnographers from fully immersing into their communities of study. By talking about being down, I hope to help shift ethnographers' methodological language away from increasingly antiquated ideas about in-groups and out-groups. We don't achieve some special status that follows us for the rest of our time in the field. Rather, our identities shift and unfold in different situations. We are constantly being assessed and evaluated by people we meet in the field. Sometimes, situations give us opportunities to show that we are down. Other times, we fail to mesh. And then there are the situations in which we are forced to confront privilege, which also shapes our interactions with the people we meet. In these moments, historical and structural realities become salient and reveal the limits of being "in" with the people we write about.

* * *

Part 1, "Becoming Rappers," looks at how young men become rappers. In chapter 1, I describe the biographies of men I met, highlighting their experiences of growing up around neighborhood gangs and violence. These stories set the stage for the rest of the book, showing how experiences with violence sow the seeds of existential urgency. These stories also help explain how hip hop became, for many, a "creative alternative" to gangs. Hip hop provided alternative kinds of masculinity that allowed people to be cool and respected outside of gangs.

From there, I transition into chapters about Project Blowed. Project Blowed was a neutral zone where young people could get together around a shared loved of hip hop. It shielded men from gangs. At Project Blowed, young men received mentoring from older and more experienced rappers. They also created friendships and collaborations with other youth immersed in hip hop. These chapters also focus on the intricacies of rhyming and show how young men acquired different skills.

In chapter 2, I analyze how young rappers learned how to rock a mic, or perform prewritten songs in front of a peer audience. In addition to developing a larger arsenal of rhymes, they developed subtle performance skills that gave them confidence on the stage and off. Specifically, they learned to energize crowds and control their breathing so the crowd could hear and feel their words.

In chapter 3, I analyze the art of freestyling. What seems like spontaneous rhyming is in fact the result of deep practice. Rappers learn to "think in rhyme" through dedication and practice. They also face different dilemmas when they showcase their freestyling skills in "ciphers," or group freestyle sessions. Here, their rhymes are supposed to be off the cuff but they are generally well-polished gems. The real improvisational magic is in making it appear that one is coming up with rhymes on the spot.

In chapter 4, I analyze battling, one of hip hop's most time-honored rituals. It's often used as a gauge of one's skill. But battles can also help resolve conflicts and moments of perceived disrespect between rappers. Thus, in addition to being a place where youth learn how to rhyme, Project Blowed was scene that transformed the larger code of the street. Young men competed for status and respect, but with rhymes rather than fists or guns.

Part 2, "Trying to Blow Up," examines the lives of young men who eventually transitioned away from Project Blowed. I show how the men organized their lives around blowin' up as recording artists.

In chapter 5, I examine how young men organized their lives around getting discovered and signed to a record label. This transition is, in part, inspired by rappers' changing relationships with senior members at Project Blowed and how they came to see these "veterans" as cautionary tales. As the young men aspire to blowin' up, they see veterans' stalled careers and begin to branch out of the scene into new social worlds and networks. They hope these relationships will launch their careers.

In chapter 6, I examine how the larger entertainment industry structures and shapes the pursuits of aspiring rappers. Different "momentous interactions" they have with people in the industry provide rappers with hope. In LA, they had opportunities to get on MTV, develop collaborations with key people in the entertainment world, and occasionally work with celebrities. All these interactions made blowin' up feel attainable and sustained these young men's existential urgency.

In chapter 7, I look at how rap dreams affect these men's commitments to low-wage jobs. Existential urgency leads them to bracket commitments and responsibilities that feel like distractions from their main goals. In addition to not seeing possibilities for upward mobility or validation in low-wage work, these men run into a number of time conflicts that lead them to temporarily ditch their day jobs in order to chase their dreams.

Chapter 8 returns to the theme of gang violence. These men were trying to blow up amid escalating racialized violence among Black and Brown gangs in Los Angeles. They feared that they would be targeted for nothing more than being Black. These fears came to a head when Flawliss was shot. Flawliss wasn't in a gang but was attacked in a hate crime. This rippled out among those who knew him from Project Blowed. His shooting was another reminder of how quickly and abruptly gang violence can derail lives.

I conclude with a discussion about the power of the arts in the lives of "at-promise" youth.[41] Project Blowed was a model for how other community institutions can engage young people with the arts and music. Instead of criminalizing and punishing youth, Project Blowed and KAOS Network more broadly show how supportive mentoring can steer at-promise youth away from gangs. Here, I move away from my research to the abstract, discussing institutional dilemmas around supporting youth with creative talents in hip hop.

In the methods appendix at the end of the book, I describe how videos enhanced my data collection and analysis. But before getting into all of that, we have to start by understanding the formative years of these men's lives. We have to understand the worlds in which these men grew up and the role that hip hop played in their lives as young people.

PART ONE

BECOMING RAPPERS

1

Growing Up in Gangland

It was a little after eight and the sun had set over Leimert Park. I was in the parking lot behind KAOS Network. On the weekends, the place was buzzing. It hosted a daytime farmers' market and music festivals. But at night it was dark, save a few patches of concrete lit by the yellow glow of street lamps.

"Choppa" said he'd be here, but I didn't see him. So I kept driving and parked near the recording studio in the back of KAOS Network. The studio wasn't anything fancy, but it got the job done. Rappers had access to a computer, recording software, a mixing board, spongy soundproofed walls, and a microphone. And Choppa basically lived here, recording or helping others do the same.

He emerged from the studio just as I parked my car. Choppa seemed less edgy than usual. The Choppa I knew was usually bursting with frenetic energy. His eyes would dart erratically as rhymes rattled out of his mouth. But tonight he seemed relaxed.

He yelled through the darkness, "Wassup, pimpin'? You still wanna do that interview?"

"Yeah, is that cool? I brought my recorder."

He nodded and motioned for me to begin. I thought we might go somewhere else, but his eyes grew wide. So I jumped right in, "Where did you grow up?" He pointed just beyond a row of Black-owned businesses on Degnan Boulevard. "I grew up right here, homie. In Leimert Park. That's why I'm Leimert's finest. Next question!"

I then asked about his experiences growing up around gangs. He had told me about them in the past. Once, while we were driving to a local liquor store, I murmured, "This area is nice." He looked at me sideways, "This is the 'hood. Don't get that shit twisted, homie. Shit goes down here. Don't be fooled by the palm trees." On other occasions, he told me about fights, drive-by shootings, and police raids. His childhood and youth were a far cry from my own experiences in the sleepy hippie town of Eureka, California.

Choppa got quiet while reflecting on his childhood. He took a drag from his cigarette, exhaled, and flicked the butt into the distance:

> You know, I was a kid in LA at a time when gangbanging was very popular. It used to be like, "What set [neighborhood clique] you from?" Like it was already established that you was *from* a set. That's what I think people don't understand. Kids were more drawn to it than not. It wasn't like they were being forced.

For the next hour, Choppa told me stories about the Harlem Rollin' 30s, the Neighborhood Rollin' 40s, the Black P. Stones, and other Crip and Blood sets. He told me about the general anxiety he felt growing up around warring gangs. Everyday routines that I had taken for granted—like walking to school or the store—were wrought with tension in his neighborhood. He also told me about friends who had joined gangs; getting "jumped in" (initiated into a gang through violence) was a rite of passage.[1] Some of these youth had been wounded in shootings and others had been incarcerated. A few had been killed.

But Choppa's life was different. He was never in a gang. He was drawn to hip hop. His older cousin, "M-16," was establishing a reputation in South Central as one of the emerging stars from the Good Life.[2] Choppa took notice:

> And when I saw my big cousin, you know, dressing hip hop, he'd be all LL Cool J'd out and shit, it was just the coolest thing I ever saw. And I knew that that was what I wanted to do.

M-16 had a big influence on Choppa. He was already one of the most recognized rappers at the Good Life, and Choppa wanted to be just like him. He wanted to rock Adidas suits and bolo chains. He wanted girls to notice him. But mostly he wanted to be known for his skills. Like M-16, he wanted to "chop," a rapid-fire rap style created at the Good Life and later developed at Project Blowed. He hoped to create his own signature style of chopping and get respect in the local scene.

Choppa explained it in simple terms: "What hip hop did for me was provide me an outlet where I could be the coolest motherfucker and didn't have nothing to do with that bullshit, being in a gang." Hip hop was a world where Choppa could make a name for himself, a "creative alternative" to gangs.

* * *

Elijah Anderson takes us deep into the lives of young Black men who grow up in working-class communities.[3] He shows how some feel alienated from schools, the labor market, and other institutions through which people often gain status and respect. Looking elsewhere, these youth become attuned to the "code of the street," an informal set of rules governing public interactions and violence. Under this code, young men win and lose respect depending on how well they can fight, how willing they are to "ride" (mobilize in violence) when someone disrespects them, and how much courage they show when confrontations turn violent.[4] By joining gangs, young men inherit the infamous reputation of their set—and by extension can make identity claims about their own toughness.

But not everyone is drawn to the street. There are other identities to which young Black men gravitate outside of gangs. Some are drawn to academic pursuits and what Anderson calls "decent" values and worldviews. They try hard in school, steer clear of gangs, and imagine themselves working to succeed in mainstream society. They believe in the possibility of the American dream and work hard to achieve their goals at schools and in the labor market.

Others are drawn to skills they imagine as springboards to upward mobility. In working-class neighborhoods, some young men are drawn to what historian Robin Kelley calls "play labor."[5] Feeling shut out of the American dream, they invest in leisure skills that might lead to upward mobility and fame. In addition to basketball, football, and other popular sports, young Black men are also drawn to hip hop culture. Like the baller whose on-court talents are recognized in the neighborhood, talented rappers enjoy elevated status among their neighborhood peers. These youth are locally respected for their skills and shielded by gangs from the street life.[6]

This chapter shows how hip hop provides young Black men with a creative alternative to gangs. While many people have written about why young people are drawn to gangs, we know considerably less about the experiences that repel and divert them from gangs.[7] And because of popular culture, we assume that hip hop is a gateway to gangs, violence, and the street life. We assume that young people mimic the lifestyles and actions they hear in gangsta rap. I look at the opposite trajectory: how hip hop shields youth from gangs.

There are three broad ways that hip hop shields youth from the gang life. Some young men are drawn to the alternative kinds of masculinity modeled in hip hop. There they find mentors and friends who endorse political and creative identities that are different from the "thug" identities of gang members.[8] Becoming a rapper, known for your creativity, is another way to become known and respected in the 'hood.

Second, some young men receive a "pass," or exemption from joining the gang. As they do for youth with athletic and academic talents, gang members recognize the creative interests of rappers, producers, and others in hip hop, and they encourage them to steer clear of gangs. The gang nurtures their talents and encourages these young people to pursue their talents and get out of the 'hood.[9]

Third, there are young men who join gangs but later experience the dead ends of that path: incarceration and violence make them question their commitments to gangbanging. These experiences are reflexive moments in the life course of these men. They have had a taste of the bleak consequences awaiting them in the gang life and they jump ship. For these men, hip hop represented a world of new possibilities outside their *former* gang lives, a space in which they could turn their lived experiences into an art form and gain respect for it.

All these examples show how hip hop represents a creative alternative to gangs. But the stories here also reveal the existential toll of gangs and violence on young men. The men I met were still exposed to the tragedies of the gang life simply by virtue of growing up in South Central and other neighborhoods with long histories of gang violence. Incarceration, injury, and murder became omens of their precarious futures and sources of existential urgency as they tried to move out of the world they grew up in.

Public Enemy and Political Masculinity

E.M.S. was never in a gang. When I met him, he was the manager at an Italian restaurant and taking courses at a local junior college. He had grown up playing football and could talk for hours about the San Francisco 49ers and "golden age" hip hop (the early to mid-1990s, when artists like Tupac Shakur, Notorious B.I.G., Nas, and A Tribe Called Quest were, arguably, at their creative primes). When we met, E.M.S. made up one half of the Middlemen, a duo he created with his friend and fellow Project Blowed emcee N.A., which stands for "No Alias."

Like many of the rappers I met at Project Blowed, E.M.S. was initially drawn to "conscious" hip hop. Conscious hip hop often contains a political message. Even when not overtly, artists in this genre rhyme about racism, police brutality, and other structural inequalities of urban Black communities. Public Enemy was E.M.S.'s first taste of conscious hip hop. The New York group was known as one of the first explicitly political hip hop groups, having put out songs like "Fight the Power," an anthem about institutionalized racism that was featured in Spike Lee's movie *Do the Right Thing*.[10] They were also known for satirical commentaries on police neglect in Black communities with songs like "9-1-1 Is a Joke." In the 1980s and 1990s, they helped turn hip hop music into an arena for political critique and awareness around the constraints of persistent racial inequality.

E.M.S. and his friends memorized Public Enemy's lyrics and recited their songs, sometimes even performing as if they *were* Public Enemy. It was part of a political awakening for E.M.S., who became inspired to think critically about race and racism. More than anything, Public

Enemy gave him a different perspective on what it meant to be a young Black man in America:

> Ya know, Public Enemy was out. And at that time, I was hanging with people who were into being *Black*! And that was cool, because a lot of us are not into being Black. But these cats was down! These were my boys! That's how I kinda got into hip hop. It wasn't just a part of my life. It was something bigger. After that, I could say, "*This* is why I listen to hip hop music!" Public Enemy created music that let us know that it's OK to be proud of who we are!

E.M.S. and his friends really looked up to Chuck D, Public Enemy's articulate front man. Chuck D made it cool to be smart, critical, and politically engaged. This identity was very different from the "thug" identity celebrated in gangs. According to E.M.S.: "Chuck D was just deep. Like real deep. Like he would say something that got you thinking. He just flipped the whole script on what it meant to be a man. Like cats were into being smart instead of thuggin'."

E.M.S. was inspired by music and by his friends to think about race, racism, and social inequalities in the United States. At the same time, E.M.S. was growing up around gang violence. Hip hop provided a soundtrack to help him make sense of gangs, but the violence still weighed heavily on him. One night when we were at his apartment, he started reminiscing about his youth. He got really quiet. His eyes went glassy, and he spoke in whispers. At first, he didn't want to tell me what was on his mind. I waited. After some quiet reflection, E.M.S. opened up about a friend's murder and how it changed his outlook on life:

> There was a time in high school where . . . there were crews that were killing each other. I lost a lot of friends. So I left, I moved to Texas, 'cause I thought I was next. I was playing basketball with this guy on Friday and he was dead on Monday. Like, what?!

The violent death of a close friend in E.M.S.'s formative years became a moment for reflection. In the aftermath, he became more keenly aware of his mortality. He realized how his own life intersected with people who were getting shot and killed. These were not random news stories of strangers murdered in his community or city. These were close friends with whom he had grown up.

Murder is a disruptive event in a person's life course. After losing someone to violence, people can suffer from acute post-traumatic stress, depression, and other mental health challenges. But murder can have longer-lasting consequences, particularly for young people, who glimpse their own mortality and learn that their future isn't guaranteed. This is an unsettling vision. But instead of inspiring despair, exposure to violence can also inspire investments in meaningful pursuits and exit strategies. Exposure to violence becomes a source of existential urgency.

Creative Masculinity in Hip Hop

Like E.M.S., N.A. was never in a gang. Within moments of meeting him, it becomes hard to imagine him being upset — much less involved with gangs. About six feet tall and 250 pounds, N.A. was soft spoken and always seemed to be smiling. A longtime producer and rapper, he loved old jazz and soul. He didn't have a car but would ride public buses to go "digging" for used records. On a typical Saturday, N.A. would hit up record shops, Salvation Army stores, and swap meets. Sometimes, he would spend an entire day sifting through dusty stacks just to find one rare gem to sample.

When most kids his age were getting into pop music or mainstream rap, N.A. was listening to jazz with his mom. He had a deep appreciation for artists like Miles Davis, John Coltrane, and Stan Getz. Interestingly, this love smoothed his transition into underground hip hop. Many East Coast artists like A Tribe Called Quest and De La Soul were rhyming over jazz- and soul-sampled beats. Underground hip hop was a natural outgrowth of his musical tastes.

N.A. first discovered underground hip hop on KDAY, a hip hop and R&B radio station in LA. He liked conscious hip hop groups like Public Enemy and N.W.A., but he gravitated toward the lyricism and rich storytelling of other underground hip hop groups. He loved old-school New York rappers like Doug E. Fresh and Slick Rick. Although they rhymed about social problems in urban Black communities, their politics were less overt. And instead of using a militant political angle, these artists used humor to tell stories about poverty, violence, and everyday life in the 'hood. "They were just regular dudes talking about life," N.A. told me once at his apartment. This appealed to N.A., who appreciated but did not immediately identify with the militancy of groups like Public Enemy.

While station hopping late one night, N.A. stumbled upon *Friday Night Flavors*, a weekly show on Power 106. The show blew his mind. He stayed up all night long, in what he says was like a religious experience: "Actually, that experience changed the course of my life! Because if it wasn't for that, then who knows what I would have been inspired to do. That was it! I had found it! I was like, '*This* is what I love!'"

The more he listened, the more he became enamored. N.A. loved the lyrics, extensive vocabulary, and humor in underground hip hop. He could relate to it and was hooked:

> With the underground, what I've noticed back then is that a lot of these emcees were rhyming like they were on some level that you didn't quite hear on your typical Kris Kross song. . . . [T]heir vocabulary was extensive!

N.A.'s growing love for hip hop inspired him to start writing. A middle school teacher noticed his budding interest and encouraged him to share his creative work with the class. N.A. was nervous but accepted the opportunity. Years later, he smiled widely, recalling the anxiety-ridden time when he rapped in front of his classmates:

> My teacher, she encouraged me to spit the rhyme in front of the class, and I did, only two people liked it—the teacher and like this other guy, he wasn't really into hip hop like that, but he was like, "Yeah, it was cool!" And like the rest of the class was like, "Man, this guy sucks." I called myself 2 Tuff. The first song I ever wrote was "2 Tuff for You."

Figure 2. N.A. at home making beats on his AKAI MPC2000

The lukewarm reception didn't get him down. N.A. started branching out into poetry. At first, he wrote humorous and lighthearted poems about his worldview as a teenager:

> They were meant to be funny, kinda like on some Shel Silverstein–type stuff. And actually, people loved it, ya know what I'm saying? And I had like books of these poems that were just meant to make people laugh!

The stories of both E.M.S. and N.A. provide an important challenge to hip hop's most vocal critics. For instance, John McWhorter claims that hip hop is detrimental to Black youth because it encourages an adversarial attitude toward authority and discourages academic achievement.[11] According to McWhorter, youth who listen to hip hop become invested in thug identities, which thwarts their academic pursuits. He believes that hip hop pushes youth into deviance and criminality and makes learning "not cool."

I'm not sure what kind of hip hop McWhorter is referencing, or the youth he claims to observe. Many of his arguments don't present much in the way of real data. And most fail to grasp the structural reasons underlying racial-ethnic disparities in education and other realms of social life. McWhorter paints too simplistic a picture.

In E.M.S.'s case, we see how conscious hip hop can inspire young men to think critically about their situation as young Black men. By listening to groups like Public Enemy and surrounding himself with peers who did the same, E.M.S. was inspired to read and learn more about Black history. His growing love of hip hop inspired him to learn more about the structural origins of poverty, violence, and other social problems facing Black communities in the United States.

N.A.'s story shows us that hip hop doesn't need to be overtly political to shield young men from gangs, violence, and the other social problems that critics attribute to hip hop.[12] In the hip hop scene, young men are exposed to a wide range of masculine identity options. Artists like Doug E. Fresh and Slick Rick didn't present themselves as gangsters or thugs, but they weren't militant or overtly political, either. Instead, they were creative, funny, talented rappers who narrated everyday life. This resonated with N.A. and other young Black men who grew up around gangs, poverty, and violence but weren't drawn to gangbanging or the street life. They saw these artists as examples of how one could be from the 'hood but not immersed in gangs—a different kind of "cool."

Hip hop also inspired N.A.'s interests in creative writing, vocabulary, and poetry. He was enthralled by what he heard on the radio and wanted to follow suit. The linguistic anthropologist H. Samy Alim shows us that Black youth pioneer complex linguistic practices in hip hop.[13] Although these practices are rarely acknowledged by musical, artistic, and literary canons, the practices themselves have had a profound influence on the men in this book. Some, like N.A., remarked on how their emerging interests in hip hop inspired them to try out creative writing. Others became invested in expanding their vocabularies and studying the dictionary. Of course, not all young people are drawn to conscious or underground hip hop. But even young men who were drawn to gangsta rap became similarly immersed in creative writing and trying to expand their vocabularies.

The real problem is that many critics like McWhorter roundly dismiss hip hop, ignoring the many ways that educators might harness young people's interests in rhyming, writing songs, and developing a more expansive vocabulary. Hip hop can become a powerful complement to the language arts and formal education. Unfortunately, for every teacher or school that supports young people's creative interests in hip hop culture, many others enforce policies that quickly marginalize youth of color, particularly those who seem like they might be gang affiliated.[14] This is particularly true for youth immersed in hip hop culture, which sometimes mimics and reproduces the clothing, language, and mannerisms of the streets. Hip hop is too often mistaken as a gateway to gangs and violence and too infrequently recognized for its potential to complement academic pursuits.

Most important, youth who become interested in underground hip hop are immersed in peer groups that are removed from gangs. In this way, hip hop culture functions like sports and other extracurricular activities, providing young people with an alternative way to construct a "cool" identity outside of gangs. And at the end of the day, hip hop does this because it is fun and enthralling to be around people listening to music and trying to write rhymes. When academics write about hip hop, they often neglect the immediate pleasures and visceral reactions that hip hop elicits among hip hop heads.[15] For E.M.S., N.A., and other young men in this book, hip hop sounded good, made them want to rhyme, and captivated their imagination.

Getting a Pass

Some young men get a "pass" out of gang life—an exemption from "OGs" (senior gang members) who recognize their talents and leave them to pursue these interests.[16] This pass works against popular images of gangs. While gangs exert multiple pressures on youth to join their ranks, they also offer some youth an acceptable way out. In some cases, gangs shield young people who show talent and interests in paths that could vault them into a high-status labor market, such as those who show talents in the classroom and star athletes who have a chance to "go pro."[17] Gangs take pride in knowing that someone from their neighborhood could make it and endorse their talents.

This was the case for Dibiase, a skinny and soft-spoken rapper and producer from the Grape Street area of the Watts neighborhood in South Central. When I first met Dibiase, he went by Diabolic. But as he got older, he started considering other names. He felt that the name Diabolic didn't really represent his personality and eventually dropped it for "Dibiase," inspired by Ted DiBiase, the Million Dollar Man, a World Wrestling Federation wrestler known for his black sequined tuxedo and flashy personality. Although Dibiase never wore such clothing, he was known for rocking fresh gear. He tended toward brightly colored Ralph Lauren polo shirts, clean Nike running shoes, and a matching hat or Bape hoodie.

Dibiase rapped, but he was also known as a producer. He made most of the beats for the Missing Page Crew, a hip hop group born of friendships at Project Blowed. On most Thursday nights he parked his faded-brown Jeep Wrangler—the Beat Jeep—at the corner and propped open the back to crank beats out of two ten-inch speakers. When he wanted to save his car's battery, he would bring a boom box and cradle it while others rapped.

One afternoon at his grandmother's house, amid piles of records, Dibiase played me some beats and talked about his life. He mentioned the challenges of growing up around Grape Street—an area near the Jordan Downs Housing Projects in Watts. In addition to coming of age in a community besieged by poverty and high incarceration rates, Dibiase also grew up around the Grape Street Watts Crips, a notorious and sprawling Crip set. They had a long-standing beef with the Bounty Hunter Bloods set in the Nickerson Gardens projects in Watts, which often resulted in fatal violence.

He recalled how many of his childhood friends were drawn to the gang. Some joined, and the gang evolved out of preexisting friendships. Dibiase was close to members, but he got a pass:

D   I used to kick it with some of the dudes before they got into gangs.
         I be hoopin' against some of them, too. Then, some of them joined
         gangs—the Avalons, Grape Street—and I just kept doing my
         music.

J   Did they ever approach you to join?

D   Shit, they know I be doing my music and they respected that.
         They used to call me "Mad Scientist."

J   What happened to those guys?

D   Shit, some of them aren't alive anymore, some of them are in jail.
         I still fuck with some of the cats who were into music back then
         to this day. But yeah, they knew I was on the music tip, so the
         homies weren't trippin' or nothin'.

Dibiase's story is important for a number of reasons. First, it invites a
more nuanced understanding of how gangs interact with local youth.[18]
Gangs contribute to violence and disorder in urban working-class communities, but they can also have an active hand in supporting youth
with recognized talents. OGs exempt some kids from joining the gang.
But those passes don't always come for free. They can also come with
strings attached. Gang members might expect the person they supported to give back to the community and remember the help they
received if and when they make it big. Similar to the social pressures
around a local star athlete who successfully goes pro, young men who
get a pass because of their rhyming skills are expected to "represent"
their community. The person who blows up, goes pro, or attends an elite
university will show the outside world that there's talent in the ghetto.
The gang and wider community take pride in knowing that "one of their
own" has done great things.

Of course, there are multiple reasons gangs give out passes. Gangs
can use them strategically, expecting returns on their support; the star
rapper or athlete who gets an exemption can be expected to "shout
out" the neighborhood gang if he makes it big. In some scenarios, gang
members might expect explicit financial returns on their "investment"
in a youth's talents.

Also, passes are a nonconfrontational way for gangs to exclude people who might not make good gang members. A young person who has other passionate interests is not an ideal candidate for the gang, which prizes loyalty and commitment to the set. Instead, OGs look for people who have a "ride or die" attitude about the gang. These people are willing to put their life on the line for the gang and fellow gang members.[19] They are also less likely to cooperate with police and are seen as a better bet than someone whose commitments might be elsewhere. The pass, then, gives gang members an uncomplicated way to exclude someone without the risk of embarrassing that person or damaging their relationship. In some situations, gangs can also give young men an "affiliate" status, which allows those people to remain socially connected with the gang without having a deep stake in the gang's illicit dealings.

But in some ways, gang motivations for issuing passes are secondary to a larger point. I once asked Dibiase if he could connect me with any of his former friends who had gone in another direction, toward the gang life. I wanted to know more about that path and hoped they could tell me about Dibiase, too. He hesitated at first but admitted that he had lost touch with most of those friends. Even though he still ran into them around his neighborhood, his time was directed elsewhere, with other youth. Over the years, Dibiase became much closer to youth immersed in hip hop. As he got older, he became closer to fellow rappers and producers he had met at Project Blowed. These friends became his primary group.

His immersion in hip hop funneled him away from the peers who remained committed to local gangs. And this alone had positive consequences, since hip hop had provided a locally accepted alternative to getting initiated into the gang.

Cold Feet

Although most of the men I met had not joined gangs, some had brief stints in them. They had joined because they wanted to become known for being "hard" and because they needed or wanted protection from other gangs. These are familiar stories in sociological writing about gangs.

But explanations for how and why young men *exit* gangs is far less clear.[20] In addition to supportive mentoring, exiting a gang can also be motivated by different experiences that make youth doubt their commitments to the gang identity and lifestyle. Some get cold feet as they approach a more serious stage in their gang careers. Different experiences make them feel a reflexive doubt that causes hesitation. They pause, wondering whether they are wholly committed to the gang identity and its future implications.[21] They worry that they aren't ready or wholly committed to their chosen path—that the next step will trap them.

For the men in this book, traumatic experiences with violence and incarceration gave them pause, jolting them away from gangbanging. Sometimes a friend or family member was killed or locked up. Other times, they got a taste of incarceration themselves. In various ways, they glimpsed the bleak futures that awaited them in gangs. Hip hop became an alternative way for them to be known and respected, to creatively represent their lived experiences and the experiences of others in their situation.

Exiting a Gang War

Flawliss, who I introduced at the start of this book, helped me understand how a person can get cold feet. He formally exited gangbanging on the eve of a gang war. But more likely, his transition out of gangbanging started when he was sent to juvenile hall after a fight at school around his sixteenth birthday. It wasn't his first offense, and in his recollection, he'd badly beaten his opponent. As he retells it, the judge "said that [the victim] was bullied and wanted to make an example out of my ass."

During his time away, Flawliss fell out of touch with members of Black Menace Mafia, a gang that he and other Black youth had established for protection from the Palmdale Peckerwoods—a White supremacist gang in Antelope Valley. The gang's membership grew during his absence, and Flawliss didn't recognize many of the new faces. More significant, the gang he had helped found had also become more violent. It had become more serious.

He saw many of these changes in his best friend, "Randall." When Flawliss got out of juvenile hall, Randall was even more deeply committed to gangbanging as a lifestyle and an identity. Flawliss was shocked to learn about Randall's latest hustles, which involved burglaries, home invasions, and an impressive arsenal:

> It was weird. Like, I was always cool with Randall, but then I went to his house and he had an AK, mini-14s with the thirty-round clip, and pistols. He had all of them up on his wall and shit—like trophies. He was showing these to me and saying how he robbed niggas and was finna smoke people who fucked with him. It was one of those weird things, because he was always on my side, but shit just seemed real serious.

Festering feelings of estrangement came to a head on the night of Flawliss's welcome-home party. Typically, at these homecomings a gang member returns to a hero's welcome, resuming his place in the gang. But that's not what happened for Flawliss. That night, Randall and other members of Black Menace Mafia had been partying before a high school football game. During the game, two members of the Neighborhood Rollin' 60s, Los Angeles's largest Crip gang, approached the girlfriend of a Black Menace Mafia member. According to Flawliss, the young woman rebuffed their advances and said she was dating a member of Black Menace Mafia. The Rollin' 60s were upset, Flawliss recalled: "So they said, 'Well, fuck you then, bitch! Rollin' 60s, fuck Black Menace Mafia!'"

The disrespect traveled quickly among members of Black Menace Mafia. A few called friends, and within minutes, a crew started to gather in the stadium parking lot. They waited, ready to jump the Rollin' 60s as they emerged from the football game. The heated argument rapidly escalated into a fight. On-site security from the sheriff's department broke up the melee and made several arrests, including Randall.

Another deputy instructed Flawliss and some friends to go home. On the way, one of Flawliss's friends received a page from Randall, who had managed to flee and was hiding in his own garage, still handcuffed.

After getting Randall out of the handcuffs, members of the Black Menace Mafia began preparing to "ride" on the Rollin' 60s. "Riding" is the process of rallying one's side for retributive violence, and it can include organizing for a drive-by shooting. It is a core part of gang life and, in many ways, a test of a young man's loyalty to his gang.[22] Young men can earn a reputation for being a rider when they consistently rise to the call of violence. Those who don't ride for their set can lose face. Flawliss was ambivalent. He never thought of himself as a rider, and he'd just left juvenile hall and wasn't eager to go back. As his gang readied to ride, he remembered:

> I didn't want to go [ride], but if I didn't go, then I'd be looked at like a punk, so for me to go, it was like mandatory or some shit. I think my boy could sense that I didn't want to ride; he was like, "Nah, I don't want you to go." He was like, "Nah, you just got out and shit. You just go to the park and wait for us."

The next morning, Flawliss got a page from Randall: "He told me that he shot this dude and police were looking for him. Everybody knew he did it." After a few days in hiding, Randall was intercepted by local police. He was eventually tried and sentenced to prison for aggravated assault and weapons charges.

At the same time, the Rollin' 60s were mobilizing against the Black Menace Mafia, and Flawliss worried he would get caught up in the beef. He imagined getting arrested, going back to jail, or getting killed. Flawliss was ready for a change of scenery. He asked his mother if he could go live with extended family in Texas:

> I was ready to go. I wanted a new beginning. I moved to Texas, and it really changed a lot for me. Basically, it put me in a new environment, where I didn't have all my fucked-up friends around me. I didn't know anybody and I was quiet. I went to a blue-ribbon school. At first, I was

kinda culture shocked. Like, people would hear me talk and say, "Oh, he sounds all proper and shit." But they didn't know that that's how Cali niggas talk. It kinda changed everything for me. I started getting good grades. I had a 3.5 GPA. I got a job working at McDonald's.

Whether we are elite prep school students or inner-city gang members, our friends offer us a sense of what we might reasonably expect for ourselves. As Flawliss thought about his life, he looked around. He was surrounded by friends who were entrenched in escalating gang violence. Some, like Randall, had graduated to more serious crimes. Randall was facing prison time as an adult. The conflict with the Rollin' 60s could turn fatal. These experiences loomed over Flawliss and inspired his exit from gangbanging. Flawliss eventually finished high school in Texas, away from his friends and an emerging gang war. Two years later, when he moved back to California, he was a different guy.

In hip hop, Flawliss saw opportunities to reinvent himself. In hip hop, he could craft a masculine identity that was still connected to the streets but removed from the activities and situations that were getting his closest friends in trouble. In hip hop, he could become a respected rhymesayer who represented the street life, but he didn't have to be wholly immersed in that life. As it does for other youth, hip hop validated Flawliss's past and offered him alternative options and the allure of a more promising future.

Exiting Gangs after Jail

People typically think of jail or prison as places where younger, less experienced criminals are mentored by more experienced inmates.[23] But interactions with more experienced inmates can have the opposite effect. Sometimes, a young man's integration into a population of more seasoned criminals can repel him from that world. It might also give him cold feet.

Of course, "cold feet" is not an experience unique to gangs. It is a shared experience many people have when they enter a larger and more competitive context for the first time. The star high school student entering the first lecture hall at a major university and the small-town actor going to the first audition in a major media market likely have the same unease as the person wondering whether he is cut out for the gang life. They all wonder whether they have it in them to continue down their chosen path. Facing a new and more competitive reference group, their confidence withers. This experience challenges one's previously taken-for-granted notions of the self.

For young men flirting with the gang lifestyle, stints behind bars can shatter the image they worked so hard to establish on the outside. Through interactions with more seasoned gang members, they learn that they might not be as committed to the gang lifestyle as previously imagined. These interactions also become omens of the future. Young men wonder whether they can handle the severe consequences that come with gangbanging.

Trenseta grew up around the Harlem Rollin' 30s Crip set. As a young man, he earned a reputation among his peers for having "heart," or courage. He was known as a tough, athletic, and gifted fighter. I met Trenseta when he was well into his thirties, but he still had a muscular, lean body, which he attributed to daily weight lifting and pickup basketball.

One quiet afternoon at the barbershop where he worked, Trenseta shared some stories about his former life in the Rollin' 30s. The sound of his broom scratching the floor was interrupted by the light hum of the TV in the background. Like other young men who had matured out of gangs, Trenseta seemed embarrassed to talk about his past. My previous attempts to get such information from him had not gone well, but on this particular day, he opened up.

Trenseta began by sharing stories about his neighborhood, a place where most of his friends were getting jumped in to the Rollin' 30s as BGs, "baby gangstas." He and his friends were drawn to the gang because older youth in the neighborhood looked like they had a lot of money:

> Growing up in the 30s was hard as hell, because you wanted a Benz! You wanted money! You wanted all that stuff, and you see the big homies got

this stuff! You come into the same place, all the people doing the wrong thing, and it just kind of rubs off.

Trenseta was jumped in as a teenager and quickly took to his role as an up-and-comer. One night, soon after his eighteenth birthday, Trenseta and other members of the Rollin' 30s were arrested and held in county jail after they got in a rumble at a night club. Although nobody had been seriously hurt and the district attorney eventually dropped all charges, the experience became a key turning point. Trenseta hated being in custody. It was a humbling experience to await a hearing alongside criminals facing more serious charges. These men showed what awaited Trenseta if he persisted in the gang life. They also made him doubt his commitments to the gang life:

> When I was young, I never thought about how you could go to jail at eighteen for doing dumb shit. Now, I'm in county, and I'm in there with everybody! I got nine, ten people with me in a cell who done more dirt. I'm in there with murderers and killers! I'm in there with people who been shot up and done much more shit—it was *different*.

After his release, Trenseta became determined to carve out another path. He was one of the toughest among his friends, but his reputation was no match for the men he met in jail. So while jail can be fertile ground for all kinds of criminal mentoring, time behind bars can also convince young men that they are not cut out for the life.

Trenseta hit another turning point when, shortly after his release, he learned that his girlfriend was pregnant. Preparing to become a father gave him even more reason to think critically about his life and future:

> I started taking life serious, man. I started looking at everything serious. No more play. I start thinking, "I need some honest money." "I need an honest way of living." When you get older and when you 'bout to have a kid, you kinda grow out of gangbanging. . . . A lot of people think gangbangers are gangbangers all their life. But most of us are just regular people who grow outta that life.

Figure 3. Trenseta taking a break at work to reflect on his life (photo courtesy of Kyle "VerBS" Guy)

Robert Sampson and John Laub explain these transitions in their study of criminality over the life course.[24] Young men exit careers in crime once they develop more serious romantic relationships, when they marry, and especially when they have children. Trenseta similarly left the gang when his life began to offer him different identities. Anticipating fatherhood pushed Trenseta further away from gangbanging. For the first time in his life, Trenseta felt completely responsible for someone else. His emerging identity as a father replaced his previous identity that was tied to the gang. Instead of hanging out on the block and "putting in work" (demonstrating one's toughness and loyalty) for the set, he became focused on making money to support his girlfriend and baby on the way.

As he reminisced about his transition out of gang life, Trenseta told me how far he had come. He didn't miss his former lifestyle:

> I'm comfortable now compared to how I was. Like, a everyday job is cool to me. Before I was running around trying to break into something, trying to look for the next scheme, trying to get some cash. But when you have a child, you change. Like, you got to do this and work.[25]

For Trenseta, hip hop represented new possibilities. While transitioning out of the gang and into fatherhood, Trenseta's focus and allegiance shifted from his gang to his family. He sought out work in the service economy to make ends meet as he shifted his energies to developing his craft as a rapper. He once said:

> I already rapped. I grew up doing it, but once I was out [of the gang], I was like, lemme see what I can do with this hip hop thing. Maybe all those hustles didn't work out, but I'ma try to do it this way then.

As Trenseta prepared for fatherhood, he set his sights on pursuing his creative talents as a rhymer and songwriter, a path he hoped would propel his family into a new income bracket. Most immediately, he became focused on finding a job that could provide for his family and planning for the future. Hip hop seemed to offer him a rare chance at upward mobility. It was a skill he hoped would transform his life.

Conclusion

Hip hop was a creative alternative for the men in this book. For some, it represented an alternative masculinity. Rappers could still be cool and respected on the streets even if they weren't in gangs.[26] Others were indirectly shielded from gangs through their participation in hip hop, as family members, friends, and other mentors inspired their creative interests. Still others were directly exempted, getting a pass from gangs to develop their talents and pursue their rap dreams. If they blew up, there might be strings attached, but for the time being, support from a gang would mostly keep them out of harm's way.

Hip hop also provides an alternative identity for youth who have tried out the gang life. Flawliss and Trenseta's stories show how former gang members see hip hop as a way to stay symbolically connected to the streets while removing themselves from the daily aspects of gang life. They see dead ends in the gang world and dedicate themselves to hip hop, which is cathartic. Hip hop is also a culture in which they can represent their own experiences. It provides young men with a rare space in which they can talk about violence, incarceration, and other traumatic life experiences that weigh heavily on young people growing up in the 'hood.

Moreover, through hip hop these men can parlay their experiences into highly sought-after street cred, which legitimizes underground rappers and popular recording artists. As Tricia Rose shows us, violence, jail stints, and other experiences that make a person appear more "street" help legitimize artists in the eyes of labels and fans.[27] This is an irony of the hip hop industry. While hip hop acts as a creative alternative for many young Black men, when they are trying to blow up, they also confront opposing pressures to prove that they are from the street or have past gang ties. Hip hop is one of the few career paths in which these men's pasts are not only validated but also celebrated as an additional kind of social capital.[28]

As all of us grow up, we get ideas about our future from the collective experiences of family, friends, and others whom we envision as reference points. We see ourselves in those around us. Their biographies become symbols of what we might reasonably expect—or at least hope for—in our own lives. From them, we glean clues about the kinds of opportunities that we might pursue, and we learn about the pitfalls along the way.

The men in this book grew up in families, peer groups, and neighborhoods in which becoming a gang member was a routine rite of passage. Growing up around gangs brings young people into close contact with their own vulnerability and mortality. Young Black men who come of age around gangs do not grow up with people whose natural youthful feelings of invulnerability are affirmed by obtaining college degrees, landing good jobs, or pursuing successful careers as adults. Instead, they grow up knowing people who have been incarcerated, shot, and critically wounded; they grieve for family and friends whose lives have been ruined or ended by gang violence. These experiences cast doubt over their futures.

All of this takes a toll on young men, creating and reinforcing their existential urgency. Middle- and upper-class young people do not typically experience this urgency. Growing up is an almost universally anxiety-ridden experience, but young people who are surrounded by successful family and friends take for granted that they, too, will land on their feet as adults. The young men I met didn't take that for granted. They saw a much more precarious path to adulthood and attached special meanings to hip hop along the way. For them, rap wasn't just a more meaningful way to transition into adulthood: it was a real, attainable way to change their lives for the better.

But before they could entertain ideas of blowin' up, they had to learn how to rap. Doing so isn't a solo project; it's something they learned and practiced at Project Blowed, a training ground that nurtured their creative talents and socialized them away from gangs.

In the following three chapters, I look more closely at how young men become rappers, which involves practice, mentoring, and immersion into the practices, rules, and local culture of Project Blowed.[29] Embarking on this process sets in motion many changes in the social worlds of young Black men, not the least of which is an immersion into the creative and collaborative scene at Project Blowed.

2

Masters of Ceremony

Trenseta was reviewing the rules when "Doze" walked on stage. "If somebody get up here and they wack, what do you say?" We mustered up a disjointed response: "Please pass the mic . . ."

Trenseta was unimpressed. "Nah, nah, hold on, hold on! This the Blowed! We at *Project Blowed*! If somebody get up here and you ain't feelin' them, what do you say?" This time, the crowd stepped up to the call-and-response and yelled, "Please pass the mic!" Trenseta looked satisfied with our energy and handed Doze the mic.

But Doze looked nervous. He strutted around the stage with his chest puffed out and yelled, "Yeah! We gonna get this shit crackin'!" And then there was silence. He waited for a beat, but nothing came. DJ Tommy Blak didn't have anything to play. Doze didn't know that he was sup-posed to bring his own beat to the open mic. He had missed that rappers were expected to show up prepared, with a song ready to go. Sure, on occasions, "veterans" (what locals call senior rappers) like Aceyalone, Medusa, Busdriver, and Abstract Rude would show up unannounced and freestyle.[1] But they had earned that right in the eyes of Blowedians. They were veterans who had put in their time and earned respect. Doze wasn't a veteran.

"Drop a beat! Drop whatever you got! I'll spit on whatever you got," Doze seemed more nervous by the moment. I thought, "This can't be good." I hadn't been in the scene for very long, but I knew how quickly audience members chanted unprepared rappers offstage.[2] Blowedians took pride in upholding the open mic's reputation for being a tough training ground, a place where everyone has to earn their keep.

Tommy thumbed through a plastic crate of hip hop, soul, and funk records. He pulled one out, scratched some drum cuts on his Technics 1200 turntables, and let the beat ride. But Doze didn't jump on the beat. Instead, he stared blankly at the ground. With each passing moment, our anticipation grew. At one point, it looked like he was counting in his head, trying to fit his rhymes to the beat. I felt anxious *for* him.

And then he started rapping. His rhymes ricocheted off the walls of the open mic. A few people started bobbing their heads. It looked like he might just pull it off, but not for long. Doze's voice trailed off at the instrumental break when he should have transitioned into a hook (a chorus or refrain). At the very least, he could have used a call-and-response to reignite the crowd. Something like, "When I say *Project*, you say *Blowed!*" could have kept the crowd engaged.

Doze didn't do this, and his performance soon turned into a train wreck. Instead of rapping a hook, he started yelling random words into the microphone: "Yeah! I get this shit crack! Uh-huh!" Afterward, he paused and recycled rhymes from his last verse. This was a big mistake and the beginning of the end.

It took a few seconds for the audience to realize what had happened. At first there was a light stirring. People started talking and somebody walked out. Then Flako Siete, a Salvadoran rapper whose ponytails draped down his shoulders, started chanting, "Please pass the mic!" He moved through the crowd, hands cupped like a bullhorn, getting people to chant with him.

After a few seconds of chanting, Tommy stopped the record, and the room fell silent. Doze's jaw tightened as Trenseta jumped back on the stage to resume his hosting duties. Like he always did when a rapper stumbled, Trenseta offered some advice: "*Get your bars up*, homie! Get a beat, write some lyrics, and practice your hooks!" Most rappers in Doze's place would try to exit the stage gracefully, taking a veteran's advice in stride. But Doze fired back, "I'm just doing me, nigga!"[3] Trenseta replied, "That's good! You do you! But we at the Blowed! Don't come up here without a song! Don't come up here mumblin' some shit you made up on the spot! This is Project Blowed! Go home, write a hook, practice your shit! Go get your bars up!" Doze didn't back down: "Oh, so it's like that, huh?! Lemme spit a cappella! Lemme spit! That beat was garbage!"

Doze kept demanding that he rhyme a cappella, but at first Trenseta wasn't having it: "You ain't up here to freestyle! You can do that outside! This is a workshop! This is where you spit your hottest shit!" Doze persisted, and eventually Trenseta gave in to his demands. Maybe Trenseta was feeling charitable, or maybe he figured Doze would fail again and embarrass himself. But Trenseta did something he rarely did: he gave a failed rapper a second chance.

Tommy picked the beat from Royce Da 5′9″'s "Boom," a classic track produced by DJ Premier, or "Premo."[4] The longtime producer of Gang Starr, Premo was beloved at Project Blowed and throughout the underground. Within seconds we were chanting, "What you gonna do with that beat?!" which we did sometimes when Tommy put on a classic. "Boom" was one of those beats that raised the audience's energy and expectations. Failing to deliver on a classic like "Boom" could get you booed offstage quickly.

It didn't take long for Doze to disappoint. He started mumbling into the mic. And then he seemed to be counting beats again. Meanwhile, the beat rumbled on. After an extended pause, he jumped into the same verse from his last try. But this time, he was *way* offbeat. The sound of his voice was out of sync with the music.

Trenseta put a stop to this: "Hol', hol', hol', hold on! Cut the beat!" Then he berated Doze, "You still ain't with it, man!" Looking defeated, Doze handed off the microphone. As he jumped off the stage, he mumbled something that caught Trenseta's ear. Trenseta looked irritated: "This is a workshop! Don't be comin' up here without a song! Don't come up here to practice your hooks! Don't come up here spittin' some weak-ass rhymes! This is the Blowed! Get your bars up!"

Doze sulked out of the workshop with a few friends. On their way out, he shouted something back at Trenseta. I didn't hear what he said, but Trenseta was fuming:

Ay, ay, ay! If your shit is wack, then your shit is wack! Simple as that! Maybe you need to go find something else to do. If you up in your mid-

thirties and still ain't got it, then you need to go do something else! Leave
hip hop alone, and go get you a little job at International House of Pan-
cakes or some shit! Leave this rappin' alone!

After Doze's crew left, Trenseta turned back to the crowd: "Put your
hands up if you thought that nigga was wack!" A sea of hands shot up.
Before the next performer, Trenseta reviewed the rules of the open mic:
Project Blowed was a workshop. Rappers were expected to perform a
polished piece of music. This was where you got critical feedback on
original music. And the crowd, which was mostly other rappers, should
be critical of performers. Nobody should get a free pass. This was part of
Project Blowed's legacy as a tough training ground in the underground
hip hop world. Before turning to the next performer, Trenseta asked
us again, "How do you expect to get better if nobody tells you that you
wack?"

* * *

The open mic at Project Blowed is a lot like a peer review. Senior rappers host it, and up-and-comers submit their best material for a crowd's
evaluation. The crowd's reaction lets rappers know whether they like a
performance. A crowd that is bobbing their heads, waving their arms,
dancing, or cheering is generally "feeling" or enjoying a performance.
At the same time, a quiet and listless crowd is losing interest. And if
an audience catches a performer forgetting their lines, stuttering, or
worse, showing up unprepared, they chant that person offstage by saying, "Please pass the mic!" This was a long-standing tradition in the
open mic and something Blowedians took seriously.

If a rapper consistently did well in the open mic, his peers would say
that he has "bars," a local saying for being a talented rhymer. Bars refer
to lines in a rapper's verse; there are typically sixteen bars in a verse,
which is followed by a "hook," or chorus. So, on the one hand, saying
that a person has bars is a positive appraisal of his or her lyrical skills.
Conversely, when someone gains a reputation for delivering lackluster
performances, that person needs to "get their bars up." As Trenseta told

Doze, telling people to "get their bars up" is a blunt way of saying that they need work on their songwriting, wordplay, and lyricism.

Marcyliena Morgan writes about the lyrical training at Project Blowed.[5] In research conducted nearly a decade before my own, Morgan describes how regulars would often evaluate one another on the basis of their rapid-fire rhyming skills. Although not everyone rhymed this way, locals treated it as a barometer of "lyrical fitness":

> At Project Blowed, the lyrical delivery style may include five to ten words, syllables, or morphemes (meaningful sound segments) in one-second intervals and beats. Only a few members of Project Blowed use this style repeatedly, though they all possess the skills to do so and incorporate them into extended rhymes. The style itself represents the height of what is known as lyrical fitness. It is not enough to speak quickly, but one should also enunciate.[6]

Lyrical fitness is just one part of what makes a skilled rapper—just one tool rappers rehearse inside the open mic. Doze had other holes in his repertoire. His lackluster performance reveals that emceeing is more fundamentally about engaging and energizing a crowd. In the 1986 classic "Eric B. Is President," Eric B. (of Eric B. & Rakim) rhymes, "'Cause to me / MC means 'move the crowd.'" If being an emcee involves inciting, managing, and sustaining the emotional energy of crowds, then Doze failed miserably.

Randall Collins writes about "emotional energy" in his theory of interaction rituals.[7] When people in crowds come together, they become attuned to one another's emotional and embodied rhythms. This collective experience leaves people feeling connected and emotionally charged. But euphoria is not guaranteed. It can be derailed by different situations. This is particularly true in live performances, where a lone person or group is responsible for engaging and charging everyone else up. Positive emotional energy can wane if a performer slips up, looks timid, or does not show enthusiasm. An interested audience can feel unsettled or, worse, embarrassed and angry toward a performer who fails in this role. No rapper — or crowd — wants that. So, becoming a rapper involves lyrical training and a more subtle understanding of "emotional conducting," or directing and controlling the emotional energy of their audience.

In this chapter, I show how rappers practice emotional conducting.[8] Aside from improving their wordplay, they practice arousing and sustaining the energy of an audience. Two techniques for this are paramount. First, rappers learn how to control their nerves so that they don't taint the audience's experience. For many, Project Blowed is the first time they have rapped on stage, in front of a live audience. This is daunting. Novices are understandably nervous performing in a scene that gives audience members the power to chant weak performers offstage. But few realize that their emotions are contagious. Through trial and error, they see how quickly their nerves can be transmitted to their audience. To control this, rappers learn to prime or warm up their audience before and during a performance. This helps keep an audience engaged, which in turn boosts their confidence. All of this helps them deliver a more energized performance.

Second, rappers practice mic control. Few have ever used a live microphone before coming to Project Blowed. As novices, the microphone is a foreign instrument that interferes with their ability to be heard. Many hold the microphone awkwardly and make mistakes trying to project into it. This leads to an equally frustrated and unsettled audience. But through practice, the microphone becomes an extension of the self. Rappers learn how to hold it and how to discipline their bodies so they can be heard loud and clear.

Through practice, feedback, and mentoring, rappers learn to embody these techniques and turn them into habits.[9] They incorporate them into a larger repertoire of moves that feel natural. This adds to their confidence and helps prepare them for what they hope will come next: performances in front of bigger audiences. This is all part of the intensive training at Project Blowed.

But first, I want to share a little more about the history of Project Blowed. A short trip back in time shows how Project Blowed and KAOS

Network are part of a much longer tradition of "creative interventions" in Leimert Park. This context is vital for understanding the significance of hip hop in the lives of Black youth in South Central.

Creative Interventions: Black Music in Leimert Park

Leimert Park became a center for Black music in 1961 when Horace Tapscott, a Black jazz pianist and composer, founded the Pan Afrikan Peoples Arkestra (originally called the Underground Musicians Association). Tapscott enlisted the help of pianist Linda Hill and trombonist Lester Robertson. Together, they spearheaded a group of jazz players, dancers, and community activists who gathered to perform at churches and community events across the city. Although the group did not regularly practice in Leimert Park, they often played for free in Leimert Park and provided loyal support to Black arts and political consciousness in the area. During the Watts riots, as business were looted and burned, the group attempted to bring calm to the situation by playing from the backs of flatbed trucks.

Black music continued to thrive in Leimert Park during the 1970s and 1980s. However, in the late 1980s, new generations of artists and musicians focused on "creative mentoring." For example, in 1989, drummer Billy Higgins (1936–2001) and the poet and community activist Kamau Daaood founded the World Stage, a jazz workshop that would bring together experienced players and youth. In addition to performances and jam sessions, the World Stage continues to host weekly workshops in which accomplished musicians provide free mentoring and lessons.

Similarly, just days before the 1992 LA riots, jazz musician and community activist Richard Fulton opened Fifth Street Dick's, a coffeehouse featuring live jazz, blues, and rap. Fulton envisioned Fifth Street Dick's as a gathering space for the entire community. Small tables throughout the space allow people to talk and to play chess, an arrangement that has been credited with creating a scene that has transformed gangbangers into poets, rappers, and writers.[10]

Taking a cue from Leimert Park, in the late 1980s, the surrounding area in South Central evolved into a home for underground hip hop. The Good Life, mentioned earlier, began operations in 1989 at a South Central health-food store operated by B. Hall and her son R. Kain (who would adopt the rap name Blaze). B. Hall started this nighttime venture because "young people needed a place to go to develop their own art. The no-cussing policy wasn't about us being uptight church people, it was about wanting the atmosphere of a serious arts workshop. Most of the crowd respected the rule, some said it made rapping more challenging, that it created more respect and brotherhood."[11]

The Good Life became the training ground for many of South Central's earliest underground rappers, including the Freestyle Fellowship, Hip Hop KClan, Medusa, 2Mex, Chali 2na from Jurassic 5, Volume 10, Skee-Lo, and other rappers dear to underground fans.[12] Interestingly, the "Please pass the mic!" chant became a point of contention between artists and organizers. Marcyliena Morgan notes that many of the emerging artists at the Good Life objected to Hall's and Kain's attempts to halt the chant, claiming that it added to their rigorous training and kept them on their toes.

The Good Life nurtured the creative talents of young Black men and women who wanted to build a vibrant underground hip hop scene in South Central. As an institution, it challenged the prevailing stereotype of South Central as an area overrun by gangs. According to Morgan, "While the rest of the country viewed LA as the center of decadence, and as a-historical, reactionary, low life, and gangsta' hiphop, the underground revolution was on. Moreover, it was the hottest thing for hiphop culture in LA, though gangster hiphop and gang activity were always in competition."[13]

Project Blowed was an outgrowth of this rich musical tradition. It was a vision spearheaded by Ben Caldwell, a filmmaker and activist who studied at UCLA in the 1970s. Caldwell earned an MA in film and television, and then later returned to UCLA for a second MA in international business and ethnocommunication. During his time at UCLA, Caldwell interned at the Brockman Gallery, a local art studio that aimed to promote the work of Black artists. After graduating from UCLA, Caldwell took a job teaching film and television at Howard University, a historically Black university in Washington, DC, where he became interested in researching the history and culture of modern music.

After three years at Howard, Caldwell moved to Los Angeles and began extensive work with other local artists and activists. Here, he connected with a long-standing group of drummers who would gather around the Watts Towers in the Watts neighborhood of Los Angeles. Caldwell was their documentarian. This experience, in turn, helped Caldwell when he applied for an "artist in community grant" funded by the California Arts Council. This eight-year grant provided the funding for Caldwell to start KAOS Network, a community center that he envisioned as a hub for supporting and mentoring local youth through the arts.

The opportunities, Caldwell thought, were too scarce within the public education system. As the Los Angeles Unified School District underwent significant cutbacks in arts and music funding during the late 1980s and early 1990s, young people in the area had fewer ways to pursue their creative interests. KAOS Network and Project Blowed specifically were local responses to those circumstances. In creating KAOS Network, Caldwell wanted to give local youth a neutral space where they could get together and learn about the arts and music away from the daily stresses of their neighborhoods. Similarly, Caldwell believed that KAOS Network and Project Blowed would represent the collective experiences of youth whose lives and interests were not always honored in conventional artistic and musical canons.

At the same time, Project Blowed's significance can be appreciated in comparison to other institutional responses to the "youth problem" in South Central. During this same era, the city of Los Angeles rolled out civil gang injunctions inside neighborhoods that the LAPD identified as hot spots of gang activity. Enacted by the City Attorney's Office with approval from a judge, gang injunctions are effectively restraining orders against gangs. At their core, they forbid gang members from engaging in different illegal activities in public, and they result in lawsuits to identify gang members. Initially rolled out by the city in the 1980s, there were forty-five gang injunctions covering seventy-two different gangs in Los Angeles while finishing this book.[14]

But in the process of criminalizing routine activities and profiling youth, gang injunctions have disrupted other forms of pro-social community life in South Central and beyond. Youth living in neighborhoods under injunctions get stopped and asked by police officers about their gang affiliation, sent home from public parks, or simply harassed while conducting other routine parts of their everyday lives in public. Some of the men in this book reported having such experiences even though they did not have ties with any gangs.[15]

Ben Caldwell had a different vision. He believed that youth could be deterred from gangs without the use of force, surveillance, or legal sanctions. Rather than punish youth, Caldwell's vision of KAOS Network—and Project Blowed more specifically—was to inspire them with art, to provide a place where they could meet other youth with similar creative interests. In addition to being a place where young people could get together around a shared love of hip hop, Caldwell wanted KAOS Network and Project Blowed to be a vehicle for friendships, creative collaboration, and mentoring. This was and continues to be a part of Caldwell's long-standing legacy in the area. It also continues a broader history of creative mentoring in Leimert Park.

Controlling Nerves, Priming the Audience

Anyone who has ever seen a nervous person stumble through a wedding toast or fumble a job interview knows how quickly a performer's nerves can infect the emotional energy in a room. If not managed well, the performer's anxiety can be contagious, leaving the audience with feelings of unease, sympathy, embarrassment, and even anger. Emotions like these create interference in a performance. They block an audience from being swept up in the moment, in the ritual.

Inexperienced rappers learned an important lesson in their time at Project Blowed: They would not get a positive reception unless they warmed up, or "primed," their audience. Priming techniques are not just ways to get the audience excited for a performance; they also pro-

MASTERS OF CEREMONY   57

vide a cover for rappers, who are less overwhelmed as the audience cheers for them. Ironically, priming had a double function: it helped charge up the audience, and it helped rappers overcome momentary stage fright. By getting the audience to cheer or show excitement, rappers would be emotionally swept up in the ritual, which quieted their own internal doubts and anxieties.

I first learned about this from Open Mike, a native Chicago rapper who often wore his hair in tight dreadlocks. One afternoon at KAOS Network, he told me about managing the anxieties of performing at Project Blowed:

> I was nervous. I was real nervous, looking out and seeing all them people and just seeing everyone who had came before and everyone that had got booed before, like, I didn't do my crowd mastery thing right. And that's something I didn't learn until later: that you kinda have to establish a presence with the crowd, even before you open your mouth. Or, before you rap, 'cause you gotta open your mouth to establish it. But you know, you gotta focus the energy on you. Like you could be great, but if you're not giving them the proper presentation, then they'll just eat you up. And I wasn't really good then. I was just a little bit above average.

Over time, Open Mike learned priming techniques to energize a crowd. He learned to gauge how he was coming across to the audience. He'd use the audience's initial reactions as a measuring stick for their unfolding energy during his performance:

> I like to tell the crowd to make noise—like give up energy, ya know? "Let's make a moment here," ya know what I'm saying? You know, "I'm about to try and really do something for y'all, I want y'all to really pay attention." That's what I'm up here doing this for—it's for the reaction. So I try and establish that from the beginning. I get them to make some noise. I get them ready to do this, you know? It's also a real good barometer for how I'm doing, like, 'cause if I make them make a lot of noise in the beginning, I hear how loud they can be. So when I'm doing my thing, and I say something that I feel should have garnered some reaction, and I see blank

faces, I'm like, "OK, so, maybe I didn't do that right." It's good for me to know how much energy they really have so I can try and keep it going.

As he gained more experience, Open Mike became increasingly aware of his audience. He learned to sense when they were "feeling" him: head nodding, dancing, arm waving, and other body movements were signs they were engaged. Silence, quizzical looks, and stirring were signs that he was quickly losing the crowd. If he sensed that the audience's energy was slipping, he would engage them in a call-and-response, get them to put their hands up, or get them to make some noise. These techniques would resuscitate the audience by jolting them into a collective rhythm.

Figure 4. Open Mike deep into his performance (photo courtesy of Kyle "VerBS" Guy)

Other rappers used humor for the same effect. Public speakers of all types know that a well-timed joke can lighten the mood and warm an audience up for a fun time. Shocace, a battle rapper best known for his "punch lines," or witty one-liners, would often start his performances with a joke. Through trial and error, Shocace learned that the hard, street image he relied on in his everyday life on the streets of South Central didn't necessarily transfer well into the open mic workshop, where audience members expected charisma.

I once saw Shocace lightening the mood before a song. He set the tone by getting the audience to laugh with him:

> Shocace gets onstage. He's smiling ear to ear and says, "What's up people, I'm Shocace, and I'm going to do a little song for you tonight . . ." The crowd is mostly silent as he introduces himself. It feels very serious in the room at this point, particularly since the previous two performers got booed off in spectacular fashion. Shocace, undeterred, opens his eyes very widely and makes a playfully aggressive face. He then says, "If anybody passes the mic on me, they can battle me outside!" This gets the crowd laughing. Shocace immediately breaks frame and goes back to smiling. He then says, "Nah, I'm just playin'." Before he introduces the song he is going to rap, he says, "But, f'real, if somebody pass the mic on me, they gettin' served outside!" As he says this, he smiles again.

Later that night, I talked with Shocace outside Project Blowed. He told me that joking before he rhymed made him feel calmer and more at ease. He said, "If people laughin' with me, they probably not tryin' to hate on me as much." Shocace also knew that the rules around his presentation of self had to change with his venue: "It's different here at the Blowed. I used to think you could come out and be a straight thug on stage. But niggas wasn't feeling it. Here, they want you to come with some intelligence and humor."

While violence, toughness, and nerve command respect on the streets, the rules were different in the open mic.[16] Here, young men won respect for their creative skills, humor, and charisma. In fact, regulars considered it a sign of weakness if a person tried to sound overly hard or tough on the microphone. People saw this as a crutch, an admission that a rapper had to coerce a crowd into liking him.

Conversely, I saw how regulars treated people who relied too heavily on a hard and tough presentation onstage. Although profanity was allowed at Project Blowed, regulars felt that people shouldn't rely on it indiscriminately. Instead, rappers were expected to develop a unique style, come up with clever rhymes, and use their on-stage charisma to win over a crowd. Many tried to distance themselves from the sometimes gratuitous violence and misogyny in gangsta rap, a genre that some regulars did not respect at Project Blowed.

One night, I saw a newcomer asked to pass the mic. He hadn't lasted long. Midway through his first verse, he started talking about "murkin' niggas." In the next line, I heard, "Fuck them niggas!" Many of his rhymes included the N-word or involved explicit references to killing and murder. He was shouting loudly into the microphone and audience members were stirring, *not* enjoying his performance.

DVS, one of the few regular "femcees" (female emcees) in the scene, was hosting that night. She shook her head and intervened: "This is how it goes down, people! If you ain't feelin' somebody, you gotta let 'em know—it's not personal or anything, it's just part of how you get better!"

The guy who got booed off was not persuaded. He seemed to get more livid by the moment. For a minute or two, he walked around the room staring down different people who had told him to pass the mic; a few times, he stopped in front of somebody and eyed him down like he wanted to fight. His actions ramped up tensions in the room.[17] Eventually, a friend tugged at his arm to leave. As they walked out, the dejected rapper yelled to his friend, "Fuck this shit, cuz!"[18] The two then stormed out of the open mic.

I was standing by E.Crimsin, a rapper who had grown up minutes from Project Blowed. He nudged my arm, laughing so hard that he had to cover his mouth with his hand. After he calmed down, he joked, "Some niggas can't handle the fact that they weak!" Aspect One, a rapper originally from the Bronx who grew up around hip hop legends like Melle Mel, added: "I hate it when people just get up there and spit a bunch of 'nigga this, nigga that' with no *style*. Like, you can be a gang-sta, and that's cool if that's who you are, but you gotta do it with some flair, you can't just get up there and start yelling loud and shit."

Ten minutes later, I stepped outside and saw the dejected rapper—who had the build of an NFL running back—walking around the corner with his shirt off, chest puffed out, squared shoulders, biceps flexing. I scanned the corner and a bunch of people were cautiously watching this guy, who appeared ready for a fight. With clenched fists, he moved through different crowds on the corner, trying to catch somebody "slip-pin'" (attempting to make eye contact with people who were obviously trying to ignore him).

I looked away to ask Flawliss, "What's up with this guy?" Flawliss shrugged. "I dunno, but he betta not try to fuck with me. He's getting all loud and shit 'cause he got the mic passed." The hostile rapper stalked about, daring anyone to look at him or provoke him. Nobody said any-thing, and everyone did their best to ignore him.[19]

Not soon enough, his friend again tugged him away, saying, "Fuck this! This place doesn't make us!" But the shirtless rapper ignored his friend's pleas, jerked his body away, and kept confronting people, flex-ing his muscles. When he was out of earshot, Flawliss leaned in, made a funny face, and echoed my question: "What's this guy's problem?"

As he prolonged this spectacle, the angry rapper seemed to forget where he had placed his T-shirt. He marched around the corner for a few more minutes, looking for a challenger, but then started frantically looking for his T-shirt and yelling at different people, "Where's my T, cuz!? Where's my T?" He flared his nostrils, holding his fists as if he was ready to unload a barrage of violent punches. He circled, anger build-ing.

When his friend found the shirt on the ground, I spied a subtle look of embarrassment on the rapper's face. His clenched jaw, stiff posture, and flared nostrils relaxed slightly as he brushed the leaves and dust off his crisp white T-shirt. He put it on and followed his friend away from Project Blowed.

Later, regulars discussed this guy's response to getting asked to pass the mic. E.Crimsin and a few others said some people are "too sensitive" and "get their feelings hurt." E.Crimsin casually recalled that several of the OGs had criticized his rapping in the past, but he explained that he was a "man first" and considered it unbecoming to show anger after being chanted off stage. When I asked him to elaborate, he explained that it's humiliating to get the mic passed on you, but even more so to respond with anger. Others chimed in, agreeing.

Although these young men still live in neighborhoods in which the "code of the street"[20] shapes interactions on the streets, they enter into a new social world at Project Blowed, one with different rules and rituals. At Project Blowed, creativity and charisma reign supreme. And unlike the streets, in which young men use displays of toughness to gain status, rappers at Project Blowed can actually lose respect if they try to come across as thugs and gangstas on and off the microphone. By trying to escalate his artistic failure into a fight, the rapper in this case lost face for not being able to "keep it hip hop."

Later that morning, he and his friend slinked away. People talked about these two as examples of how *not* to act at Project Blowed. Although the rapper appeared angry to the casual onlooker, part of me wondered if he was also embarrassed after getting asked to pass the mic and misplacing his T-shirt. Although hosts invite people to come back, I never saw these two again.

In addition to providing them with a creative outlet and an alternative way to become known, Project Blowed provided a social setting in which young men practiced deference to their peers. To last at Project Blowed, a person needed to be open to critique and manage their reactions to failure. This logic runs counter to the "code of the street," which requires that young men respond to personal slights and challenges with "nerve" or the threat of violence. Instead, young men who wanted to be respected at Project Blowed were discouraged from "catching feelings," or taking critiques or failures too personally.[21] And under no circumstances should a person respond in anger. Doing so casts a person out from the local community. This stoicism was not just superficial, either. The young man who lost his cool in the face of critique was effectively admitting that he was not confident in his skills as a rhymer. Project Blowed nurtured these responses, socializing young men to be open to critique. It also placed them into contact with other young people who were invested in a scene that prized charisma and creativity over a tough and hard presentation of self.

Rockin' the Mic

Although it seems intuitive, rappers also practice "rockin' the mic" inside the open mic. Many have vague ideas about how to hold and use the microphone, but enter the scene without ever having used one. At most, some have rapped for a small group of friends in freestyle sessions, or "ciphers," but have not developed the subtle dexterity to confidently use a live microphone.

This was a steep learning curve for some people. Many held the mic too far from their mouths. Others held it too close. Still others inherited the bad habits of popular cultural representations of famous rappers who "cuff the mic" (placing their hands over its head), reducing the surface area designed to capture sounds. Rappers who couldn't clearly project through the microphone were at risk of losing the attention and engagement of their audience, which would typically lead to chants to get them off stage. Once while playing me beats at his apartment, N.A. explained, "If people can't understand what you're saying, you could be the illest guy ever, but if we can't hear you, it's just not happening."

The veterans see these challenges and give novice rappers feedback during the open mic. Choppa, for one, was adamant about teaching mic control. One night, he paced back and forth near the front of the stage, stared down the audience, and gave a quick tutorial on how to hold the mic and project into it. At first he spoke into the microphone loudly, clearly, and confidently: "This is how you hold a mic! For all of you young-ass rappers out there who think you bad and shit, you need to learn how to hold the mic right first!" Next, he lowered the mic about six inches and, in a distant and barely audible voice, announced, "Too many of you rap like this." His voice trailed off into an unintelligible string of utterances and sounds. He then pulled the mic up to just beneath his chin, so that it was nearly touching his lips. Now his voice boomed throughout the room, creating a loud and unpleasant distortion in the speakers: "Some of you rap like this!" I looked around, and some of the audience members were cupping their ears. Finally, he lowered the mic to just a few inches below his chin and proclaimed, "*This* is how you hold yo' muthafuckin' mic!"

To further encourage good habits, veterans would turn down the volume on the receivers that channeled the sounds from the stage mics back into the speakers. This forced rappers to be especially mindful of using the mic. The logic was simple: rappers would learn to be heard despite built-in hurdles; they would develop a stronger repertoire by performing in suboptimal conditions. If they could be heard here, they'd have less trouble being heard with a better microphone setup.

This was one way Project Blowed helped train rappers for future endeavors. Aspiring rappers who want to take their career to the next level benefit greatly from being resilient and open to learning in these situations. By training in suboptimal conditions, rappers develop an inner confidence in their own abilities to pull off a performance—even in spite of various unfavorable circumstances. Like marathon runners training with ankle weights, rappers at Project Blowed gain confidence from persevering under suboptimal conditions.

But the challenge of being heard is also one of poor breath control. Over the course of a song—often more than a few minutes—rappers move around, dance, and try to hype their audiences. This exertion is another key difference between their performances in the open mic and their past, informal performances.

I learned the pitfalls of poor breath control on my first night at Project Blowed, as I stood in the middle of the audience watching a two-man group onstage. I didn't know who they were, but their failure helped me understand the different layers in a performance. Not only were audience members judging a rapper's lyrics and song-writing; they were also paying close attention to how loudly and clearly a rapper sounded. I wrote:

> They start rapping. I can hear the first guy fine. He raps loudly and clearly. I can also hear the second guy, who seems to be mostly a "hype man" in the first verse. After the hook, the second guy launches into his verse. He starts off strong but quickly begins to fade. He seems to be running out of air at multiple times in the verse; some of his words sound strained as they hurriedly come out of his mouth. At some points it sounds like he's

off the beat, just trying to get all his words out. As the verse unfolds, he seems increasingly uncomfortable and out of breath. This continues until the end of the verse, when Flako [Siete] begins walking through the audience, chanting, "Please pass the mic!" He walks through the crowd with his hands cupped around his mouth, saying it repeatedly. As he walks through the audience, people begin to join him in chanting, "Please pass the mic." Within 3–5 seconds the crowd has taken over, both of the performers' body language drastically changes; both stop moving around the stage and look like deer caught in headlights. [Then] 2–3 seconds later the DJ stops the record abruptly, and both MCs understand that they are supposed to hand the mics back to the head MC.

Shamir, a Project Blowed veteran, offers commentary in between rounds. He tells the second guy in the group, "You need to breathe! You can't get up here and spit sixteen bars in one breath! When your body tells you to, you need to breathe. . . . [S]imple as that." He then tells the audience, "You need to stop being scared to say 'please pass the mic'!" . . . Continuing, he talks about KRS-One from the South Bronx, and notes, "KRS would tell you to your face, 'Yo skills are wack, you just don't got it! Leave hip hop alone!'"

Becoming a rapper, like acquiring any new skill set, involves different types of awareness and learning. For example, aspiring rappers have to first master a number of micro-level skills that are part and parcel of any performance. The most fundamental of these is breathing. Although everyone knows how to breathe, and does so without much thought, rappers have to learn how to do this under new kinds of duress. The anxiety of performing onstage and having to project into a microphone adds strain to an otherwise taken-for-granted action.

Until rappers fully embody these skills and they become second nature, they are overwhelmed by what the philosopher Michael Polanyi described as the "subsidiary awareness" of action.[22] In brief, every activity we do requires a number of competencies. For example, while hammering a nail, a person most immediately attends to connecting the tip of the hammer to the head of a nail to drive it into a piece of wood. This is the "focal awareness" of action. At the same time, though, the person is able to hammer only because he or she has mastered a

number of other tacit skills, and these represent the subsidiary awareness needed to complete the action. For example, while hammering,
the person unconsciously attends to the grip on the handle and on overall balance. As people become more adept in something, they are able
to screen out many of the tacit skills to perform the action competently.
For rappers, until they embody these tacit skills, they are caught up in
trying to breathe and hold the microphone a particular way. Their attention to these subsidiary actions takes them away from what *should* be
the focal point of their attention: connecting with the audience.

Explaining Failure

At Project Blowed, getting chanted off stage is part of the learning
curve.[23] Although most have been asked to pass the mic, many are still
guarded when asked about the experience. They failed, and that memory threatens their cool, skilled presentation of self. I first learned about
how young men make sense of being told to pass the mic from June
One, a soft-spoken black rapper from Compton. He denied ever having
had to pass the mic.

I met June at Project Blowed early in my days there. He was wearing
a dark blue Los Angeles Angels hat, black-framed glasses, and baggy
jeans. He saw me approaching him and nodded: "Wassup, fam?" We
gave each other daps. When I jokingly said, "I see you always *pass the
mic* on people!" June went from smiling to looking defensive. He must
have thought I said he always got the mic passed on him, because he replied, "Who? Me? Nah, man, I never had the mic passed on me." After
I explained that I meant I had noticed him chanting other people offstage, he sighed with relief. "Man, I was about to say! I never had the
mic passed on me! I was like, 'You must have me confused.'"

Other rappers admitted that they had been asked to pass the mic,
but qualified their failures.[24] For example, during the first few months
I spent at Project Blowed, I met up with CP, a rapper who often wore
different colored LA Dodgers hats with matching T-shirts and a bright
gold colored chain. Although he had been born and raised in "the 40s,"
a neighborhood near Leimert Park, CP was living with his grandparents
in Baldwin Hills when I met him.

While hanging out in his bedroom, I asked about his experiences rapping at Project Blowed. CP told me he was asked to pass the mic on his first night. He understood it as the audience rejecting the beat, not his rapping:

> I only been asked to pass the mic one time. And it wasn't 'cause I was wack or nothing like that. Like I didn't get asked to pass the mic because I wasn't comin' hard, or because I was weak or some shit. People told me afterwards that they passed the mic because they weren't really feelin' the beat.

CP's account points to a common defense mechanism that rappers used when talking about past experiences getting asked to pass the mic. Instead of talking about personal shortcomings and mistakes, many are quick to note how audience reactions were shaped by many factors beyond a person's skills as a rhymer. Failure and temporary setbacks become easier to manage when people deflect responsibility away from themselves.

Other rappers blamed the audience's unrefined taste. Like artists who brush aside critics for not "understanding" the esoteric brilliance of their work, some rappers transform a failed performance into a moment of self-righteous distinction. "J-Dub," for example, was a rapper in his twenties who often used big words in his rhymes during his frequent appearances at poetry slams and open mics. More seasoned rappers often felt that his lofty vocabulary was just a glossy crutch, and he was often asked to pass the mic. One night when I caught up with him, J-Dub offered his take:

> Too many people in here are haters, man. I swear some of the cats in there are so close-minded when it comes to music! . . . I've been going to this poetry slam and people there actually listen to what I'm saying when I rap. And it's nothing but love over there, man. Like everybody there is about peace, love, and buildin'! Here, I feel like there are a lot of haters.

Some rappers asked to pass the mic claimed that they were the victims of "scene politics." Even though hosts encouraged crowds to be honest and forthcoming about their critiques of other rappers, some felt that there were unspoken rules about not passing the mic on certain people in the scene. I learned about this from Nocando, who was widely considered the best freestyle rapper and battler at Project Blowed. A few years after I met him, he went on to win the prestigious Scribble Jam, an annual freestyle rap battle that is effectively the US championship of rap battling.

Nocando lived in "the 60s," a neighborhood about twenty blocks south of Leimert Park. He was asked to pass the mic on his first night at Project Blowed. This was a blow to his self-definition. He was one of the top rappers at his high school and had arrived with high expectations. Afterward, he attempted to pass the mic on a rapper who was widely known and respected in the scene:

> I thought that if somebody sucked, you know, get them off of there. You know? But you know there was like favoritism and all that stuff. And I got—he started saying, you know, trying to battle me from the outside. So then the host like "shut it down." Like, "What we're going to do is have a battle then. If you think you're so tough." And he called me up on stage. And my head was really big anyway just because I was the guy, I was that "battler to beat" at my school. Or at least, I was better than all the cats in my school. But I mean, so I battled that dude, Raffi. And then I won. Then I battled some other guy. They just kept bringing up people. And I won.

Beneath the surface, asking someone to pass the mic can be a way for regulars to distinguish who is and who is not a Blowedian. It can be a way for regulars to draw in and out groups in the scene. This is one of the interesting tensions in Project Blowed. While emcees are quick to talk about their rights to be original and rap about what is personally meaningful, there really *are* unstated local scene politics at work.

Later, Nocando told me how regulars will relax their harsh criticism when the person is a longtime regular or friend to others in the audience:

> Some people are just like garbage, and then since everybody knows them, they don't want to boo that guy. You know, or they don't want to please-

pass-the-mic 'em because, like, you don't want to hurt the guy's feelings, you know. Some people have been there for a long time and really impressed people back in the day, so it's like a respect thing.

Additionally, audience members are also not always accepting of hip hop that strays too far from the local, underground aesthetic that places a high emphasis on lyricism and "choppin'", a sped-up delivery. I once asked E.M.S. if he had ever told someone to pass the mic. He thought long and hard and replied:

> Where I may be a critic is if you're on some "killin' nigga, cut his head off, and I worship Satan, and all emcees are wack!" [Laughs.] Ya know, like, if it's something just totally negative. There was one cat like this not too long ago who came in there like that. Then, I was like, "Please pass the mic!"

E.M.S. wasn't alone. Other rappers were also protective of what they considered the legacy of Project Blowed as an underground hip hop mecca. Aspect One, a key member in the Missing Page Crew and active in LA's underground hip hop scene, told me that he'd pass the mic only if someone was "wack." So I asked him what made a wack emcee:

> Wack shit to me is all that jiggy dumb shit that these motherfuckers come to the Blowed with. Like you can quote me on this, I'm not really feeling Flawliss and CP and them. It's like the stuff that you hear from Death Row or some shit. Like, to me, that's not the epitome of Blowed.

In comparison, Aspect One described his influences, which were mostly artists who identified as underground emcees. He counted De La Soul and Freestyle Fellowship (who hailed from the Good Life and later Project Blowed) as key influences:

> But as a fact of being an emcee and being able to represent the Blowed, I know that they can give me that title because of the shit that I'm doing. ... As far as the styles that I'm emulating, I look up to Posdnuos from De La Soul. Like, you're very fuckin' dope, and I want to rhyme just like him.

> Same thing with Aceyalone. I always looked up to him. They're both dif-
> ferent but on the same plane. They just as introspective about a lot of shit
> and they really add another dimension, lyrically.

This analysis underscores the importance of the open mic in the lives of young Black men trying to become better rappers.[25] It was a place where rappers eagerly tried to showcase their written materials and stage presence. It was also a place where rappers could showcase their talents for a crowd of their peers. But in addition to being a proving ground, young men also used the open mic to draw boundaries around who was and who was not down in the local scene. Regulars at Blowed were notoriously hard on newcomers. Many considered it a point of pride to chant someone offstage, and they would use that power to humble outsiders. All of these things cast doubt on all the talk of the open mic as a democratic space in which people evaluated one another solely on their skills.[26]

Together, the stories in this chapter underscore the importance of reputation to young men at Project Blowed. In urban working-class neighborhoods, young men often have fewer chances to develop positive identities for themselves. Those spaces in which they *are* afforded such chances, like sports or hip hop, therefore take on elevated importance. They become sacred areas of a young man's life. Hip hop, in this context, also becomes an important setting for young Black men to transcend dominant, limiting stereotypes about them as gangstas, hustlers, and thugs. A failure at the open mic, then, is not a momentary failure in one's development. It can be a crushing experience that can ruin a young man's self-image and identity.

Conclusion

The open mic workshop is a training ground. Novice rappers workshop their music in front of a critical peer review. Rappers get help with their lyricism, rhyme schemes, and overall songwriting. When OGs and hosts implore less experienced rappers to "get their bars up," they mean that the person is lyrically weak and needs to improve his or her skills.

Beyond this training, though, rappers are learning how to be confident onstage and gain valuable practice in energizing and moving an audience. These sensibilities they gain are key to their ongoing careers. They must learn to prime, sustain, and occasionally resuscitate their audience's energy. They practice holding a microphone, projecting into it, and controlling their breath.

Although these skills become part of a rapper's repertoire, they are not necessarily unique to rappers. All performers are sensitive to the ebbs and flows of their audience's energy. Stand-up comics, religious leaders, and political orators use different techniques to engage audiences in a performance. The good ones are also sensitive to the energy of an audience and adjust accordingly. And a person's ability to use these techniques seamlessly comes across as charisma. But charisma is not an innate attribute. It is a learned emotional intelligence, something people practice and cultivate over time.[27]

Project Blowed is also place where rappers gain a measure of humility. Inexperienced rappers commonly are told to pass the mic. Although everyone readily admits that failure is just one part of developing as a rapper, people have different ways of dealing with the experience. Some speak openly about their failures but distance themselves from a previous self who was less competent. Others create accounts that shift the responsibility for failure to things that are ultimately out of their hands. They contend that the audience was ignorant to their talent or the beat was lacking or scene politics shut them down during an otherwise excellent performance.

Being told to pass the mic puts a dent in a rapper's local reputation, but graceful acceptance is a far better outcome than "catching feelings" and trying to escalate dismissal to violence. Indeed, young men who revert to the code of the street and cannot "keep it hip hop" risk losing more face by breaching the implicit emphasis on charisma and creativity in the scene. As we'll see in the following chapters, young men who cannot control their emotions are quickly marginalized by their peers.

Ultimately, at the open mic workshop young men begin undergoing an identity transformation. The setting places them into challenging situations that trains them for the next steps in their careers. As young men begin to feel themselves overcome these challenges, they develop swag, more confidence in their abilities. They begin to feel more comfortable on stage and can develop unique ways of engaging their audience.

3

Freestyle

Open Mike looked possessed whenever he freestyled. He'd close his eyes and rock his body. His fingers twitched and crawled like spiders, vibrating to the sounds and syllables coming out of his mouth.

In high school, Open Mike and his friends started experimenting with rhyming and b-boying.[1] As a young adult, Open Mike still rapped, was a huge professional wrestling fan, and mentored youth at one of KAOS Network's after-school programs. He usually wore a neatly trimmed mustache, a goatee, and shoulder-length dreadlocks. When I asked about his eclectic personal style, he told me he'd never really been into gangsta rap, gravitating instead toward indie rock as a youth:

> I like hip hop when hip hop was fun. When people got to talkin' about "shoot 'em up," that was lost on me. I remember specifically when *Menace II Society* came out. Everybody had the *Menace II Society* soundtrack. There was nothing interesting about that to me. I was off on the whole grunge thing, that whole Seattle thing.

By the time I met Open Mike, he spent most Thursday nights freestyling with Psychosiz, a rapper who lived in "the Jungles."[2] Psychosiz was a self-described "video-game nerd" and was known for the high register of his voice and creative rhyme schemes. Sometimes, he'd wear long, droopy beanies that made him look like a wizard. The two were original partners in a group called Parts Unknown.[3] Years later, they helped found Thirsty Fish and the Swim Team—hip hop groups that grew from friendships made at Project Blowed.

One night I walked up to the corner and saw a cipher—a group free-style rap session—forming around Open Mike and Psychosiz. The crowd was loving it. Open Mike rhymed:

> And leave you froze,
> like an ice cube with polio,
> fucked up like Valentine's Day with lonely folk,
> that's next week,
> I flex heat,
> like loose leaf,
> my fashion sense is unique,
> not really,
> I'll blow the spot silly,
> MCs are tryin' to get a hot milly,
> in the rap game,
> eat 'em like pancakes,
> open up like oysters and clambakes,
> down into the middle,
> I'll rip a little,
> on my shoulder,
> just like a little fiddle,
> but they can't take the last line to this riddle,
> Open is gonna kill it,
> and my rhymes are tight like Psychosiz,
> but my mic they might . . . blow . . . shit . . .

Open Mike's voice trailed off. Then, tenths of a second later, Psychosiz picked up:

> And I come through with that dope shit,
> that off-the-dome dopeness,
> make 'em bend backward like multiple sclerosis,
> no it's off the brain,
> hit you like a train,
> oh! It's too sick,

wipe the stain,

so it don't stick on the,

what am I wearing now?

hit you with the veritable style,

I'm a veteran, bow!

to the master here,

when I come through,

I be like pass the sphere,

and pass it here . . .

Just as his voice trailed off, "Random"—another regular at Project Blowed—jumped in. And so it went for the next half hour. Different people in the cipher took turns, jumping in when another person started to trail off. Onlookers cheered and gave rappers props.[4] Occasionally, some people left the cipher and were replaced by others looking to freestyle. Like a game of hot potato, people worked together to keep the cipher going.[5] Abrupt stoppages in the action were felt by everyone, not only the person who couldn't keep rhyming. As such, rappers tried to avoid these breaks, keeping the fun alive. Their words seemed to magically leap from their brains, or, as Psychosiz rhymed, to come straight "off the dome."

* * *

Freestyling—the ability to improvise rhymes—would seem to resemble what psychologist Mihaly Csikszentmihalyi calls flow.[6] Csikszentmihalyi writes that people experience flow, or "optimal performance," when they become intensely absorbed in what they are doing. They become wholly locked into the moment and, in turn, capable of spontaneously extraordinary feats. Famous athletes, like Michael Jordan, have helped mythologize flow by describing moments when they felt at "one with the game," as if they were playing by pure instinct, unable to fail.

At a glance, rappers like Open Mike, Psychosiz, and others seemed to come up with poetic, thought-provoking, and sometimes hilarious rhymes on the spot. It seemed like the words, inflections, and entire rhyme patterns were magically rolling off their tongues. Many people have even referred to the act of freestyling as flowing. But freestyling is *not* a purely spontaneous activity—at least not in the ways that emcees, fans, and journalists have constructed it to be. Freestyling, like Jordan's legendary basketball skills, is the result of long and varied kinds of practice. By the time a rapper jumps into a cipher, he has encountered the same words and rhymes many times over. These rhymes have been rehearsed, rehashed, and remixed, often in private.

In a similar vein, David Sudnow sheds light on the intense work that goes into learning improvisation in his reflexive study of jazz piano. Before he felt confident playing in front of others, Sudnow spent long hours practicing, memorizing, and drilling basic piano scales. Over time, his fingers became attuned to patterned movements. He developed a "stockpile of places to go."[7] This background training, in turn, gave him the confidence to improvise. It gave him a foundation from which he could spontaneously combine rehearsed sequences and scales.

Rappers undergo a similar kind of cognitive training. Through repetition, they learn to think in rhyme. In dingy notebooks and in the corners of their minds, they develop a stockpile of words and rhyme patterns they can deploy in the heat of the moment. They figure out transitions that will give them time to think of their next rhyme while they're digging for something clever to unleash on an audience. Rappers' monastic devotion to practice helps them develop the ability to quickly mix and match words, styles, and other vocalizations into a seamless freestyle. This skill set is not far removed from what public speakers, ministers, pickup artists, sales representatives, and others develop through repetitive performances in front of audiences.

Rappers also practice with and learn from others. From rhyming sessions at work to everyday practice with friends, aspiring rappers find different ways to integrate freestyling into the day to day. They learn even more when they start freestyling in ciphers at Project Blowed. Like battles (covered in the next chapter), ciphers are fun, but they are also a high-pressure performance situation that places them in contact with other people who have their own rhymes and style.

The cipher is a unique training space, though, because rappers face a dilemma. On the one hand, rappers want to put their best foot forward to impress their peers. To increase those odds, they may draw from a stock of prewritten rhymes, pulled together to elicit a warm response. But they have to be careful not to overdo it. A person who comes across sounding too polished can be accused of "spitting writtens," or trying to pawn off prewritten rhymes as extemporaneous. Indeed, unlike the open mic, where people are supposed to come ready to perform polished music, rappers in a cipher are supposed to at least maintain the *appearance* of spontaneity. To be in the moment, lyricists should play off one another and make their rhymes responsive to the unfolding action in the cipher.

And here is the great irony of freestyling in a cipher: Everyone draws from a stock of old and recycled rhymes. Everyone has logged long hours writing rhymes, learning rhythms, and stringing together great lines. But nobody wants to be found out. Being known as someone who indiscriminately recycles old rhymes can diminish a rapper's reputation and status. Rappers are therefore walking a tightrope, drawing from old techniques but trying to make them appear wholly new. Thus, the *real* improvisational magic is in finding ways to use stock rhymes without getting caught.

Thinking in Rhyme

Freestyling is one of hip hop's most time-honored skills. Rappers and fans treat it as a benchmark skill, much like "scratching" for turntablists.[8] A refrain among many turntablists is "What is a DJ if he can't scratch?"[9] Rappers have a similar perspective on freestyling and critique emcees who aren't good at it. This was especially true at Project Blowed, an underground scene with a rich history of freestyling. Long before I started hanging out in the scene, Project Blowed had established a worldwide reputation as a training ground for freestyle rhyming. A previous generation of rappers from the Good Life—Aceyalone, Myka 9, P.E.A.C.E., Ellay Khule, Medusa, 2Mex, and Abstract Rude (among others)—had carved out a large base of underground hip hop fans who were drawn to the fast-paced, esoteric, and lyrically complex brand of freestyling.

These mentors were also part of Project Blowed and kept the rich freestyling legacy alive. Young rappers who came into the scene were eager to impress their storied mentors and worked hard at learning the craft. When I asked Open Mike to tell me about freestyling, he talked about how he had developed an arsenal of stock rhymes through repetition and practice in quiet, everyday moments: "I practice in the car, in the shower. Whenever I'm alone. Not *whenever*, but a lot of times, I'll end up just freestyling when I'm by myself." I asked him why he'd practice alone:

> I'm more likely to push it somewhere when I'm by myself. 'Cause there's no risk factor. If I mess up, it's just messing up to me. You know, if you're in the cipher, there's like twelve people listening to you. Even if you kinda wanna have that fortitude to say "fuck the risk," you might not a lot of times.

Over time, Open Mike became increasingly comfortable freestyling. He developed lyrical dexterity. Through repetition and drilling, he began to automatically make word associations and vocalizations that he could string together without hesitation:

> **OM** You start thinking in rhyme to a degree, and like, like right now, even sometimes when I'm talking, I'm hearing the last syllable that I say, and some part of my mind is thinking of some word I can rhyme with it, and after a while you get to this point where you seen just about every syllable chain at least once, ya know? And so even if it's not something you've written, you kinda start to get a catalog of words that rhyme with other words. . . . [W]hat becomes new is how you put them together. The stuff in between, ya know?
>
> **J**   . . . So, if I said the word *down*?
>
> **OM** Yeah, you get *frown, drown, clown,* you know, *mounds, pounds* . . . . You know, my thing now though is like how many syllables can I do? So you get syllable, your fillable, lyrical, ya know? Just, ya know, trying to stretch it out like that, because that's when it

sounds real good. Just like, get out there and do freestyle for like five syllables, ya know what I'm saying? That's when it sounds real potent.

Hours and hours of repetition led to a refinement of his craft. As he became more comfortable thinking in rhyme, Open Mike's rhyme schemes became more complex. Instead of just rhyming the vowel sounds at the end of words, he had come to rhyme multiple syllables and vary the focal point of his rhyming (for instance, *syllable* and *fillable* rhyme in three places and carry a matching rhythm).

VerBS also practiced alone. Originally from the Mar Vista Gardens area (a low-income housing project in Culver City), his accounts echoed Open Mike's. While hanging out in his bedroom listening to music, I asked VerBS how he practiced freestyling:

Sometimes I be listening to something and I get inspired. I be watching a TV show and I get inspired. Or I'll be just walking down the street, listening to some shit, and I'll get inspired. Like walking down the street, I just start rapping and think of some shit to rhyme with. Sometimes I'll just listen to instrumentals and just go on a writing tangent for a couple minutes and just start rhyming. People walking by probably think, "This guy's talking to himself." In the shower. Especially when I know I'm gonna be going to a battle that day, I just get so hyped and start rapping in the shower. Like, just try to think of some punch lines that I can recycle and use in the battle.

In addition to these flashes of inspiration, VerBS was methodical about his training. He spent many evenings expanding his vocabulary and creating word associations. One night on the corner, VerBS told me about his nightly ritual:

I go home every day, and I'll like find a page in the dictionary and start writing out a bunch of words. Then I'll try to write out as many words as I can that rhyme with each of the words. So one day, I might start off in the like middle of the dictionary and just try to find as many words that rhyme with "row." The next day, I'll do the same thing and just keep doing that 'til I got like a bunch of words that just rhyme with whatever I'm sayin'.

This practice, which included copying the definitions of thousands of words along with making lists of words that rhyme with them, gave VerBS a tremendous vocabulary—another part of developing lyrical dexterity. Much as they are for writers and poets, words are the building blocks of a rapper's craft. As wordsmiths, rappers strive for an expansive and intuitive command of language, storing away new and interesting words, idioms, and other vocalizations. This vocabulary stockpile gives rappers more resources to draw on.

Rappers also spend a lot of time practicing with others, even in the midst of other routine activities. For example, when we first met, VerBS had just graduated from Hamilton High School in the Mid-City area of Los Angeles. He was eighteen and still learning to freestyle, along with his friend CP. The two enjoyed cruising around the city, freestyling in CP's car.

On weekends, CP would pick up VerBS at his mom's apartment and

Figure 5. VerBS taking in the sites and sounds of the corner (photo courtesy of Kyle "VerBS" Guy)

the two would drive to Crenshaw Boulevard. It was the place to be. They'd often freestyle right on the boulevard. Back then, this area, featured in the film *Boyz n the Hood*, was a popular spot for cruising.[10] The lowriders, women, gang members, and patrolling police officers became part of a larger experience that spurred their creativity.[11]

VerBS also practiced at work. It helped him pass the time, working long hours in the stockrooms of clothing stores. There he'd practice with Alpha MC, a close friend and collaborator. VerBS and Alpha MC freestyled while picking up, passing, and unloading boxes of clothing. I got a five-minute taste of this game one night as I drove VerBS and Alpha MC home from Project Blowed. The two were living together at the time and constantly practicing. We were cruising on I-10 when they started freestyling in my car. At a break in the action, VerBS explained how they practiced:

> Talk to anybody at the Abercrombie & Fitch in Santa Monica, they be like, "That dude in the stockroom, all he does is rap!" Like people'll be talkin', like they'll say, "We need a stock check," and I be like, "Stock check, I'll drop sets, hot wet, I'm lyrical styles, you can't be killin' Kyle ..." Like I just be rapping anytime anybody says anything. I just start rapping about it.

Not all of his coworkers enjoyed hearing VerBS freestyle:

> One day, I was at work, I forgot what happened, it was this Latino cat I worked with, and I was freestyling about his name and he was like, "Man, if you don't shut up!" He got hot at me! He was like, "You shut the fuck up! I don't wanna hear you rapping all the fuckin' time!" I was like, "My bad, dog. I was just trying to pass the time." That's all I do at work is freestyle.

His incessant rhyming invaded other dimensions of his personal life. VerBS's friends could get frustrated: "That's how I am when I'm on the phone with people, too! Like the other person will say something, I'll repeat it, and I'll rap with it. People'll be like, 'Man, you rhyme with everything! What the fuck?'"

VerBS would forget to stop rhyming—even during romantic encounters with women, whose sweet nothings would set off a string of word associations. This became an issue one night, when his girlfriend caught him trying to rhyme responses to her intimate requests. "Wait a minute," I interrupted. "So you were hooking up and rhyming at the same time?" VerBS could barely contain his laughter: "Yeah, that's some shit, right? Sometimes I be doing it and don't even know."

* * *

Rappers practice freestyling obsessively. Much of this is done privately, away from others. Long showers and other quiet moments become impromptu practice sessions. Rappers begin to experiment with words and slowly building their confidence. And even though rappers eventually branch out and freestyle with others, practicing alone remains important in later stages of the career, too. It provides space to try out new ideas and modes of expression without risking public failure. Alone time provides a creative cocoon in which rappers can continue to evolve, pushing themselves and experimenting with the craft.

Over time, freestyling becomes a practice that organizes and animates their lives. Words and sounds encountered in conversations, at work, and in other mundane settings become springboards into free word associations. Some become so attuned to freestyling that they forget to stop thinking in rhyme and free associating during the most personal encounters.[12] This is all part of a deep habituation into freestyling.

But while practice is an important part of developing one's skills, rappers can improve only so much on their own, in private. To get better, they put their skills to the test at Project Blowed. Rappers looking to gauge their skills against others could be found hanging out on Thursday nights, freestyling in the ciphers (group sessions) on the street corner outside of Project Blowed. This marks another developmental milestone in the careers of aspiring rappers.

Enter the Cipher

There are typically between two and ten people huddled together in a cipher, but some of the largest ciphers I witnessed had twenty or thirty people clustered together in a circle. Some people rhyme a cappella, and others rhyme over instrumentals blasting from someone's car. Others rhyme over a person beatboxing, or creating a backing track of percussive noises with nothing but their mouths.[13]

Although ciphers can seem to flow effortlessly, there is a lot of co-ordination involved in making one work.[14] Group members develop and rely on local conventions that help facilitate and organize inter-actions. At Project Blowed, there are no formal time limits and no official order by which rappers take turns in the cipher. To transi-tion in and out of turns, people use verbal cues (like *yo*, *uh*, and *lis-ten*). They might also step slightly into the middle of a cipher, tap another rapper on the shoulder, or just start rhyming. All of these are ways rappers signal that they want a turn. Then the person cur-rently rhyming is expected to finish his or her last thought and stop rapping, providing space for the next person to rhyme. When people cooperate, these transitions feel seamless. It's hard to detect when one person starts and another finishes. But on occasion, these tran-sitions can be contentious and lead to battles (which I turn to in the next chapter).

Ciphers usually last from a couple of minutes to an hour. I've seen some last more than a few hours but others that sputtered in seconds. And they aren't just fun ways for rappers to spend time with their friends. Much like the open mic, ciphers allow rappers to showcase their talents and evaluate one another. Rappers keep tabs on others' performance over time, sizing themselves up against potential collabo-rators and competition.

* * *

Once they enter a cipher, rappers face a dilemma. Rappers come to the cipher armed with a stockpile of words, rhyme patterns, and other lyri-cal tricks—lifelines if they feel they're "falling off," unable to sustain a smooth and unbroken freestyle in the cipher.[15] A failure here is a great source of embarrassment and can work against a rapper's local repu-tation. But as I mentioned earlier, rappers also run the risk of an even more serious knock against their reputation: being mocked for "spitting writtens"—the equivalent of being painted as a fraud—if they rely too heavily on their stock rhymes.

Nocando, who was known for his ferocious freestyling skills, told me, "Everybody, I don't care who you are, or how dope you think you are, everybody falls off now and then—it's just, I mean, it's part of free-styling. Everybody has their go-tos and premeds." But rappers are care-ful not to use the same premeditated rhymes too frequently or around the same crowd. They have to selectively pull from different catalogs of words, rhymes, and styles that have less chance of being discovered by their audience. The trick, then, is learning how to *perform* sponta-neity, disguising years of practice as spur-of-the-moment inspiration. As VerBS explained:

> Every MC does this. You will think of some dope-ass punch lines that could kinda go to anybody. And you will use it repeatedly. I've used punch lines over before, against one dude, and then you got to a battle somewhere you haven't been before and you use it against another dude. Cuz people be like, "He said that the other day! This nigga's wack!" No offense to Diablo, but he spits the same sixteens [bars or lines] every time he's in the cipher.

Rappers use various techniques, mostly based on misdirection, to dis-guise their writtens as spontaneous. At the most basic level, rappers will subtly pause while freestyling so it appears that they're thinking, searching for a rhyme. Flawliss told me, "Yeah, I mean, the most basic shit is when you, like, say your rhyme and then you stutter or pause. This shit kinda makes it look like you don't know what you're saying. Like, it's some real sneaky shit."

Strategic pauses and stutters only disguise so much once rappers have used their rhymes publicly. To further camouflage their writtens, rappers will bury their stock lines in different rhyme sequences, making it harder for casual listeners to spot them. In the following examples, E.Crimsin used "You can't understand that. / Like the Dow Jones and the NASDAQ!" in two different freestyles. In the first cipher I recorded:

E.Crimsin is rapping to Bobby, Nupe, Savage Terrain, and a few other regulars next to Bobby's Maroon Toyota Camry. He's really amped tonight and projects his voice over the beats playing from Bobby's car, "Super serve, homeboy, spit you out like chew toys! *You can't understand that. Like the Dow Jones and the NASDAQ!*"

Then, nearly a year later, I recorded:

E.Crimsin is rapping with VerBS, Alpha MC, Sahtyre, and a few others on the curb. Alpha MC is in the middle of "chopping," a style of rapping where the emcee raps doubly fast to produce a very quickly syncopated style of rapping. E.Crimsin enters the cipher abruptly, "Haaaadoooken! I'm the levitator, serve you now and later. Nigga! *You can't understand that, like the Dow Jones and the NASDAQ!*"

I was curious about this and asked E.Crimsin if he ever recycled rhymes. Wary at first, he insisted, "I always spit frees [freestyles]." So I stepped back and asked instead about other rappers' reusing lines. Then he was happy to oblige:

That nigga Flawliss always be sayin' things like [imitating his loud, shrill voice], "You don't want it with me!" [laughs]. I don't know, niggas be havin' they things, my nigga. Like, I'm trying to drag out my words now. Like, that nigga, Steelo, does this a lot. He'll say like [imitating his slow, growling voice] "ground and pound." This gives me a little time to think of what the fuck I'm 'bout to say next. Or I might just say, "Fuck it, I'ma freestyle," or just something that buys me some time.

So in addition to stringing together various rhyme schemes, rappers pull from a series of linguistic devices to buy themselves time. They use stock phrases or elongated syllables to provide a moment of thought about the next rhyme sequence or phrase.

As I asked around, though, rappers at Project Blowed remained understandably tight-lipped about using writtens. Not only is getting caught embarrassing; it also discredits the positive face-work they've done to establish themselves as freestyle rappers. Rappers know their rhymes are always under close scrutiny. They know their peers can become suspicious if their freestyling sounds too polished or coherent. I witnessed this one night on the corner when "Dro" was wowing a crowd of onlookers with his freestyling. "Crayze," however, wasn't impressed. He suspected that Dro was spitting writtens. Dro rhymed:

> My motto is survival,
> rivals get locked down in the gang modules,
> members only, killin' phonies,
> I got my own homies turnin' on me,
> tryin' to dome me,
> it's street prophecy,
> real's inside of me,
> ghetto prodigy,
> teachin' lethal philosophies,
> possibly intoxicated,
> can't near nigga fade me,
> I'm stayin' shaded,
> I pack heats like incinerators,
> meet ya fate like full grown from the chrome,
> the same nigga ya told on,
> got rolled on,
> follow me to mortician's like autopsies,
> I will smash your shit bags like colostomies,
> run with monster beat,
> elites and squadrons,
> breakin' laws and dentals causin' major problems.

Crayze whispered to me, "Dude can rap, but he ain't freestylin'. That's some writtens." Choice, by contrast, was completely sold: after Dro dropped from the cipher, Choice gave him daps and said, "Dayum!" Dro peered over at Crayze and said: "It's all free, though, my nigga. Ain't nothin' but some free!" This is a typical announcement made by rappers to downplay people's doubts about their freestyling authenticity. The truth of the promise is secondary. Instead, these kinds of meta-commentary are ways rappers try to control the situation. They actively construct their rapping as spontaneous—"off the dome."

Interestingly, the close relations between rappers lead to another dilemma around calling each other out. Rappers listen closely and develop a working knowledge of other people's tendencies. This is part of learning and developing within a communal scene like Project Blowed, and it can be a strategic advantage in battles. I first learned about this one night, standing on the outer edges of a cipher with CP. We were listening to Flawliss freestyle. I later recorded the following:

> CP is standing toward the back of a cipher, listening to Flawliss rap. He turns to me and says, "These sixteens are really helping Flawliss."
>
> Confused, I ask CP, "What are sixteens?"
>
> CP continues, "Well, Flawliss is a lot like me; he'll write four bars [lines], then actually freestyle, then use another four, and then freestyle."
>
> Clarifying his description, I ask CP, "So you freestyle and then draw from stuff that you've already written?"
>
> CP nods along, "Yeah . . . exactly . . . he's cool and all, but he ain't comin' off the top."

Over time, I started noticing this more. With Flawliss, I learned that he liked to say things like "You don't want it with me" as a stock phrase to set up any number of rhyme combinations. Once he rhymed, "You don't want it with me, / You got a better off chance having sex with your knee." On another occasion, "You don't want it with me, / You probably fall asleep from the weed." This was just one of many stock phrases Flawliss would combine with alternate follow-up rhymes.

Ironically, these same relations between rappers also prevent many from calling each other out. Close-knit communities rely on unspoken allowances between group members, and calling someone out would shake up the existing relations and could damage a reputation. If a person has been caught on previous occasions, then he might now be seen as a repeat offender, a fraud.[16] So calling someone out is a heavy move, and one that young men who see each other weekly don't take lightly.

Moreover, the person who gets exposed might feel betrayed, particularly if he had helped the person calling him out save face in the past. When this happens, the person called out is likely to lose trust, realizing that the relationship with the person who called him out was not what it appeared to be. In many ways, calling someone out violates what Erving Goffman describes as "protective face work,"[17] the general rule that family and friends tend to look out for one another and help each other save face during potentially embarrassing situations.

Finally, rappers are concerned about how *they* will be seen after calling out multiple people. The scrutinizing can backfire. Regularly exposing others for "spitting writtens" risks inviting reciprocal scrutiny. Rappers who regularly police others worry that their own rhymes will be scrutinized and audited more closely by others. Most rappers don't want to risk being a target in their own scene. All of these dynamics discourage rappers from calling one another out all the time.

Still, rappers occasionally toss out the accusation, even if in jest. One night, "Sheena G," one of the few female regulars in the scene, accused CP of spitting writtens. From where I was standing, it felt like Sheena G was playfully ribbing CP, who seemed embarrassed and upset that she would call him out. According to my notes:

> CP, Sheena G, VerBS, and SS are all sitting in Sheena G's white sedan rapping with each other. CP is using a line that I've heard him say in other ciphers and battles, "As for music, the raps is stupid, fuck fallin' in love, cuz I'm clappin' cupid, unless she lookin' like Stacey Dash in *Clueless*, a vibrant thing, but I don't act like Q-Tip . . ." Sheena G starts grinning ear-to-ear at first, and then pretends to be writing something with her right hand. . . . This irritates CP, who stops rapping for a moment and insists that he's freestyling. Sheena G starts laughing now and asks CP, "Why you spittin' writtens?" CP frowns at her and then they get into a heated argument as to whether or not his rhymes are "written" or "off the top."

I asked Sheena G about this incident a week later while she, SS, and I were hanging out beneath the awning of the Vision Theater (a performance theater next door to Project Blowed). She explained that she had heard CP use the "Stacey Dash in *Clueless*" line several times before but had never said anything. She said she'd been partially kidding around with CP but quickly realized he didn't find it funny.

* * *

The cipher is a testing ground for rappers who wanted to make a name for themselves and earn the respect of their peers. Rappers knew that they were being evaluated and were eager to put on a good showing. Most inevitably drew from a well of prewritten rhymes, part of a larger repertoire of techniques a rapper uses to avoid "falling off," or not being able to freestyle without stopping.

Minor mistakes and imperfections were not held against rappers, so long as they didn't completely fall off. In fact, rappers usually gained a degree of respect for a person who could maintain their flow despite gaffes and other minor disruptions in their flow. They earn respect for their resiliency in the face of adversity. The key, however, is for rappers to camouflage their prewritten rhymes with different techniques. Some use writtens only when they absolutely need them, whereas others use them sparingly and around different people. Others try to dispel suspicion by announcing that they are freestyling or coming off the top. And then there are those who pause, stutter, or creatively mix and match their rhymes to conceal them from discovery. All of this is part of the *performance* of spontaneity.

But by the rules of the scene, rappers who use their prewritten rhymes indiscriminately run the risk of being called out for spitting writtens. It's one of the graver accusations in the scene, exposing cracks in rappers' lyricism and self-presentation. Rappers face various social sanctions for getting caught. The person who comes across cool, collected, and creative in ciphers is suddenly cast in a new light: he looks like a fraud or a cheater.

Further, those who call a person out are making a bold move. In one fell swoop, they risk damaging their relationship with the person being called out. Plus, regulars remember when they've been called out. If people call out others enough times, they invite intense scrutiny back onto themselves, making their own lives more difficult in the process.

Freestyling is a fun, spontaneous, invigorating practice. Ciphers provide a proving ground with less pressure than an open mic or battle, and they let rappers flex their lyrical dexterity. But the informal social rules that exist around acknowledged but unstated prewritten rhymes and the process of calling someone out or being called out make ciphers a tricky social space, too. Friendships are forged and fractured in freestyling.

Biting and Flipping

Rappers are quick to assert that their rhymes are original. This is a big part of the underground world, and I saw it time and time again at Project Blowed. Rappers talk about themselves as rugged individualists, always staying true to themselves. Once, when I saw "JR" complimented on his freestyling, he replied, "It's all *me*, my nigga. That's just how *I* do."

Extending from this, rappers also try to avoid "biting," or plagiarizing one another. Biting is a serious offense in hip hop culture.[18] It can delegitimize a person's claims to skills. In "Just Don't Give a Fuck," Eminem rhymes, "You wacker than the motherfucker you bit your style from / You ain't gonna sell two copies if you press a double album."[19] Biting is a violation of the implied ethics and norms among underground artists.

But there's some irony here. Although most rappers are against people completely biting their lyrics or style, they do routinely borrow ideas from one another. Like research teams who develop ideas together and work on complementary projects, rappers who rhyme together borrow ideas from one another. The cipher is a great incubator of spontaneous creativity. A person gains exposure in the cipher, able to access multiple rappers who have different styles and rhyme patterns. As such, rappers build on each other, taking words, phrases, rhyme schemes, and even styles of rhyming from other rappers. They "flip" rhymes and styles. The key difference between biting and flipping is that biting is wholesale plagiarism of rhymes, schemes, or even styles. Flipping is a *selective* use of another person's rhymes or style, a soft version of borrowing another person's ideas. "Flipping a rhyme" is loosely derived from the way drug dealers talk about "flipping" a large sum of drugs by cutting the drugs to a less pure version in order to make additional profit. In both cases, a person takes an original product and infuses it with his personal touch, putting a personal stamp on it.

I saw this one early one morning, when most of the "tourists" (non-regulars) had left the block. The remaining core regulars seemed to relax and ramp up their efforts once they were among their fellow Blowedians. Flawliss, CP, Open Mike, Flako, and others were in a cipher next to CP's car, a gray Honda Civic customized with "Lambo" (Lamborghini) doors. The doors flew open, resulting in a mini-spectacle. We all stood by admiring his ride. Beaming with pride, CP popped an instrumental CD into his stereo and cranked up the volume, flaunting the power of his subwoofers and providing a backing track for the cipher. I pulled out my camera and documented the next hour of freestyling. In the following cipher different rappers borrow words from each other that help ignite their own creative process. Moments when rappers are rhyming at the same time are in italics, and moments when they "flip" each other's rhymes are also in italics. In the following exchange, note how Flawliss uses the word *world*, which Open Mike then picks up and flips. After that, Open Mike introduces the word *astronaut*, which Flawliss picks up and flips in his next turn:

F   . . . I wanna introduce y'all niggas to Flawliss*world*, nigga, I am nice like Flawliss girls, I hold it down like I got Flawliss curls, like '88 baby, I'm bustin' the 8 crazy . . .

OM   And I'm doper than all the *worlds*, put me at the top, like I said, 'cause I'm in the cipher, or the fucking sky like an *astronaut*, I'm at Mars, lookin' at these cats that drive cars, I'm way far away from that, I'm a crazy cat, to show you that the place you're at is not where you need to be, you're not at the right frequency, so you can't deep frequency, so you can't be as deep as *me* . . .

F   *Yo*, my nigga say he high like an *astronaut*, well I'll beat you up
chew you like after snot, after the Glock, after the cop, I come
back and beat you with a half of a rock, that's horrible, nasty
gruesome shit, Flawliss got hoes like the deuce-some, newsome
twins, gluesome, newsome . . . somebody better go elusive . . .

Later, CP introduces a rhyme with a reference to *B-12* and *C-12*. Open
Mike flips this idea and references the Detroit-based rap group *D-12*:

CP   I still driving, hand me the coop, fuck it I'll hang myself, hand me
the noose, nigga I can see Satan, waiting in hell, after that they
waitin' with shells, I don't care man, I wait with the twelve, *B-12*,
details, same color as a *C-12*, as a seashell, I don't know, nigga you
can see this, fuck yeah man, *email* . . .

OM   *And* it's Bizarre from *D-12*, and my record will be shelved, I'm
not independent, Open is fuckin' interdependent, that means
I'm dependent on symbiosis, my rhymes are way past dopeness,
I'm fuckin' ferocious, Tyrannosaurus Rex, takin' their whores'
cassettes and put 'em in my pocket, I got power like fucking . . .
eye sockets . . .

And finally, CP later introduces the idea of people "passing" marijuana
around to smoke in his rhymes. Flawliss flips the term and uses the verb
pass to jump-start his turn:

CP   *Yo*, I hop like a six-four, bounce like a hundred, watch CP and
[unclear] smoke sumptin', yes nigga got me an ounce in the sack,
after that you can take an ounce to the hat, now spring back, puff,
puff, puff, *pass, pass it me*, after that *pass* me a beat, 'cause I'll *pass*
up a free, never *pass* up an offerin', after that niggas all lungs
coughin' in . . .

F   [indecipherable] Y'all *passed* up the coffins when, when I come
back and offer them, Flawliss I got more life to offer them,
offer twins, matter fact offer brothers too, matter fact I never

s-s-stutter fool, matter fact my flows are so butter woo, but you don't understand that, so pick another move . . .

In different ways, all the emcees were borrowing words, ideas, and phrases from one another. For example, in his first turn, Flawliss rhymes, "I wanna introduce y'all niggas to Flawlissworld." Open Mike plays off the world theme to rhyme, "And I'm doper than all the worlds, put me at the top, like I said, 'cause I'm in the cipher, or the fucking . . . sky like an astronaut." Flawliss grabs *astronaut* and jumps into his next turn: "My nigga say he high like an astronaut." In the next turn, CP rhymes, "I wait with the twelve, B-12, details, same color as a C-12." His use of *twelve* becomes a springboard for Open Mike, who rhymes, "It's Bizarre from D-12, and my record will be shelved." In the excerpt just above, CP rhymes, "Puff, puff, puff, *pass, pass* it me, after that pass me a beat," from which Flawliss springs to "Y'all *passed* up the coffins when." Words, idioms, and other themes introduced into the cipher become creative springboards for everyone to borrow and use.

In addition, rappers are inspired by styles. Some will temporarily mirror a fellow rapper's cadence or overall flow to launch into their turn in a cipher. During one session, Wildchild, Big Flossy's younger cousin who lived minutes from Leimert Park, began rapping in double-time (shown in italic text), speeding up his delivery to about twice the speed of other rappers. This inspired Flawliss to do the same:

w   *Bullshit, cuz I pull quick, 45 hollow tips in a full clip, leave a nigga*
    bleedin' from his upper region, both of these slugs go through his heart
    he, see me in the street, hope he touchin' that heat in the chest . . .
f   All right, you gotta do it like this now emcees . . .
w   *. . . walkin' in the house . . .*
f   *Better, rip that better, get that better, bust that, bust that letter, Flaw,*
    Flaw, drif draff, I forgot the letter, bust that shit, I divide that shit,
    I decline that shit, when I climb that shit, my mind is sick, I'm back
    double-double-timed the shit, whoa!, better slow that, slow that,
    hold back, slow that, slow that, give it back and f'dumb to do that,

> do two better flow that, all I do is bust shit 'til your shoulders clap,
> hold that back, mold that back, show that fact, and I gave you that
> punch line show that black . . .

Wildchild's double-time rapping inspired others to continue that tempo. Flawliss soon announced, "All right, you gotta do it like this now emcees," then rapped in double-time himself. It's common for rappers to piggyback like this.

But the collaborative structure of ciphers can also be constraining. Rappers who want to jump into the cipher are expected to build off the person who rhymes before them. They feel a pressure to sustain what the person before them set in motion. Starting something anew is not only abrupt but also shows a person's lack of lyrical and stylistic flexibility. This means that rappers should at least match the skills of a previous rhymer or create a seamless blend between their turn and the previous one. Like other skills, rappers need to learn how to flip someone else's rhyme, and then pull the cipher toward their own style.

A similar thing occurred when Wildchild introduced a new rap style in the cipher that caught Flawliss's attention. Although Flawliss rarely, if ever, "chopped," he wanted to keep the cipher's flow. By rapping like Wildchild, Flawliss was showing his appreciation for the other rapper's skills and bridging his turn by temporarily adopting Wildchild's style. Flawliss helped reduce the abruptness of his own transition. In this way, rappers collaborate to create an ongoing, seamless flow in ciphers. Though the young men are all competing for attention and respect, they are also collaborating on a shared project: a memorable cipher they'll talk about in the future.

* * *

Robert Faulkner and Howard Becker note that jazz players often abandon their own ideas in favor of the "best" or most interesting idea that emerges from a group.[20] These ideas usually come from the player everyone else considers the most central figure (often—though not exclusively—the most experienced person in the group). In coming together, members agree to let that person dictate how a group plays and will then follow his or her lead. Thus, jazz groups work only insofar as members all subscribe to these working rules. Individuals have to suspend their personal interests to play within an evolving group framework and create something that swings.

Although rappers commonly defer to each other in a cipher and let the person before them shape the style, tempo, and even content of the cipher, there is also a subtle face-work in the act of following another person's lead. These are not just selfless actions to keep the cipher flowing smoothly: switching one's style or adopting another person's suggestions can be its own kind of self-aggrandizing. These are moves people use to display their lyrical dexterity.

Rappers borrow snippets of lyrics or rhyme styles and add a signature twist to make it their own. Thus, in addition to working together and deferring to senior members or those with good ideas, there's a moral dimension to how to sample another person's work. When it's done well, flipping is as much a reputation booster as rocking the crowd at an open mic.

Conclusion

Rappers at Project Blowed take pride in their ability to freestyle. At the core, freestyling is part of the rich history at Project Blowed. Up-and-coming rappers look up to old-school veterans who paved the way for freestyling and have worked hard at their craft.

Freestyling is also a way for some rappers to distinguish themselves from mainstream artists, whose music is often critiqued (if not dismissed) in the underground. During my time at Project Blowed, many young men would tell me that they "weren't feeling" mainstream hip hop because it was filled with misogynistic, violent, negative, and stylistically simple lyrics and hooks. It was a common sentiment, and it helped differentiate what was happening at Project Blowed from anything else in mainstream hip hop.

Still, while freestyling is an awesome skill, emcees, fans, and people writing about freestyling tend to romanticize it. Following the lead of emcees, these collective accounts treat freestyling as a type of pure, spontaneous rhyming. Rappers seem to magically come up with words and rhymes on the fly. Audiences eat this stuff up. But a careful look at how people *learn* to freestyle reveals a different picture and, perhaps, an even more impressive skill set at work.

Although rappers can experience moments when they seem to connect words together magically, aspiring rappers usually spend countless hours practicing, drilling, and learning how to think in rhyme. They become obsessed, and the obsession helps habituate them to the art of freestyling. Some, like Open Mike, rap during alone time, when being in a quiet, private setting allows them to push their creative limits and try out new things without fear of immediate peer judgment. When routine practice becomes an obsessive activity, rappers can forget to turn it off. They continue thinking in rhyme, even around people who are not rappers or interested in freestyling. Over time, though, rappers develop stock word associations that they can use to avoid falling off when they're handed a mic. They become comfortable improvising from a well-worn catalog of rhymes.

Rappers also face a dilemma: they want to do their best in ciphers to gain the respect of their peers. This means that they inevitably will draw from a deep reserve of rhymes. But they can't do so indiscriminately. If they come across as sounding too polished or rehearsed, they can be accused of spitting writtens, a source of shame. Likewise, it's easy to miss how much and how freely rappers borrow from one another. Underground rappers are vehemently opposed to biting or wholesale plagiarism, but they aren't opposed to selectively flipping each other's ideas.

In the bigger scheme of things, freestyling leaves an imprint on the lives of young men at Project Blowed. Sure, each is looking to shine in the cipher, but all the young men are primed for collaboration. Ciphers work only when everyone takes turns and works to sustain the cipher. Rappers have to bow out gracefully, jump in when the action stalls, and look for ways to build and sustain the session. This kind of socialization is part and parcel of what many young people experience in sports teams, clubs, and other group settings, but it's not readily available to young men who grow up in resource-scarce areas like South Central LA. The cipher—and hip hop culture more generally—is a context in which young Black men who live in such areas develop a sense of camaraderie and teamwork. This stands in stark contrast to gang culture, which promotes confrontational and adversarial interactions on the streets. In this safe space, rappers can express themselves, express admiration for one another, and find fellowship in the act of rhyming together.

4

The Battle

It was 10:30 on a Thursday night and Dibiase was out on the block. He was bumping beats out of his little white boom box, covered in peeling stickers. People were freestyling and everyone was relaxed. The mood was light and the cipher was humming along. Then "Bugsy" showed up.

At first, he stood at the edge of the cipher, gazing into the action and bobbing his head. Slowly, he crept closer to the middle, looking for a way to squeeze into the mix. As he weaved through the huddled crowd, I noticed Lyraflip roll his eyes. Flawliss asked, "Is that him?" Lyraflip nodded and mumbled something about Bugsy walking around the corner trying to battle everyone. He was a newcomer and seemed to be trying too hard. Lyraflip and others felt that Bugsy was "fucking up the vibe."

As Bugsy entered the cipher, Flawliss announced, "Man, I'ma serve this nigga! You say he dis you?":

All right, look, you fuckin' Puff Daddy
You 'bout to have a rough badly
Day, Baby's daddy
He look like everybody's fuckin' baby's daddy
'Cept he's only 5′2″
I'ma try not to rip you from jiu jitsu
Look at your glasses
Look at him he's handsome
He's moving around wit' half of a suit on [Bugsy holds in his laughter]
Nigga betta go before I get half of a shoot on!

Flawliss mimed shooting Bugsy in the chest with a machine gun. A few people laughed, but Bugsy still had a chance to redeem himself. Who knew? Maybe he could hold his own.

But Bugsy looked and sounded shook. Most of his rhymes were hard to hear, and the more he rapped, the more he seemed to be outmatched. I felt embarrassed *for* him. Flawliss jumped back in, swiftly ending the battle in the second round:

Like he really wanna try me?
This muthafucka got a suit on
and a muthafuckin' dirty-ass white T!
How the fuck does he spite me?
You ain't gotta like me,
but bitch bite me!
I'm the best on the block,
you betta come through,
and niggas like you,
I wrestle a cop,
just to get over that nigga,
make the rest of you pop,
fuck ya face—nigga, make the rest of you stomp!
Everybody in this bitch do the A-town stomp! [Flawliss starts dancing]
Nigga I'm the best nonstop!
How the fuck ya gonna see me though?
This nigga rappin' like this nigga got a suit on—under it he got a Speedi-o!

The "Speedi-o" line got everyone laughing. Even a perfectly timed rebuttal would have fallen on deaf ears. Bugsy gave Flawliss daps, conceding the battle. After a few exchanged words, he slumped away in defeat.

A few hours later, Flawliss, E.Crimsin, and I were talking on the corner. Flawliss was still basking in his glory: "Man, you shoulda been here earlier! I served this nigga bad! He got all quiet and shit!" E.Crimsin smiled, "That's crazy. You always servin' out here!" I added, "You also started dancing! That was awesome!" Flawliss kept laughing, "Yeah! That's right! I almost forgot about that! I started doing the 'A-Town stomp'! Sometimes I don't even be realizing what I do!" We all shared a good laugh.

* * *

In the previous chapter, I showed how rappers cooperate to make ciphers work without formal rules. They take turns so that everyone gets a chance to rhyme. They use different phrases and utterances to transition to their turn. And perhaps most important, they become a familiar face on the corner. Although newcomers are sometimes viewed with suspicion, regulars will defer to their peers. Blowedians give each other small allowances in the cipher, letting other regulars interrupt them and take a turn without sanction.

But despite these conventions, there are still moments when rappers feel disrespected while rhyming together. The loose structure of ciphers makes them ripe for conflict. A rapper can feel "cut off," like another person is "hoggin' the mic," or like someone is "throwing subliminals," or indirect disses, at them. In these situations, the offended party might call out or challenge the person with whom he has a problem.[1]

The person who gets called out can rise to the challenge and step to his opponent, ready to battle—or he can back down. But young men risk losing face if they shy away from being called out. The person who backs down comes across looking shook, unsure of his abilities.

In these ways, battles are a creative twist on the identity challenges Elijah Anderson describes as part of the "code of the street."[2] According to this code, a young man who is disrespected and verbally challenged must show "nerve" and the willingness to become violent if challenged. If he does not respond that way, he gets a reputation for being a "punk" or someone who can be "rolled on" and attacked by others. The rise of easily accessible firearms and other weapons has made these identity challenges dangerous—even fatal.

Hip hop and battling transform the methods through which young men negotiate perceived disrespect. People who come into the scene are quickly socialized into these rules and learn from Blowedians that violence is not locally tolerated. In battles, young men rely on their lyrical skills, creativity, and humor rather than their fists or guns. Young men who "catch feelings," or try to escalate battles into physical violence, lose face. They are frowned upon for not being able to contain their emotions or match their opponent's skill. Anger and other emotional outbursts tarnish a person's reputation in the battle rap scene. People who become upset are seen as not confident in their rhyming abilities. And in an inversion of the street code, locals see such a person as someone who has to resort to violence instead of "keeping it hip hop."

In this chapter, I dissect battles, showing how they begin and how people seize advantages. I conclude by looking at the collaborative work done by rappers and their audience that keeps battles from escalating into physical violence. For young men who are otherwise surrounded by violence, wars of words are important ways to resolve perceived disrespect.

You Wanna Battle?

Feeling Cut Off and Hoggin' the Mic

I first learned what it was like to be "cut off" while hanging out with Flawliss in Long Beach. It was a sunny Saturday afternoon and we were sipping iced coffees outside a café. He was scheduled to enter a round-robin-style battle later that evening. Unlike the street corner rap battles at Project Blowed, this one was on a concert stage to compete against other rappers for a money pot.

I asked about his experiences battling on the corner outside Project Blowed. Flawliss explained that most battles could be traced back to disputes over turn taking in the cipher. In his account, a turn-taking rhythm arises fairly organically in a cipher. People watch and then estimate how long each person is rhyming for. It isn't an exact science, but people who want to rhyme get a sense of how many bars, or lines, they should let others have before jumping in. When he didn't get the time others were getting, Flawliss felt cut off:

Figure 6. Flawliss feeling good after a freestyle session on the corner (photo courtesy of Kyle "VerBS" Guy)

So, say everybody is spitting sixteen-bar lines in a cipher. You know when it's your turn, you got sixteen bars to spit. And say I spit, like, four bars, and some dude jumps in and starts rapping loud. When that happens, I feel like I didn't get to say what the fuck I was about to say! It was my turn, fairly, and he cut me off—like some kid cutting you off at lunch and shit when you're in high school. Like, "What the fuck you doing? I'm right here, homie!" [laughs]. So that's how that it is with that shit too, ya know? You don't want nobody cuttin' you off, so then that causes beef because I feel, like, just disrespected. So now, I'ma say something!

As I described in the previous chapter, rappers use verbal and non-verbal cues to show that they want a turn. The sting of an interruption can be softened when a rapper prefaces his turn by saying "yo," "uh," "listen," or other utterances that signal a transition. In truth, rappers can say just about anything to communicate that they want a turn. The cues give the person rhyming time to finish their thought and transition out.

But sometimes rappers will not cue themselves in, and their entrance is abrupt. Cutting others off raises the likelihood of a dispute. Flawliss remembered:

> The hardest thing that I've had problems with is when you just come to a cipher. Like, if there's already a cipher going on, niggas don't know what's going on, they just walked up. "I walk up, and I feel like rappin'! I'm all amped and shit!" Like this one time, I walked up, and I jumped right in. I didn't know how long the other guy had been rappin'. He might have just said three words before I walked up, and I just cut him off. After that, he wanted to battle me, ya know? But I didn't know, I just walked up!

Rappers also call out people who hog the mic. Mic hogs dominate the cipher, but most rappers believe that everyone should have a turn to rhyme. The person who rhymes too frequently violates this tacit rule, says Open Mike: "You can't mic hog. If you rapping and somebody else is ready to come in, you have to let them get their turn. If you keep rapping over them, then, you mic hoggin', you know, you're trying to start something. That's disrespectful."

I saw "Cane" call Flawliss out for mic hoggin' one night on the block. Cane wasn't a regular in the scene but would always jump into ongoing ciphers. He had a husky voice and was known for identifying more as a gangsta rapper. Flawliss and a few others were in the cipher when this happened:

> Cane leans forward into the cipher and starts rapping, "I leave a nigga depressed . . ." Flawliss does not stop rapping. Cane grimaces toward CP, who's standing across from him. He waits for a few more moments and starts rapping again; this time both Flawliss and Cane rap at the same time. After about ten seconds where both are rapping at the same time,

Cane stops and looks over at CP again and starts grumbling about Flawliss: "C'mon, I'm not even trying to battle, open it up!" Flawliss stops rapping a few moments later, after which time Cane starts dissing Flawliss,
"But see, everybody trying to spit some hot shit, but this nigga [points at
Flawliss] always wanna control the topics!"

After a few more failed attempts at rhyming, Cane called out Flawliss
for mic hoggin', although Flawliss didn't seem to take Cane's subliminal
challenge seriously. He laughed it off but quieted down quickly, giving
Cane the stage. Flawliss's nonresponse skirted a battle.

There are subtle differences between these two pathways into battles.
The first is temporal. Unlike the cutoff, which occurs in one particularly charged moment, mic hoggin' is an offense that accumulates over
time. For example, Cane's irritation with Flawliss increased after his repeated attempts to come into the cipher. The conflict wasn't contained
in a single instant—it had festered.

Cutoffs are also interpersonal offenses, whereas the accusation of
mic hoggin' is (at least ostensibly) a collective one. Those who feel cut
off are upset that they aren't being allowed to finish what they started.
While rhyming, rappers develop creative momentum and feel that
they are "heating up," or getting into a lyrical groove. When someone else hurriedly transitions into a turn, rappers can feel irked that
they didn't get the chance to ride out their creative wave.[3] In contrast,
a person upset at a mic hog is bothered that a rapper isn't sharing the
stage or is robbing others of their chance to rhyme. Interestingly, the
person who calls out the mic hog is often the one who most immediately feels that he or she isn't being given a chance to rhyme. Flawliss
would later tell me, "Usually the person calling someone out like that
[for mic hoggin'] is the person who wants to rhyme. They just do it
that way, so it looks less selfish." In one move, then, the person who
calls out someone for mic hoggin' can give off the impression of being
a moral actor who cares deeply about preserving the collective rules
and rituals that organize the cipher. But there are multiple and perhaps competing motivations that compel someone to call out another
person this way.

Allowances for Friends

How a rapper responds to an interruption is also shaped by his relationship with the person interrupting him. Rappers make allowances for friends and close collaborators that they wouldn't freely extend to others. A stranger's interruptions hold different meanings than a friend's. Among friends, there's a rapport—they may rap together often or know one another from outside the scene. Instead of treating these interruptions as a form of disrespect, rappers let friends and other regular acquaintances have their turn.

Newcomers and other outsiders, however, get little leeway. Near the end of my first year in the field, I hung out with CP, Big Flossy, and "SS"—three friends who often freestyled together because, as CP explained, "We just vibe together." For months, I hung around these three and a few other revolving emcees. They'd get together and freestyle for hours without interruption.

All of this changed one night when "Lil E" (a short Latino rapper) tried to get into their cipher. I had never seen Lil E rhyme with CP and his crew. He showed up unannounced and started bobbing his head outside the cipher. Without forewarning, he started rapping. Big Flossy reacted swiftly. "Hold on, man! You need to stop! You a bitch nigga, dog! I can make it pop! Don't you know I'm a gangsta, nigga?! Don't you know I could break you, nigga!?" Surprised, Lil E tried to muster up a response. But after stringing together a few unimpressive rhymes, he slumped away in defeat.

The following week, Lil E showed up on the block. Big Flossy nudged me and said, "That nigga needs to leave rappin' alone. He always gettin' his ass served!"

I replied, "Yeah, you really served his ass last week!"

"Man, you already know, Jeeyoung! I hate doin' a nigga like that, but sometimes he ask for it! He shouldn't be gettin' in there with the big boys when he can't spit!"[4] Big Flossy went on about Lil E's rhymes: "He kept trying to get in when we was just vibing, doing our thing. He ain't cool with us like that, so he should've gone somewhere else."

Here was one of the unspoken tensions on the corner at Project Blowed. Although young men talked about how everyone should have a chance to rhyme, there were plenty of situations when this convention was not observed. Friends gravitated together. Young men who have a shared history together on the block also rhymed together. Sometimes, they treated these sessions like they were closed to the general public, becoming irritated when others tried to come into *their* cipher and join in on *their* fun.

Similarly, some of them also believed that less experienced rappers and newcomers should defer to more experienced regulars, that newcomers would stall the creative energy generated in a cipher. This happens particularly when a cipher is gaining creative momentum. Rappers' playing off each other seamlessly leads to a kind of collective effervescence, and a rapper who cannot match the others' skill level can dampen the vibe and draw the ire of others.

Rappers liked to talk about ciphers as open group freestyle sessions. But there were tensions between what people said and what they did in practice. Although ciphers were group freestyle sessions, they also became sites of exclusion, where groups closed ranks and shut out others who weren't part of their social circle.

Subliminals

I first learned about subliminals while hanging out with Flawliss. "Major L"—a lanky Black rapper in his late twenties—stood opposite Flawliss. When Flawliss rapped, Major L made pained faces, like he was unimpressed with everything coming out of Flawliss's mouth. Major L waited for Flawliss to finish his turn and responded with a line that came across as an indirect challenge: "I'm tighter than all these niggas!" When he said this, he glared at Flawliss, evidence that he was challenging Flawliss without formally calling him out.

Flawliss nudged me. "Oh, OK. This guy wants to battle. He finna get served!" Major L overheard him and stared again at Flawliss, dropping three more indirect challenges: "Niggas think they dope, but they really not. I step up in the cipher and I rule the spot!" Major L wasn't explicitly calling out Flawliss, but Flawliss was sure the rapper was "throwing subliminals," or indirect disses, his way.

Flawliss squared his body to Major L, showing that he was ready to battle. Once Major L was done rhyming, Flawliss responded with rhymes that played on Major L's Grambling State University sweatshirt: "Nigga got a jersey like he just *rambled!* Your hair [pointing to Major L] is nappy, it looks like some eggs got *scrambled!*" Major L looked pissed off. Nodding, he waited for his chance to respond. The battle was on.

Flawliss had responded to Major L's sideways disses with his own, and both had come to an impromptu understanding that they were going to battle. Major L nodded at Flawliss and announced, "OK, this fat nigga wanna get served." The two went back and forth, round and round, rhyming and responding.

This battle opened more insights into how one-on-one battles work outside Project Blowed. Rappers often say indirect things in the cipher that provoke others. Sometimes this is intended, and sometimes it is just chance. Many rappers like to boast in their rhymes, so it's not always clear if a person is in fact trying to indirectly lure others into battles, or if he is just supremely confident in his abilities. In either case, rhymes that could come across as passive aggressive disses can escalate tensions, shifting the cipher closer to an explicit war of words. The person who feels dissed or offended at another person's rhymes often responds with his own indirect comments, ramping up the situation even closer to a battle. As this is happening, both parties face a number of interesting choices: they can forge ahead into battle, coming back with more and more disses; they can walk away; or they can try to defuse the situation, apologizing and clearing up any misunderstandings.

Rappers faced with a rhyme that feels like a subliminal sometimes put out "feelers," or rhymes meant to leave some room so that they can figure out their would-be opponent's intentions.[5] Was it to provoke them? Putting out feelers gives the offended party a chance to figure out whether the person was trying to offend or whether it was a simple misunderstanding. Until a person has officially called someone else out, both parties still have an acceptable escape plan.[6]

One day, while hanging out in his one-bedroom apartment in "the 40s," Big Flossy explained how feelers work. He told me how he would gauge another rapper's intentions before calling them out to battle:

> Back then [in high school] I had one battle with this cat who had been rapping a long time and everything. Everybody was like, "He was one of the hottest!" He was new at the school and stuff. He had said something to me in a cipher. You know how you'll say something that's towards that person, but it ain't really towards that person? Like, a subliminal. . . . He said something about me, but it wasn't to me. Then, I went ahead and did the same to him, to see if he was tryin' to start something. And it just ended up as a battle. He came back like he really meant it and shit. Then, we just kept going back and forth, back and forth, back and forth.

Feelers, then, open up various options between parties teetering closer to a battle, including a chance for people to conceal and change their intentions. Maybe the guy throwing subliminals actually wanted to start a battle, but when his target put out a feeler, he can decide to reverse course, feigning innocence if he realizes he's in too deep or the other person has taken their subliminal too personally. He may opt to defuse the situation. But feelers can also *instigate* a battle. The person being issued a feeler might take the feeler as a sign of disrespect, or feel upset that the other person would question him.

Ciphers are competitive interactions fraught with ambiguous moments. Even if it goes unsaid, each person wants a turn to shine. This dynamic invites a competitive tension that can lead to conflict. According to Open Mike:

> Freestyle rappin' is a very egotistical sport. So half the time out there you got everybody saying that they're the greatest person to ever hold a microphone, ever. And, there's only certain ways that you can say that, and not make it sound like you're not talking about everybody standing around you right there.

In the most general sense, battles are lyrical duels and dissing contests. Opponents take turns dissing each other or hyping themselves up. Winners and losers are determined by audience reaction—cheering, waving hands in the air, laughing, and other gestures that show approval and support of one or the other rapper. The rapper who gains a more visible and audible audience support wins the battle.

But battles are much more than this too. Beneath the surface of lyrical braggadocio and dissing, battle rappers use different techniques to read their opponent's intentions and gain advantages—all without explicitly committing to a battle.[7] There is an artfulness and complexity to how this is done. Much like skilled fighters, chess players, and others trained in competitive combat, battle rappers are masterful at manipulating roles in situations.[8] In addition to provoking opponents with techniques that leave them the option of backing out, they have ways to bait their opponents into calling them out. Rappers who do this subtly provoke their opponents. In a subtle twist, this makes the person doing the calling out look overly aggressive and desperate. The skilled battle rapper can chip away at his opponents' public reception *before* the battle even starts. By tricking an opponent into calling them out, rappers come across looking like someone just defending their own honor.

Seizing Emotional Dominance

Lyrical skills are just one part of what rappers use to sway their audience. Rappers are emcees, and one of the skills they develop is hyping up an audience. In a battle, each is trying to seize emotional dominance against their opponent. They want the crowd cheering *for* them and they want the audience laughing at their punch lines against an opponent. Winning over the crowd, though, isn't just about a person's rhymes. It includes subtle techniques to corral audience support and disrupt the confidence of one's opponent. These techniques include projecting "swag," or unflinching confidence, and "flipping the script," or turning an opponent's dis into a resource.

Swag

The best battle rappers ooze swag. They never look defeated or unsure. They seem unimpressed by their opponents, not only to intimidate but also to buy themselves some time to keep a level head and drum up confidence under stress.

Joseph Schloss writes about similar kinds of confidence in his book on breakdancers.[9] In dance battles, "b-boys" and "b-girls" are judged not only on their style and skill but also on their outward confidence. This is best exemplified by Ken Swift, a b-boy pioneer from the Rock Steady Crew in the South Bronx. Swift was known for "mean mugging," looking tough or unimpressed no matter what his opponents brought to the floor. Mugging became part of his signature look and helped Swift harness both his own emotions and the crowd's in battles.

Rappers use similar strategies. Nocando once revealed to me how he worked himself up emotionally to battle. This was not only to intimidate his opponents but also to help him channel the right energy to win the battle. He would seize emotional dominance by becoming angry and impressing the audience with his ferocity:

> Here's my trick. I become angry, like "Don't fuck with me!" I make them feel like, "You have no chance, why would you want to wake a sleeping monster!?" This is the character that I use . . . or little tricky ways to make it seem like you're under control. This makes it so you're like not folding, like you can always win.

Rappers use swag on three levels. First, a rapper outwardly performs swag to sway an audience's support in his favor. This is particularly useful if a rapper is matched up against someone who lands an impactful rhyme. By remaining stoic, a rapper can convince his audience that he is not outmatched or in trouble. Second, a rapper can use swag to intimidate his opponent. A rapper who remains visibly unbothered by another person's best rhymes can break (or at least chip away at) his opponent's confidence. Third, and perhaps most important, a rapper can use swag to drum up self-confidence. Swag is more than bravado put on for an audience. It is a performance that can make a rapper feel better about his chances under duress. Swag tilts the emotional power of a situation into a rapper's hands, making him feel that he is never completely out of the fight.

But this performance can be emotionally draining. It takes a lot of energy to channel and project swag. Open Mike once confessed that the confidence and emotional energy needed to battle weighed heavily on him:

> You know, I haven't battled in a long time, 'cause the energy that it takes to battle somebody is real dark energy. It's real, you gotta be almost ready to fight but not ready to fight. You can't be passive. It's a real apelike, chest-beating, domination thing—you gotta be ready to talk over somebody, get in they face. And I'm not really that kind of person, so it's real difficult for me sometimes to do that. I used to get in battles, I used to win battles, I used to be able to channel into that and separate myself from that. . . . After that battle, even if I won or everybody says I won, I still feel the adrenaline, the fight [or] flight syndrome. I feel messed up for the rest of the night. I can't relax, like I was tensed up all night. That place you gotta go, it's just real hard for me to like, get in and get out—and act like nothing happened.

In battles, young men often flirt with a precarious line between play and more serious activity. A big part of battling is being able to toe this line without catching feelings, or taking things too personally. The ability to stay cool under pressure and respond without breaking the "play frame" of the battle are valued by rappers at Project Blowed. As Big Flossy put it:

> The feeling—I ain't gonna lie to you—the feeling inside of somebody getting you, it messes with you. You'll feel like, "Man, this dog is really getting me!" You know what I'm saying? But you don't want to show that 'cause that's what takes over, if you show it. You could serve me and be dissing me and I'ma still be waiting like, "OK, whatever, whatever." And it could be really getting me inside my mind but I'm not gonna show

you. I'm not gonna let you see it. You know what I'm saying? I can be real pissed off at you but I'll come up and shake your hand and smile and say, "Wassup, man?" You'll never know I'm mad because I don't want nobody else to get the victory over my happiness. See, when you mad, you give that other person the victory. Then they know, "OK, well, he mad so I *got* him." And that's one thing people can't take from me, is my happiness.

Moreover, in addition to keeping a steely outward appearance under fire, rappers also need to keep their swag when they win. The rapper who appears unaffected in victory maintains a supremely confident image. He shows that he *expected* to win. Even if he revels in victory among peers, he might avoid showing this to his opponent, because paradoxically, doing so would validate his opponent as a worthy one. All of this points to a high degree of emotional control in battling. The control that rappers cultivate in battles is a far cry from the popular image of gangstas who work hard to show that they are "crazy," beyond reason, or "down for whatever" in gangs and other aspects of street life.[10]

Flipping the Script

Rappers can also seize advantages by flipping the script on their opponent. Flipping the script is the art of turning someone's dis into a weapon. It is an "offense through defense" strategy in which a rapper hijacks a rhyme, phrase, or concept used by an opponent and recycles it, often directing it back at the original user. In a single move, rappers show that they are lyrically adept and break an opponent's confidence and momentum. Nocando once walked me through the art of flipping the script. Contrary to what I believed, it wasn't always about one-upping an opponent. Sometimes, it just meant being able to match an opponent's intensity and garner a similar audience response. This alone could help someone flip the script, or reverse the collective emotional impact of an opponent's rhymes:

If somebody's really on point and they have the momentum, just by hanging with them you can seem better than them. You can seem like you did better or just by topping them by a little bit. Just because the crowd is already warmed up. Pretty much the other person got them ready to re-act. So a rebuttal—like if you rebuttal something that he or she said you get a point for that. And if you come with a hard line just as hard as one of his hard lines, you get a double point for that. You're taking the crowd like higher. You're building up the drama. And he left it right here, like a point on this step. And you're pretty much taking it from where he put it on a higher step. And crowds are like, "OK, let's see if you can reach higher than you just got right there."

Flawliss was also good at flipping the script. Many opponents targeted him because of his size. Over time, he learned to anticipate that opponents would revert to "fat jokes" against him, so he often responded to a fat joke with one of his own, stealing the thunder of his opponent's dis:

> It's easy to battle me! Anybody can battle me, 'cause you can spit a fat joke, and win. I've had a dude who just can't rap, beat me in a battle, 'cause he said a funnier joke. He had more ammo than me. He could just come up with the fuckin' basic skin of the potato, and be like, "You're fat! Look at your back! It looks like a Big Mac on crack!" And they'll start laughing, because it's funny. . . . I'm fat, that puts me at a disability. I come into the battle with a minus one; a regular-looking guy comes into the battle plus one. I'm trying to switch spots with you; you know, I gotta win the crowd over, I gotta make them like my fat ass!

During my first year of fieldwork, Flawliss and Nocando faced off for the first time in a heated street-corner battle just outside Project Blowed. They were among the most highly respected and decorated rappers in the scene. In this battle, both flipped the script on each other (in italics), leading to a tightly contested back-and-forth. Early on, Flawliss rapped:

> C'mon, James [Nocando's first name], you don't really want it with me.
> . . . *C'mon, you're like a half, I'm like a hundred MCs! That's a whole big diff,*

that's a whole big blip. And your hair is nappy, you got a whole big stiff!
Nigga get half, you don't stiff, nigga you so small, I make yo' body get lift,
nigga get buffer, the flow's a gift, and yo ass ain't nothing.

Nocando easily parried Flawliss's rhyme about Nocando being a "half"
and Flawliss being a "hundred MCs":

Ah! You suck dick, bitch fuck it . . . *The only hundred you are, are Mc-
Nuggets—kick buckets.* Had the speakers, but the sound is off! The song is
gone and the power's off. I won't stop it! You grab balls from the board,
like you're so Rodman. So fuckin' change your hair, dye a scare a guy,
I came not to Pterodactyl, just to terrorize!

Flawliss faced a potentially devastating dis about his weight. But he
swung the emotional energy back in his favor, transforming Nocando's
flipped reference to McNuggets into a weapon:

C'mon, James, you don't really want it with Greg [his own first name].
It's Friday, it look like a bunch of spiders having a meeting on your head!
What's wrong with this guy? What's wrong with the Clyde, *yeah, I'm
supersized nuggets, but you a smallest of fries,* what the fuck? Nigga you
don't wanna take it there, I rape yo' bitch in the naked air! And do it again,
nigga, and make it fair. You never stop me dog, just braid your hair, what
the fuck!

Rappers flip the script on each other not just lyrically but also stylistically. When rappers start to "style," or switch up a rhyme scheme or
cadence, they are issuing an informal agility challenge. This isn't a direct dis, but rappers who can wield multiple styles win favor in the eyes
of their peers. If an opponent has a more limited range or can't quickly
switch styles, he will come across looking weak and unskilled in comparison. Styling is especially important among Project Blowed rappers,
who look up to the OGs who developed "chopping" and other esoteric
styles of underground rhyming.

* * *

In the sixth round, Flawliss was styling on Nocando. He slowed down his delivery (slowed-down tempo in italics), sounding like the late Houston rapper Paul Wall, who was known for the slow hip hop style "chopped and screwed":[11]

> C'mon, dog, [unclear], the fat He-Man versus Skeletor! How the fuck you gonna rap with me? And this nigga couldn't battle unless he swings his naps at me. So when he fuckin' raps when he, c'mon, dog, don't fuckin' frown, just fuckin' laugh with me, and yo ass will get beat up quick, this nigga look like a Slim Jim, he chewed up quick, [unclear recording], and get your screwed-up clique, I'll beat you to it slow down, like you *screwed up clique* . . . [unclear recording], cop with me, I'll beat you so bad, call with go inside and call the cops quickly.

Not to be outdone, Nocando flipped the script on Flawliss's styling. He sped up and slowed down his rhymes, showing that he too could vary his tempo:

> Ey, but fuck Gilbert Gottfried, I'm bringing the nice poems. I got a question guys, "Who ate Mike Jones?" I've got a question guys, "Who ate Mike Jones?" I'm about to make you spit in one lonely night home, *you're bettin' on groupies, way you can do me, screwed up and slowed down, with a dope sound,* you weigh four-forty pounds, this is my hometown, I keep goin', this man eats abominable.[12]

Rappers use different techniques to corral audience support. The person who uses humorous punch lines might seize an early advantage against his opponent, but critical audiences at Project Blowed listen for much more than just cheap laughs. When facing a skilled opponent, rappers must have an arsenal of weapons to seize emotional dominance. The rapper who can flip the script and keep his swag shows not only that he can win a battle but also that he expects to win *every* battle.

Between Play and Violence

Some disses have the power to humiliate, offend, and enrage. In battles, there are no clear boundaries around what is and is not fair game. For instance, it's common to hear "yo' mama" jokes in a battle, but these jokes might deeply offend some people—especially if they are sensitive about jokes involving their mothers, or if their mother has passed away. June One, a rapper living in Compton at the time, once told me, "I'm a pretty mild-mannered guy and you can say what you will, know what I'm sayin'? But, man, if somebody talk bad about my mama, then it's on some *other* shit, know what I mean?"

While battling, it's also common for rappers to simulate and talk about violence they would or could exact upon their opponent, and this is all usually within the realm of fair game. But rhyming this way can initiate an inadvertent frame shift, sliding the lyrical battle into a confrontation that tilts closer to physical violence. One night, I observed CP battling "Skrills." CP was outdueling Skrills, who seemed irritated with CP's bravado:

CP   Yo, I'll end one battle in the same day. Somebody don't wanna see things the same way. Even when we was back, if we was in the same grade, if we was in the same age, we still wouldn't be the same page. My money'll be much more, I got on my hustle early. This nigga, I dunno, somebody go wake up Shirley. Callin' for Sam, callin' for me, I'm the king of the streets, this nigga's king of the weaks.

S   [speaking normally] How much money you got in your pocket?

CP   [continuing to rhyme] He's not even worthy of battlin' a nigga that's worthy of battlin' me.

Skrills walked over to my camera and waved his hand at the lens: "Don't believe that fake shit, listen." He then addressed CP again: "How much money a man got in his pocket? How much money you got in your pocket?"

CP   I got sixty in my back pocket, three hundred in the car . . .

S   . . . sixty dollars?

CP   . . . I got like three Gs in the bank, I can still go even more far . . .

S   How much you got in your pocket?

CP   . . . Trust fund and another savings account that's not somewhere in Cali . . .

S   [rolls his eyes and shakes his head] That's why I don't do this battlin' shit.

CP   . . . What the fuck, this nigga's broke! He ain't funny like John Salley.

Skrills pulled out a wad of bills, flipping some over and claiming he had a thousand dollars. CP didn't look impressed: "Thousand dollars couldn't even buy one rim on my whip!" "Chaos Unlimited" covered his mouth and laughed. Although Chaos Unlimited was one of CP's friends, he always tried to remain impartial when watching battles. Afterward, he would often analyze the battle with CP and others, offering his frank ideas about how people did. I couldn't tell whether he was laughing at CP's brazen attitude or if he genuinely thought the comeback about his car's rims was hilarious. In either case, Skrills didn't seem pleased. CP continued:

> Nigga, I'm still shittin' doors lift up when I wave at you when I'm passing. Nigga, one crack, one casket, one body bag, nah, just one aspirin. See, he done got CP pissed off, I'll smack this nigga and tell his chick to go buy me some lip gloss!

Skrills had resisted being drawn into battle thus far, but he became noticeably upset at CP's last remark:

> Lyin' like a motherfucker. I got one hand [the other is in a cast] and I'll knock yo ass out! Don't even play that old shit. I got one hand and you will get knocked out.

CP kept rhyming as Skrills issued a warning: "C'mon, stop playing all that fake shit, I'll knock yo' ass out." CP didn't publicly apologize, but he seemed to sense Skrills was not playing around. He slowly walked away. Chaos stepped between Skrills and CP, cutting the tension with a joke aimed at Skrills: "We a little older now, I'm thirty! He's nineteen, twenty, you know how you was when you were that age . . . high . . . just spittin' whatever comes to mind, you know we too old for that shit!" Chaos laughed nervously, but Skrills nodded in agreement. He relaxed a bit and seemed to cool down.

Crowd members like Chaos Unlimited play an important part in keeping battles from escalating to physical fights. They pay close attention to the body language and emotional energy of rappers and intervene when needed. In this case, Chaos defused the situation by downplaying CP's comments. He reasoned with Skrills, explaining that CP was young and immature. He broke the tension and warned against getting too caught up by suggesting that he and Skrills, in their thirties, were older and wiser.

Although Project Blowed was a creative sanctuary away from gangs and gang violence, young men still lived in neighborhoods and had friends around whom they had to respect the code of the street.[13] Nocando recalled "serving" (lyrically dominating) a gang member in front of his friends in the gang. Nocando's victory was a painfully embarrassing moment for his opponent and almost led to violence:

> I think I was irritating them because they had a really big ego. Plus there was a gangbanger cat. So he's around his homies. And it pretty much turned into "this is what happened, you know, when rap will turn to scrap." And that was his last line. And he started taking off his jacket. And so, you know, I stood there, and I didn't back down because I was figuring if anything, this guy is my size. Even though he's got friends, I would try to knock his teeth out before they can hit me once. Anything else that happens after that, it doesn't matter. But then one of his boys came in the middle and broke it up.

Moments like these were sobering reminders of how quickly play can get serious. In some situations, dissing can closely resemble "hoo ridin',"[14] a way that gang members challenge one another on the streets. Hoo ridin' sets up a violent sequence: participants know that gang members use it as a lead-in for violent encounters.

On another night, "Spyda" got into a heated battle with "Chavy," a Latino male in his twenties, who escalated the battle by hoo ridin' and saying the *n*-word (its use is generally taboo for non-Black men). I wrote in my fieldnotes:

The onlooking crowd of about twenty erupts into laughter after Spyda calls Chavy a fag. Chavy seems particularly embarrassed by this and starts hoo ridin' on Spyda, "Nigga! Where you from!?" Spyda, who was laughing along with others, quickly becomes serious. He fires back, "Don't say nigga again! You can diss me on whatever you want, but remember where you at, homie!" There are some murmurs amongst onlookers, who wait to see how Chavy is going to respond. Instead of apologizing or downplaying his comment, he reasserts his question, this time a little louder than previously, "I *said*, nigga where you from!?" Spyda is fuming now and while walking back to his car, he announces, "Nigga, I'ma show you where I'm from!" He opens the passenger door of his car, reaches into the glove compartment, and pulls out a black .9 mm pistol. He cocks the gun once and walks back over to Chavy. Onlookers start to scatter at this point. Spyda holds the gun up and points it at Chavy's face. Spyda continues, "Now what's up!? You ain't sayin' nothin' now!" A couple of Chavy's friends grab him by the arm and drag him away from Spyda.

Regulars were quick to reprimand Spyda for "pulling his heat"—brandishing a gun. Spyda listened attentively but also defended the act, saying that he was not really planning to attack Chavy.

Looking back, this interaction reveals important moments that threaten the play frame of the battle. First, Chavy broke from the play frame and threatened Spyda with a gun. Unlike other kinds of bluster, aggressive hoo ridin' and brandishing a firearm leave less room for negotiation. Once a person "goes there," the other person's options are limited. Regulars worried that Spyda's reaction could have initiated a far more violent turn of events.

Second, Chavy further offended Spyda when he used the word *nigga*. Although non-Black young men might regularly use this epithet among Black friends who know them, the same courtesy isn't extended to non-Black newcomers—their use of the term evokes much deeper feelings of racial animosity.

Third, Spyda issued an ultimatum that Chavy transgressed. After Chavy yelled, "Nigga, where you from!?" the first time, Spyda cautioned him. Chavy repeated himself, undermining Spyda's moral authority on what was, ostensibly, his turf. This defiance ratcheted up the tension. Spyda would lose face if he backed down or begged pardon. Chavy had made violence a viable option in order for Spyda to save face.

A few weeks later, Spyda told me more about his night with Chavy:

> I was battling this one cat. I believe he was Hispanic or so. And I mean, as far as me, man, I don't care what words you use, we're rapping, we're having a great time and that's it. He was using the word *nigga*. Now, I have lots of friends who call me nigga. I use the word too, so I can't really blame nobody else for using it. I'm not like these cats out here, he used that word. Naw, man. A lot of people do use the word and they mean it as, "What's up, homie?" You my boy and I can call you that because we know each other. And I didn't mind him using it, but when he kept using it, it became personal, because it seems like he's not saying it as if he's saying "What it do, homie?" He's more saying it as "You a nigga and I'm dissing you and I'm disrespecting you now."

When I asked why he pulled heat on Chavy, Spyda laughed. He said he'd forgotten he was on the corner rapping and slipped back into his gangbanging past:

> I have my ignorant ways too. I'm ignorant too sometimes. And I popped the trunk and I showed him, "You get at me, on me, I'll pop you." You know what I'm saying? So, I mean, I was wrong on my behalf on doing it but I was so upset that I wanted to show him, "Homie I don't fear nobody!

I'll get at you!" You know what I'm saying? 'Cause I'm a real cool person. I respect everybody and I just want the same respect. You know? And don't take it personal if I'm serving you out there.

Battles straddle a thin line between play and violence. The play frame of a battle can change in a flash, particularly when rappers feel that an opponent has really disrespected them. In South Central, such verbal challenges and disrespect aren't taken lightly. In this setting, young men see disses as fighting words, springboards to more serious kinds of violence.

Sometimes disses have the power to deeply offend and provoke because they hit too close to home; other times a rhyme or hoo ridin' jolts one person out of the battle and into a different frame, like when Chavy's insolence irritated Spyda. One dis became two, and suddenly Spyda faced the choice of looking like a punk or trying to seize back control over the situation. The crowd becomes especially important in "keeping it hip hop." They look for light pushing, shouting, and other signs that participants have broken frame. When it happens, crowd members intervene and try to defuse the situation, as Chaos Unlimited did with Spyda and Chavy. And regulars place sanctions on the hotheads: rappers who catch feelings lose face. If a rapper regularly loses control over his emotions, he can become an outcast. No one wants to be known as the guy who can't keep it hip hop, who turns to violence because he doesn't have self-control or lyrical weaponry to do battle with words alone.

Conclusion

The informal structure of ciphers creates opportunities for conflict between rappers. But instead of immediately resorting to violence, young men battle verbally in these moments of perceived disrespect. It is a creative way for them to transform the code of the street. At Project Blowed and in the hip hop underground more generally, young people turn the rules and rituals of the streets on their head. Instead of winning respect for showing their mastery over violence, they win respect for being crafty and creative with their words. They become known as "curb servers" who have a superior command over lyrics, flow, and other highly prized rap skills.

But the meanings of battling changes as rappers gain age and experience. Early in their careers, some believe—or at least hope—that battles will become stepping-stones to bigger and better things in their careers. Indeed, most of the young men I knew could recite the stories of Notorious B.I.G., Eminem, Cassidy, and Jin—hip hop artists whose stellar battle performances launched their careers as underground artists. The young men I followed saw these stories as blueprints for and beacons of their eventual success.

However, as they aged and learned more about blowin' up, I saw many young men mature out of battling. Some of the attrition can be chalked up to life experience. For example, as young men get older, they have less to prove on the corner. They may acquire more friends and experiences that show them other ways to prove their skills. This was the case for Nocando, who wrote poignantly in *LA Weekly* about his departure from the very battle rap scene that had helped make him a recognized name.[15]

In addition to outgrowing the rules and rituals of battling, some men also start to see battling as a dead end. They realize that the skills that they've honed for freestyling and battling aren't necessarily transferrable to the next stage of their careers. Once they set their sights on attracting an audience *outside* the corner, many notice that even successful battle rappers are unsigned. They're great on the corner, but they don't have lucrative (or even promising) prospects as recording artists.

For instance, people who win many battles are typically great at using lots of punch lines in their rhymes. They can deliver devastating disses. But dissing does not always transfer well into songwriting, which requires the ability to weave a compelling story into a particular beat. Philadelphia rapper Cassidy once reflected on this tension:

> Yeah, that's a hard adjustment to make. That's why a lot of battle rappers can't elevate to making good records and good songs. . . . When you battle rappin', like a "bar," one, two, three, four. So when you battle rappin', your

bar might not necessarily have to fall on that four. It might be six beats. Or three beats. Ya know what I'm saying? So, if you say it to a beat, it'll be off-beat.[16]

Indeed, this is one of the core tensions in an aspiring rapper's career. If rappers start off focusing a lot of energy on becoming talented free-style and battle rappers, they develop a skill set that might not easily transfer into the skills they need to "blow up." In many ways, this is similar to street basketball players who realize that the skill set that gained them notoriety and respect in the local scene might not trans-late into professional basketball prowess, where different rules and an entirely different team concept enter the game.[17] Coming to under-stand that raw talent is not the same as marketable skills pushes these men toward alternative courses of action. Getting to the next level is a big leap.

PART TWO

TRYING TO BLOW UP

5

Cautionary Tales

Chaos Unlimited motioned for me to follow him. We moved across the street to his car, where he said, "How do you think it feels to be one of the most talented rappers on the planet and still be on the same corner for the past ten years?" Chaos's question floored me. I had never thought about "Dru the MC" in this way. He continued:

> Imagine if you saw CP, Nocando, or Flawliss out here in ten years. Dru was the Nocando of his generation. He was supposed to be the next one to blow up. You might not believe me, but Dru was the guy out here everybody said was gonna blow. Now he looks like another crazy person you might see begging for a dollar on the street.

Chaos's words forced me to confront a difficult reality. I didn't know the numbers, but I knew that it was rare for an underground rapper to get signed to a major record label. Chaos wasn't alone, either. In different ways, many of the men expressed similar doubts. Even if they did not talk about it openly, they knew that blowin' up was hard to do and that most people—regardless of their talent—wouldn't be signed. To be sure, some were content with a career as an underground artist. But in different moments, others who aspired to blow up expressed uncertainty about their future.

For some up-and-coming rappers, Dru came to represent a stalled career in the underground. He was well respected at Project Blowed but hadn't developed a career outside of the scene. He was stuck and had gone as far as he could go. For instance, once while talking about Dru,

Big Flossy told me that he respected him as a person and artist but was more critical of his musical style: "If you up in the club with yo girl or yo boys, you don't wanna hear all that noise, you feel me? You wanna hear something you can dance to."

* * *

When novices are learning how to rap, they look up to veterans like Dru.[1] Veterans give them feedback on their songwriting, critique their lyrics, and help them become more confident performers. Much of this happens in the open mic workshop. But it also happens on the corner in ciphers and battles.

As up-and-comers gain experience and confidence, some develop different goals. They focus on recording music, performing in new venues, and becoming signed recording artists. This marks a turning point in their rap career and changes how these young men think about hip hop, their future, and their relationships with veterans. Their mentors no longer have the expertise to guide them in this phase of their career. For those who want to be signed to a major label, veterans come to represent the limits of an underground career. They become "cautionary tales."[2]

This chapter examines the changing nature of the mentor-mentee relationship at Project Blowed. While up-and-comers look up to veterans and seek their approval while learning to rhyme, many seek out new mentors once they have developed their skills and gained respect at Project Blowed. This is a natural career evolution. Most rappers maintain ties to the scene, but those who become focused on blowin' up shift their time and energy to new activities and relationships. Instead of trying to get props in the open mic or one-up other rappers in ciphers and battles, these men record full-length albums, perform in new venues, and network with people in the entertainment world. They do these things with the hope that they will be discovered and signed to a record label.

This begins a more general process of branching out. Aspiring rappers enlist the help of new mentors who introduce them to the challenges in becoming a signed recording artist. In different ways, these new mentors encourage them to think about their music in entrepreneurial terms. At the same time, these collaborations often introduce new identity dilemmas. To increase their chances of getting signed and appealing to a wider audience, rappers cede some of the creative control over their image and music that they cherished as fledgling underground rappers. Thus, this stage of the rap career brings young men into contact with the sacrifices they will have to make to become commercially viable.

Becoming Cautionary Tales

Some of the up-and-coming rappers saw Dru as a cautionary tale. As a young man, he had been a member of the Harlem Rollin' 30s. He never talked about this openly, but he was quick to remind people that he wasn't someone to be "messed with" and wasn't scared to "get down."

When we met, Dru had already left this life behind. He was a veteran and mentor to many up-and-coming rappers at Project Blowed, and frequently hosted the open mic. He spoke his mind freely and was quick to give younger rappers opinions about their performances. Often, he'd tell them to hold the microphone differently or project their voice more. Occasionally, he'd chastise rappers for looking "shook," urging them to have more swag. He was very opinionated and didn't hold back in his harsh critiques of rappers.

An original member of the Good Life (which preceded Project Blowed), Dru learned how to rhyme with Aceyalone, Myka 9, and others who were part of a "golden era" of underground hip hop in South Central. Many of his contemporaries were signed to independent labels, went on tours, and built fan bases beyond Project Blowed. But Dru hadn't had the same luck. Well into his thirties, he was still a regular at Project Blowed, laying into younger rappers. Many would listen because they respected Dru's knowledge and experience. He was abrasive, but he knew what he was talking about.

However, as they got more experienced and developed confidence, some in the younger generation of rappers stopped taking Dru seriously. They came to resent his sometimes hostile comments. After a

Figure 7. E.Crimsin, who remained a regular even though he branched out of the scene (photo courtesy of Kyle "VerBS" Guy)

few years in the scene, E.Crimsin had earned the respect of his peers and was starting to dream of bigger things. He started to envision goals beyond just being a "curb server" or getting props in the open mic. These affirmations were still great for him, but they didn't carry the same weight. As he looked around, he realized that many of the veterans—including Dru—had not blown up. They were still rapping on the block. It was the beginning of E.Crimsin's shift away from veterans and Project Blowed.

During this same period, E.Crimsin started dating a Latina singer and songwriter named Bianca. Bianca had already toured nationwide and was recording music videos. She became a new mentor who helped him think about the entrepreneurial side of his rap career. Once, he told me some of what he'd learned from her:

See, niggas at the Blowed don't understand certain things. I watched Bianca and her street team promoting her as a *product*. She told me all the time, "You gotta brand yourself" and see yourself as a brand. That's why I wear that black beanie and that trench coat—I see it like being a wrestler, like one of those fucking *luchadores* with the mask. You gotta keep an image in people's minds. Most of the niggas at the Blowed just sit on the corner talking about how they gonna be the next ones or how they gonna do this or do that. None of them know that this is a vast world and that there is a lot more to it than just being on that corner.

In addition to seeing himself as a brand, E.Crimsin went with Bianca to her video shoots and started interacting with music industry professionals in her network. He relished these opportunities and felt inspired. Although this process unfolded over several months, I witnessed a revealing episode one night when he was back on the block. That night, he was freestyling next to Dibiase's Beat Jeep. Dru was standing nearby, listening. I wrote in my fieldnotes:

Dru is standing with his hands on his hips, watching impatiently and listening to E.Crimsin rap. He shakes his head and mumbles, "Nigga is off-beat." E.Crimsin keeps rapping, apparently unaware of or undeterred by Dru. Dru, however, begins to hit the back of one hand in the open palm of the other—kind of like a baseball player who is throwing a ball into a mitt. Dru synchronizes the slapping sound of his hands to the beat. With the sound of his hand accentuating the beat, it becomes more noticeable that E.Crimsin is *off* beat. Dru then announces, "Here's the beat, nigga. Here's the beat." E.Crimsin keeps rapping, "Fuck you up like Lucky Charms, I'm the Spawn, you get check-mated on." He places an emphasis at the end of each sentence, which doesn't fit the meter of the beat. Dru continues using his hand like a metronome, and says again, this time a bit louder, "This the beat!" When he sees that E.Crimsin isn't changing up his tempo or delivery, he shakes his head and turns away from the cipher. "Psh. Youngstas ain't got no style."

Later that night, after people were finished rapping, Dru turned to E.Crimsin and told him that he needed to learn how to rap. E.Crimsin's eyes grew big. "That's just how I rap! You do what you do, nigga! I do what I do!" he yelled. Dru looked surprised and said, "Nigga, it ain't about you doing you or me doing me! You off beat! Ain't no two ways about it!" I wrote:

> E.Crimsin replied, "Niggas actin' like I don't know how to rap and shit."
> Dru raised his voice, "You ain't on beat. You can't rap. You need to slow that shit down and really listen to the music."
> E.Crimsin rolled his eyes, "Nigga, *you* are the one who can't rap and shit."
> Dru turned away, throwing his hands up in anger. "I try to help niggas out, but they don't wanna hear nothing."

At about three in the morning, E.Crimsin invited me to his apartment to play some video games. After stopping at Yum Yum Donuts—a twenty-four-hour shop just north of Leimert Park on Crenshaw—we arrived at his pad, a second-story walk-up that straddled the border of the Rollin' 40s and Rollin' 30s Crip gang territories. We sat in his living room and played *SoulCalibur* on his Xbox. In between bouts of beating me up in the game, where we fought as warriors from different historical periods, E.Crimsin expressed his frustration with Dru and other veterans at Project Blowed:

> I mean, it's one thing if that nigga was *somebody*. But who is he? Most nights that nigga looks like a bum! It's been the same shit for years and years. Niggas on flyers [are depicted in ads for concerts], but niggas ain't pushin' nothin' [have full albums to sell]. Fuck that performin' shit and bein' all at the Blowed rappin' to the same niggas. Unless I got some product, it's a waste of my breath.

We played games for the next hour or so. E.Crimsin kept talking about his changing feelings toward the scene. He maintained a deep respect for the veterans and said he would always "rep the Blowed," but Crimsin was at a crossroads. As he thought about his path, he realized what so many others have as they pursued their own rap dreams: He didn't want to spend years of his life rhyming in the same scene for the same audience. He wanted something more, and he was determined to branch out.

Career Inertia

Many veterans were in a difficult situation, grappling with doubts and a looming sense of inertia. Some felt stalled because they were not advancing in their career. Others felt the weight of being left behind by mentees whose careers were passing their own. Both experiences led to identity dilemmas. As the veterans' importance in the careers of up-and-comers faded, some felt uncertainty about their own careers and how to interact with their mentees.

To be sure, career inertia is not only felt by the individual. It's a collective experience that is felt and interpreted by all who are around a person. After seeing their mentor struggle, some mentees would pause and reflect on their own choices and paths. They would distance themselves from mentors who had not blown up. Having become a cautionary tale, the mentor was still an adviser, but now in a way he didn't anticipate.

All of this points to how definitions of self are situated within evolving social relationships. People come up with ideas about who they are in relation to others around them. The mentor's identity, in essence, hangs on the existence of mentees who require his help and expertise. In some professions, like education, there are always new mentees to replace those who no longer need the mentor. With each incoming cohort, teachers get a fresh supply of mentees who replenish their identity. But in other careers, a mentor who lacks the expertise that mentees seek out becomes obsolete—or worse, a cautionary tale.

* * *

One night, I met up with Choppa at his apartment. He was a veteran who was widely respected by the younger generation of rappers at Project Blowed. He had earned this respect helping rappers record their music in the Project Blowed studios and was afforded respect because he was one of the few veterans who was consistently at Project Blowed, mentoring and helping younger rappers learn the craft.

But as time went by, Choppa began to feel that his contributions had not blossomed into appreciable advances in his own career. Adding to this, he didn't always feel appreciated by younger rappers, who were starting to branch out of the scene in search of new opportunities. During a midnight beer run, he groaned about feeling that younger rappers were passing him by. This was especially frustrating because people he taught to rap were now getting opportunities to perform, record, and tour.

While cruising the streets around his apartment, Choppa said, "Customer Service [a rap group from Project Blowed] went on tour when they were twenty-one!" He stopped to make this point more dramatic. "This past summer was my first time going on tour! I put in too much work and time, man. I was supposed to have a shot a long time ago."

As we walked back to his apartment, he described the frustration he felt hawking CDs and DVDs along Crenshaw Boulevard:

You know how it makes me feel when I go up to people and I got the James Brown greatest hits or a Tupac CD? You know how it feels when people say shit like, "Yo, Choppa, you spit harder than anyone I know!"? That fucks with my mind, Jooyoung. I'm not supposed to be selling bootlegs and shit, playing cat-and-mouse with the security guards. I'm supposed to be changing the game![3]

This was a revealing conversation. Beneath his sometimes eccentric front, Choppa was grappling with career inertia. Approaching thirty, he was probably past his creative prime, at least in the eyes of the mainstream music industry. This is one of the cruel parts of the mainstream music industry. It takes many years to become a skilled rapper. Developing a unique style and rockin' a mic aren't skills that people just acquire. They take practice. But the wider industry isn't necessarily interested in signing the most lyrical or complex rappers. And the mainstream music industry's preference for younger artists who can appeal to the large teenage consumer demographic puts additional pressure on artists to get discovered quickly. Often, industry gatekeepers are looking for someone who is marketable and fills a popular niche. The hard work of aspiring rappers is sometimes out of synch with the realities of the industry.

And although getting signed to a major label wasn't his only goal as a recording artist, Choppa—like most rappers—entertained the idea of getting signed. He reasoned that it would allow him to make music full-time (which was a plus). But at his current age, he was quickly aging out of contention.

Later that night, Choppa cleared a space for me on a small black sofa that doubled as his bed. He turned on his computer and played me some of his music. The beat rumbled violently out of the speakers, cracking and popping as if a woofer were about to blow. While one song played, Choppa explained that he wrote it after being excluded from a Project Blowed anniversary show. The annual end-of-year concert features veterans and a few emerging artists: "I wrote this song right after the tenth anniversary. For some reason, they didn't think I was dope enough to put me on."

Later, "Steelo"—his roommate and collaborator—joined us in the living room. Steelo was also a veteran of the open mic and had earned his reputation as a fierce battle rapper. In the late 1990s he had won a prestigious rap battle that put him on the radar of some A&Rs (artists and repertoire executives). But in the time since then, Steelo hadn't experienced the kind of career advancement he had hoped for. He too opened up about his own frustrations as an aspiring artist. He explained the tensions between trying to stay true to himself as an artist and blow up. These goals were often at odds:

> So I had a meeting over at Def Jam West, and I was sitting there, this white boy A&R was bobbing his head. He's all getting into it, and then tells me that he doesn't know how to market me.

Both laughed as Steelo bobbed his head in imitation. "His advice to me was, rap about drugs, bitches, and gangbangin'. . . . 'Get more bass in your tracks.'"

And then Choppa put me on the spot. "From an outsider's perspective, what do you think I need to do differently to get noticed?" I paused. Was he asking for my honest opinion? Or was he hoping that I'd say, "Change nothing—you're great!"I just started talking. "Well, I've heard some people say that the whole 'chopping' style [rapid-paced rhyming style created at the Good Life] is too hard to follow, like people can't always make out what . . ." Choppa interrupted, defensively, "Yeah, but people be feelin' Aceyalone and them!" He added that Busdriver, a local rapper with a unique style of chopping, had been signed to Epitaph Records (an independent label focused on punk bands). "C'mon, how you gonna tell me that his stuff doesn't go over people heads, and then say mine does?"

Later, Choppa told me that he had recently started softening his views about mainstream hip hop. Like many at Project Blowed, Choppa had been intensely critical of much of mainstream hip hop. On most occasions, he would rail against artists on the charts, saying their music was "bullshit" that lacked creativity. Now Choppa was beginning to think a person could have multiple styles of rapping for different occasions. Choppa said he was going to try to create a more mainstream-friendly alter ego: "Skinny Swagga." Skinny would record catchy, dumbed-down club songs to appeal to wider mainstream audiences. That, he hoped, was how he would finally blow up.

* * *

Career inertia need not be an accurate or objective reading of how one is doing or progressing in a career. It is a looming sense of doubt about one's chances in a chosen path. This daunting feeling can lead to desperate actions.

What's more, career inertia is also a dilemma that transcends racial, ethnic, gender, and class lines, but a person's circumstances can amplify the intensity of this frustration. Young Black men like Choppa and others perceive themselves as having few fallback options. As I examine later, many have firsthand experiences in dead-end service industry jobs. Blowin' up, in many ways, appears to be their best option for achieving a desirable future. For these young men, a sense of stagnation takes on much greater meaning. Stalling out, and realizing it, casts a dark cloud over how they imagine the rest of their lives.

And, as mentioned earlier, inertia is a collective experience. Mentors share their struggles with mentees, who start thinking more critically about their own paths and the larger structures that prevent talented rappers from achieving their dreams. Seeing their mentors grapple with inertia inspires aspiring rappers to take a different course. They start to think differently about their careers. They become more attuned to what sells or what might attract the attention of the wider music industry, which in turn inspires them to relax some of their previous ideas about "keeping it real" or creative authenticity.

Ironically, though, this new critical awareness ends up becoming a personal critique of mentors. Mentees see the larger structural hurdles that thwart talented artists in front of them, but they do not place equal weight on the structural impediments to blowin' up. Instead, they focus most of their critique on the mentors' decision making. They try to figure out where their mentors went wrong and trace mentors' struggles back to poor choices that led them awry. This is mostly a response to the larger realities of the industry. By framing mentors' struggles as the outcome of individual decision making, mentees keep the hope alive that their future might be different if they manage it differently. In the end, this shift in sense making becomes the start of how mentees redirect their efforts and distance themselves from their mentors.

From Gs to Gents

Once they become serious about trying to get signed, some rappers distance themselves from veterans and seek out new mentors. Their new mentors help them branch out and inspire them to think about themselves and their music in new ways. While many of these new mentors have direct ties to the music industry, most are not actual A&Rs or record label executives, who hold the most decision-making power over who gets signed to a label. Instead, their new mentors are often people who work in the music industry or who have direct ties to signed artists, producers, recording engineers, promoters, and other key people involved in the creative process.

But in creating these ties, the young men encounter new kinds of identity dilemmas. As they become more serious about trying to blow up, they feel the lingering effects of what Elijah Anderson calls the "iconic ghetto."[4] The iconic ghetto is a historical stigma that follows young Black men of all classes. It is rooted in racist, stereotypical depictions of young Black men as "thugs" and "gangstas" who pose a threat to public safety. When they go into public, strangers are uncritically weary of young Black men, fearing that their own lives might be at risk.[5]

Rappers experience a version of this stigma as they branch out of Project Blowed and seek the attention of the record industry. In some settings, their new mentors encourage them to downplay aspects of their identities that might give off the impression that they are from the "ghetto." When they interact with A&Rs, potential investors, and other people at industry mixers and other professional events, they are encouraged to come across courteous, nonthreatening, and "professional." This is rarely mentioned explicitly, but the allusion to the "ghetto" carries with it both racial and class implications. Artists are supposed to act less "Black" and "working class" in these moments. Mentors juxtapose the ghetto identity to the professional identity. They encourage aspiring artists to act more White and to emulate and adopt the manners of professional businesspeople. This is supposed to signal to gatekeepers and potential investors that they are "serious" and "organized" about their pursuits. All of this requires a makeover that conceals their connections to the "ghetto."

At the same time, aspiring rappers feel an opposite force. Those who want to get signed to major labels feel *musically* pigeonholed into the stereotypical identities of the hypermasculine "thug" or "gangsta." Mentors, producers, and others involved in the writing and recording of music encourage them to play up their connections to the streets for marketing purposes. The message is clear: artists are supposed to downplay any connections to the ghetto in their face-to-face interactions with gatekeepers but should highlight—even exaggerate—their connections to the ghetto in their music, which will reach more fans. This poses new dilemmas for young men who want to build a meaningful creative identity. While many have grown up seeing hip hop as a creative alternative to gang identity, they now confront an industry that seems to reward those with a connection to that lifestyle.

I first observed these tensions while spending time with Big Flossy and his younger cousin, Wildchild. The two were virtually inseparable and were in a rap group called PTP, or Prime Time Playaz. One spring afternoon, we met up at a small barbecue just outside of their friend's cell phone store in South Central. Given that it was a high foot-traffic area, Big Flossy and Wildchild were planning to hawk their CDs to passersby.

I got to the barbecue around three in the afternoon and saw both of them unusually dressed up, holding briefcases. Big Flossy was wearing a blue-and-white-striped collared shirt, baggy jeans, and a pair of shiny blue Stacy Adams shoes. He had a Los Angeles Dodgers hat "on tilt." Wildchild sported a black blazer with its collar popped, a tan-colored undershirt, jeans, a black hat with a cannabis leaf on the front, and his own Stacy Adams dress shoes.

I parked my car across the street and walked over to them. I yelled, "Wow, you guys look like some big ballers!" Big Flossy grinned from ear to ear, "You already know!" Wildchild adjusted the brim of his hat, struck a pose, and put his hand out for daps. "That's how we do, my nigga! Wassup, Jee-young!"

Big Flossy told me they'd been thinking a lot about veterans who seemed stuck in the underground. They felt that their careers were a preview of what might happen to them if they didn't branch out of the scene and manage their careers differently:

> Usually, we're the rappers and that's basically it and all, you know what I'm saying? We do our songs and that's the part of the rapper, right? Now we're actually doing the part that's more to it, and that's the business part—communicating with rich folks and stuff. People that got money,

and telling them, you know, our occupation and what we do. Him [Wild-child] jumping on the computers and stuff, networking, you know, we're building websites, the Myspace. Look, you gotta get a picture of us.

After I took a few photos, Big Flossy talked about how some rappers never learned to interact with people outside of the open mic or their immediate peer group. He saw that isolation as a huge limitation in a rapper's career development:

> We now rockin' "the gentlemen look" and talking to people like you who got sense and like you ain't always been ghetto. And I've always said that that's the difference between people like me and my cousin, and like for instance, I'ma put a name out there, Choppa. You could never see him do this. Going to talk to White folks and million-dollar people about, you know, what he do and stuff, 'cause it wouldn't work, you know what I'm saying? 'Cause he believes what I used to think, you know, that it's Choppa and that's all there is: "I don't care about nothing else, my way or no way."

Big Flossy and Wildchild had begun working closely with "Big Dweezy," a self-styled entrepreneur who saw them performing at a low-rider convention in Southern California. Dweezy had helped produce and distribute urban lifestyle and lowrider DVDs and was, at the time, the president of a lowrider club. He had amassed an impressive list of contacts with other artists, photographers, videographers, and various creative industry types with connections to lowriding.

Dweezy became a mentor to Big Flossy and Wildchild. He saw potential and wanted to help them take that next step in their careers. He started by taking them to music industry mixers at clubs across Los Angeles, Hollywood, and San Diego. He encouraged Big Flossy and Wildchild to change their look so that people they met at these events wouldn't see them as gangstas or thugs. He stressed, "You gonna be meeting with White folks who ain't down with a couple young brothers wearing white tees and brims. You gotta look respectful and present-able—professional. Leave that 'hood shit' at home."

Figure 8. Big Flossy and Wildchild before going to an industry mixer

On a sunny Saturday afternoon not too long after the barbeque, I met up with Big Dweezy, Big Flossy, and Wildchild at Dweezy's house in the 60s. I walked around back into a shed Dweezy had converted into a storage space for all the DVDs and CDs he was promoting. While helping package some of their newly pressed albums, Big Flossy started telling me about all the stuff Big Dweezy had planned for them. Big Flossy explained, "At first, he was like, 'Hey, jump in the suit. You know, make it a little different, when you go talk to people who ain't ghetto, you can't come across ghetto.'" Flossy went on:

> [Big Dweezy's] been telling us to just get out like every night or every other night. We just grinding and really focusing on the business part now, so it feels good. It feels like we on the right path, meeting all sorts of people who got money and who know we about business.

Wildchild joined the conversation:

> Finally, we be moving in the right direction and we actually able to see the direction we going in. It makes us feel a little more comfortable, you know what I mean? It's just knowing that if we stay on our grind and keep doing what we doing, we gonna end up successful. We gonna end up somewhere.

Big Dweezy had coached Wildchild and Flossy on developing a more entrepreneurial approach to their identities and their music.

Big Dweezy chimed in, turning the conversation to the importance of investing money back into their creative work. Instead of spending profits, Dweezy encouraged them to think about making smart investments:

> That's wrong with a lot of people, too, today. They don't invest back in they self. It's like this, you go get a deal, right? They give this, hypothetically speaking; I'm not saying no names. But they give you a deal for $100,000. You don't take the $100,000 and go buy you a Bentley and a house and you don't invest back in yo self. You see what I'm saying? You don't do that. A smart businessman is not going to go do that. You take that money and you invest back in your project. So when the labels see you they will respect you more. "You spending the money I gave you and you come up with four more projects instead of this one." That's when they gonna say you a smart businessman.

Big Flossy and Wildchild told me later that now they always carried the briefcase with pressed and packaged versions of their albums. Wildchild said, "You gotta stay ready, so you don't gotta get ready." Everyone laughed, but Big Flossy explained, "You know, in the past we didn't always have our CDs all pressed up and nice. We didn't always have our stuff. So, you never know who you gonna meet when you go out. And if you don't got your stuff on you, you ain't ready to make moves yet, ya feel me?" Big Dweezy had drummed home lessons in self-promotion that would help the Prime Time Playaz gain listeners and improve the probability of getting their music into the hands of someone who could invest in them or pass their music to someone in the industry.

Beyond just clothing, Big Dweezy worked with Big Flossy and Wild-child on their physical image. He encouraged them get into shape, citing the careers of gangsta rappers like the heavily chiseled 50 Cent. Big Dweezy began picking up Big Flossy and Wildchild from their houses for morning exercise routines. He'd arrive before eight in the morning to drive them to local public parks and trails for hours of running and other exercise. He floated the idea of giving the rappers special detox juices:

BD It's healthy, my nigga. You gotta try this shit. Next time, I'ma take you to this place where you get the juice. It's wheatgrass, ginger, lemon, man, energy, and pomegranate. It's healthy. One-ounce shots. Look how Dr. Dre looking now! Y'all see how 50 [Cent] is built? Y'all see his body? The labels like that. You gotta be in shape. You can't be no soft-ass nigga. Y'all better get healthy out here, man.

BF I'm willing to do whatever it take.

W We're dropping like flies over unhealthiness now.

BD You better get it together, man. Don't live on McDonald's.

BF What's funny is I ain't been having no craving for no McDonald's or nothing.

W Me neither.

Over the course of an afternoon, I got to see firsthand how much Big Dweezy was influencing Big Flossy and Wildchild. His mentoring had little to do with their rapping abilities—they'd practiced and culti-vated those skills at Project Blowed with the help of veterans. Veterans had not, however, taught them about building a rap career: network-ing outside the Blowed, rubbing shoulders with creative industry folks and fans outside their peer group. Neither of the two had given much thought to their image as artists, either. Now these were central con-cerns.

At the same time, their story reveals some of the challenges that young Black men face as they begin "branching out" and trying to blow up. Paradoxically, men like Big Flossy and Wildchild were encouraged to change their outward appearance so that they wouldn't appear "ghetto" to industry gatekeepers who could help finance parts of their dream, or who had connections to people that could get them signed.

However, both Big Flossy and Wildchild also received mentoring that propelled them in the opposite direction. Big Dweezy knew that the music industry had a narrow image of what makes a marketable Black body—and more broadly, what makes a marketable Black masculinity. He reasoned that the two would have a better chance of getting the attention of an A&R or label rep if they were physically imposing and ripped. Dweezy held up heavily muscled rappers like 50 Cent and Tupac Shakur as models. So while the two were told to suit up, they also learned that having an imposing body is part of a subtle claim to one's authenticity as a street rapper. The buff, physically imposing body in the 'hood is a symbol that one may have served time in prison or, at least, that one is not to be messed with.[6]

Tricia Rose writes about paradoxes like this in her work on how the record industry selects and reproduces a "tragic trinity" of Black identities.[7] In addition to channeling women into stereotypical roles as overly sexualized "hos" and "gold diggers," the music industry plays up longstanding caricatures of young Black men as gangstas and pimps. This "hypergangstaization," as she calls it, is part and parcel of the product marketed to an ever-widening fan base of young White teenage consumers drawn to sensational and pathological images of Blackness in hip hop. The identity dilemmas Rose describes were playing out in front of me.

At the least, these experiences revealed some of the confusion that rappers face as they branch out of the underground. As they set their sights on getting signed, they come across what often feels like inconsistent, mixed messaging. In some situations they are encouraged to downplay parts of their identity that might signal to others that they are from the "ghetto." In other situations, particularly when it comes to their music, they are nudged in the opposite direction and encouraged to highlight their connections to gangs, drug dealing, and other street activities.

Veterans Who Continue Mentoring

Not all veterans become cautionary tales. Some flirted with blowin' up and have firsthand experiences in the music industry that give them a continued relevance in the unfolding careers of aspiring rappers. These veterans have collaborated with recording artists and know the pressures and identity dilemmas that younger rappers will face, and they can segue into new mentorship roles as those rappers branch out from Project Blowed.

Trenseta, who was already in his thirties when we met, was one of these veterans. Like many at Project Blowed, Trenseta learned how to rap at the Good Life. He was one of the youngest then. After it closed, he became one of the core members at Project Blowed. Over time, Trenseta had a series of promising leads as an artist. In July 2003 he was named "Unsigned Hype" in *The Source* magazine, a monthly honor bestowed on an unsigned rapper on the rise: "Trenseta possesses the skill, charisma, frame of reference and basically the overall package one needs to be successful in the music game. It's only a matter of time before the music industry starts to follow his lead."[8] But the closest he came to signing a deal was in 2005, when he had a record contract offer from Sony–Epic Records.

One afternoon in his small personal recording studio in a rented office space above Crenshaw Faders (a barbershop where he worked), Trenseta told me how the A&R at Sony Epic called him in for a meeting. There he'd been told the label wanted to sign him but needed him to change up his image and style. He claimed that the A&R wanted him to be "more like Chingy," a mainstream rapper whose commercial debut single "Right Thurr" had peaked at No. 2 on the Billboard commercial charts.[9]

Still, despite their commercial success, rappers like Chingy are not often well respected by underground rappers. Many rappers in the underground see artists like Chingy as an embodiment of all that is wrong and corrupt with the mainstream hip hop industry. They criticize simple, watered-down lyrics and say the music lacks creativity and is overly violent and misogynistic.

Trenseta said being asked to sound more like Chingy felt like an insult. He was young, confident in his talents, and didn't want to "dumb down" his lyrics. He believed in his skills and didn't want to "sell out." What's more, Chingy was a Southern rapper whose style epitomized the regional aesthetic coming out of St. Louis. This A&R wasn't only insulting Trenseta's pride in his own lyrical talents; he was suggesting that he abandon his own regional style, which he was immensely proud of. Trenseta, like many others from Project Blowed, would make it a point to represent their lineage and connection to Project Blowed and South Central LA more broadly. And so Trenseta turned down the deal to pursue what he hoped would be a better one.

* * *

David Grazian has written about similar career concerns among blues musicians in Chicago.[10] At the core, many want to stay true to their own artistry, but they face stiff competition for paying gigs. To have a vibrant local career, artists must forgo some of their own creative ideas to draw mainstream audiences. Indeed, blues players who hope to get gigs in locally known clubs are expected to play songs that everyone knows, covering other artists' tunes.

Rappers' choices can involve similar kinds of trade-offs and artistic dilemmas. Like most aspiring musicians, rappers also have to juggle the competing demands of artistic freedom with commercial viability. While many aspire to make meaningful music that reflects their personal and artistic circumstances, most have to make certain sacrifices if they hope to get signed. But unlike blues players, rock musicians, or classically trained artists, rappers cannot get paid for covering other people's music at local venues. There's no market for that. In fact, there are added pressures in hip hop around "keeping it real" and producing original music. Likewise, there's no popular, citywide industry devoted to celebrating the contributions of hip hop artists to a city's past—

where blues singers in Chicago or St. Louis are seen as part of a proud cultural tradition and marketed to tourists, rappers in South Central LA or the Bronx are dismissed or lumped in with a seedy image most cities would rather gloss over.

Trenseta's hoped-for deal—one that would let him keep it real and be himself—never came. His story helps us see how an artist's ideas around selling out can soften over time. Younger and more idealistic artists still believe in themselves and think more opportunities are on the horizon. Their hopes have not yet been dashed by the feeling of opportunities closing off to them. Over time, rappers can come to see selling out as a necessary evil if they want to make a life out of making music.

On a warm spring afternoon, I met up with Trenseta and CP at Crenshaw Faders. Trenseta pulled CP aside to talk about his career and pitfalls to avoid while trying to blow up. That day, Trenseta criticized many of CP's peers at Project Blowed for their blind aversion to mainstream hip hop music. He questioned the tendency of underground artists to see commercial success as a sign of selling out.[11]

Looking back on his own career path, Trenseta softened his critique of major record labels. Although he turned down a deal that would have required him to significantly change his image and musical style, he seemed to understand the precarious nature of opportunity within a competitive field like the music industry. Although he did not talk openly about whether he regretted his choices, he often gave emerging rappers like CP advice that he did not follow:

I feel a lot of people at the Blowed start to sound alike. They dis the industry, 'cause that's what you do when you underground—"Fuck the industry!" Nah, hell nah! That's what you want! Underground rap started from rappers who couldn't get record deals. I remember when people were saying, "Fuck the industry, this is the underground!" It's 'cause their demos kept getting rejected by the record companies! So we need to be professionals about this. You know, they [the underground rappers he came up with] didn't know how to make a hook [a catchy chorus]. They didn't know how to format a song. It's easy to just freestyle and say a whole bunch of stuff, but I tell them [emerging rappers] to keep it going and just make a song. It's hard to make a "song," with a hook and a verse and a concept, so I tell them to challenge themselves.

CP listened closely. Later, Trenseta talked about his own growth and maturation, which he pegged to touring as rapper Skee-Lo's "hype man" in the mid-1990s, after Skee-Lo released his hit single "I Wish." Hype men have a simple role: fire up the audience before and during a live show. The most famous hype men (like Public Enemy's Flava Flav) stand alongside the main performer and engage the audience in call-and-response, get the audience cheering, and simply engage the emotions of audience members. Trenseta's time on the road with Skee-Lo was pivotal. He learned a lot about the challenges of being a recording artist:

> It wasn't my style of music, but I got a riff of what it's like to go on tour, hit tours, and have to be up and go to the show and do this and everything. And publishers and all that type of stuff, and interviews—I was a part of that. I wasn't the head man, but I was a part of that, 'cause I was helping him with the shows, and we was on stage, hype man and all that, and that's when I was like, "Damn, this is for real." Like, "You could really be a star."

In addition to learning about the challenges of performing multiple times in multiple venues, Trenseta learned about the personal and social challenges of touring, the work that goes into promoting the tour and the music, and the different relationships professional artists have to cultivate in order to blow up and then stay popular. He saw the larger process of sustaining a successful career and the tremendous work and commitment people pour into converting one big hit into a lifetime of hits. He walked away from the tour with a new appreciation for mainstream recording artists.

Now a veteran, Trenseta extended similar opportunities to emerging rappers in his personal network. At one point in my fieldwork, a concert promoter invited him to open for E-40, a platinum-selling rap artist from Oakland. In the weeks before the show, Trenseta prepared CP and Big Flossy to be his hype men. Another afternoon in the barbershop, Trenseta and CP planned for the show, talking about the promotional flyers CP would pick up and distribute and how Trenseta thought they should make a grand entrance by "rolling up in a stretched black limo with groupies." CP sat quietly and took mental notes: Trenseta wanted everyone in matching "Trenseta" T-shirts on stage, and CP said that he might know some women who would be interested in coming on the stage and being part of the entourage.

Although Trenseta was still hanging out at Project Blowed, emerging rappers saw him as a continued source of advice about how to best navigate the music industry. In addition to performing in big shows, Trenseta was collaborating with famous, signed artists. When he had opportunities, Trenseta shared them, giving younger artists a taste of the action. For Trenseta, it was a matter of returning some of the experience he'd gained from touring with Skee-Lo years before.

Again, not all veterans are relegated to irrelevance by aspiring rappers. Veterans can guide emerging rappers through the different challenges that await them as they begin to transition away from Project Blowed. Trenseta continued to play a mentoring role in the careers of Big Flossy and CP because he was actively recording and performing with artists outside of the Project Blowed network. Giving younger men a chance to collaborate was an extremely valuable form of mentoring; while performances as "hype men" might not seem like much on the surface, they give emerging rappers a taste of performing in front of larger audiences away from their local scene. This, on its own, can help demystify the next steps that aspiring rappers take in their careers.

Conclusion

When they are still learning the ropes at Project Blowed, young men look up to and even idolize veterans. Like coaches and faculty advisers, veterans are responsible for helping these men learn the foundational skills that are central to their art. They teach emerging rappers how to hold a microphone, different ways of hyping an audience, how to manage their breathing, and so on.

However, at different points in time, young men start to outgrow their mentor-mentee relationships. Emerging rappers become less reliant on the advice and approval of veterans, who come to represent the stalled careers they hope to avoid. Once valuable mentors, emerging rappers begin to see veterans as "cautionary tales," thirtysomethings whose careers never took off outside of the local scene. Although they still respect veterans for their technical knowledge and experience, novice rappers who want to blow up focus on building relationships with new mentors.

For the young men at Project Blowed, becoming a veteran can come to represent career inertia. As they refine their skills and become more proficient rappers, they begin to focus more intensely on what they think will launch their careers as recording artists. As they seek out new mentors in a major shift in their rap careers, things become less about coming regularly to Project Blowed and trying to be the most respected freestyler or battle rapper. The new relationships give them access to a broader world of connections that exist far outside their everyday lives. They stoke their dreams of becoming signed recording artists.

These ties also introduce new identity dilemmas. Mentors might encourage rappers to become more entrepreneurial and to reproduce the racialized, hypermasculine gangsta and thug identities that are so prevalent in mainstream hip hop culture. The distinct styles that had helped the young rappers distinguish themselves in battles and ciphers might now be critiqued as industry types look for dance club hits with catchy choruses and relatable—or at least decipherable—lyrics. The identities of success are shaped by a larger industry that reproduces narrow caricatures of young Black men. By fitting in, aspiring rappers hope they might blow up. By staying underground, they fear that they will become veterans whose careers don't materialize beyond the local scene. This tension inspires their decisions to continue branching out.

6

Almost Famous

We had just finished watching a bootlegged copy of *American Gangster*.
Flako had gone home, and I was about to leave, too. But E.Crimsin motioned me into his den. He saw me checking out his wall of comic books.
"Most people don't know I collect these," he said, smiling. He was right:
the guy I knew liked lifting weights and taking selfies with his pit bull.
He often wore black tank tops, sunglasses, chinos, and a beanie with
his name embroidered in Old English lettering. Sometimes, he'd top it
all with a black trench coat. From afar, he looked like a cross between a
goth and a gangbanger.

While browsing social media, Crimsin showed me one of his online
friends, an Asian American guy whose hair was shiny from a thick gloss
of gel. "Who's that?" I asked. "That's 'Derrick Hwang,' he's a music video
producer. He's worked with big-name people," Crimsin said, smiling
proudly. We then looked at Derrick Hwang's page together. I immediately recognized the song loading on his page. It was E.Crimsin's "Donkey Kong Pimp." "How did you hook that up?" I asked. "Shit, my nigga,
I got connections! Niggas don't even know!"

I laughed, "How did you get this guy to bump your shit?" E.Crimsin
smiled:

It's funny. I know this nigga, "Jerry Kim," at LAX. He tests out the weight
of all the planes and shit. My nigga, Jerry, is friends with Derrick. Apparently they went to school together. Derrick heard my song from Jerry and
asked him about it. So Jerry told him about me, and then Derrick put it
up on his page.

Although Crimsin had met Derrick just once and emailed with him a few more times, this online gesture meant a lot. It *felt* momentous. It gave Crimsin hope about his chances of getting discovered. In his mind, he was on the right track, meeting people who were in the music industry. Blowin' up felt attainable.

As I got to know Crimsin, I learned that this was not an isolated incident. Sometimes, he met famous people at work—as a porter at Los Angeles International Airport. Celebrities would pay him to push their belongings out of the terminal. At one of his late-night after parties, he beamed with pride and told me, "I just pushed out Al Jarreau." Crimsin must have seen me looking confused and explained that Jarreau was a multi–Grammy Award jazz singer.

Curious, I asked, "Oh really? Who else have you helped?"

"Lemme see . . . I helped Snoop Dogg the other day. I told him that I represent Project Blowed."

"Did Snoop know about the Blowed?"

"Yeah, he knew about the Good Life and all that shit."

"How did Snoop tip?"

"Shit, Snoop hit me with forty dollars, nigga! I told him that I fuck with [am a part of] Project Blowed and he said, 'That's what's up!'"

Crimsin retrieved his photo album. He turned the pages with care, telling me stories about different celebrities he'd met at LAX, nightclubs, and in other random moments in his daily life. He must have thumbed through ten pages of photographs—many of which showed him standing with movie stars, musicians, athletes, and reality TV personalities. He posed with Snoop, Kiefer Sutherland, E-40 (an Oakland rapper), and a long list of others. The album could rival a collection of framed celebrity photos at a local dive bar. As he closed it, he smirked, "I'm making moves!"

Momentous Interactions

Los Angeles is a unique place to pursue rap dreams because hopefuls can feel close to fame. Since the city is home to the world's grandest entertainment industries, young hopefuls have opportunities here that do not exist in most places. Aspiring entertainers often "know somebody" or "know somebody who knows somebody" in the industry. They can rub shoulders with people in the business. And this access isn't exclusive to the middle class, elite, or even well connected. The young men I followed had fleeting encounters with celebrities as well as more lasting collaborations with people working behind the scenes. The young men felt close to the action, even though the interactions rarely led to significant advances in their careers. In different ways, each brush with fame inspired hope and made their rap dreams feel attainable.

These are what I call "momentous interactions," or encounters that leave people feeling excited and hopeful about their future. Momentous interactions do not need to be rational calculations about the future. People read what they want into interactions and form their own ideas about what the incidents do and do not mean. The person who believes he met his soul mate on an online dating site and the college student whose professor encourages her to pursue graduate studies both feel swells of momentum. They feel excited, enthralled, and hopeful about achieving some desired future. Similarly, this momentum sustains their commitments to certain people and activities, even if those commitments seem crazy or irrational to outsiders.

In this chapter, I describe three types of momentous interactions. First, the young men I studied gained exposure through popular media in and around Los Angeles. Second, they struck up collaborations with people working behind the scenes in the entertainment world. These relationships were instrumental in advancing their careers, but also springboards into larger networks of "support personnel" working in the entertainment industries.[1] Third, some were able to develop working relationships with celebrities. All these interactions *felt* momentous. They left young men with hope that they were closing in on their dreams—or at least they were on the right track.

Randall Collins provides the theoretical scaffolding for these ideas. In his theory of interaction rituals, Collins argues that interaction rituals leave people feeling happy, excited, and charged up with "emotional energy."[2] Birthdays, concerts, weddings, and other social events are energizing. People leave these events feeling rejuvenated. In similar ways, rappers left their interactions with people in the entertainment world feeling aglow with positive emotional energy. In addition to filling them with hope and excitement about their career prospects, the interactions propelled them deeper into their rap careers. They encouraged rappers to keep hustling and trying to find new angles into the entertainment world.

Ultimately, the stories here provide an important addition to my idea of existential urgency. While urgency is caused by experiences that foreshadow vulnerability, it is also *sustained* by interactions that inspire hope. Chances to be on TV and rub shoulders with people in the entertainment world make faraway dreams feel attainable. But there's an underside to these interactions. Although the men here had real advantages over other aspiring rappers without access to the entertainment world, the allure of being close to fame can be its own trap. The ease with which young men could strike up these relationships sustained their hopes in blowin' up.

MTV and Momentum

MTV has long promoted hip hop culture and music. On one hand, the televised promotion of hip hop gave young Black artists unprecedented access to popular media exposure and new audiences. Shows like *Yo! MTV Raps*, hosted by Doctor Dre (not the Dr. Dre from N.W.A.) and Ed Lover from 1988 to 1995, signaled a new era. Artists who were able to get onto MTV saw their popularity skyrocket overnight. For the first time, audiences across the nation could tune in and watch music videos for new Black artists from places like Compton, South Central, Long Beach, Inglewood, Brooklyn, Queens, and other epicenters of hip hop culture.

At the same time, hip hop's rise on MTV signaled a change in artistic control over a musician's image and identity. With the rise of new technologies and ways of consuming and promoting music, artists had to negotiate their identities with producers and television executives who were often motivated by different interests. Executives would routinely distort the identities of Black hip hop artists to fit stereotypes of

Blackness that were popular among the predominantly White, teenage, male consumer base. During this era, hip hop music took a turn toward what Tricia Rose calls the tragic trinity in hip hop: artists who portrayed gangstas, pimps, and hos received a disproportionate share of airtime, becoming the staples of hip hop's changing public image.[3]

By the late 1990s, MTV underwent changes and restructuring, shifting from music to reality TV programming. This created new hurdles for artists who wanted to get discovered. Between 1995 and 2000, MTV played 36.5 percent fewer music videos than it had in the previous generation.[4] The network's president commented: "Clearly, the novelty of just showing music videos has worn off. It's required us to reinvent ourselves to a contemporary audience."[5] Shows like *The Real World*, *Road Rules*, and other reality programming preempted video countdowns and musical guests.

Still, MTV continued airing shows connected to hip hop culture. For instance, from 2004 to 2007, MTV studios in Santa Monica produced *Pimp My Ride*, hosted by longtime gangsta rapper Xzibit. The show was an ode to the Southern California car culture in which cars were given tricked-out makeovers. MTV also featured *Yo Momma*, hosted by television celebrity Wilmer Valderrama, between 2006 and 2007. It featured contestants "playing the dozens" and rappers like Method Man, Chingy, Jadakiss, and the Ying Yang Twins.[6] The short-lived show helped modernize the dozens and represented MTV's continued role in promoting hip hop–related shows.

* * *

Although MTV's main studios are located in New York City, the channel has a branch in Santa Monica. During my fieldwork, project scouts would occasionally visit Project Blowed to recruit folks for shows in pilot or production phases. Although these interactions were rarely, if ever, motivated by interests to showcase untapped talent, they still represented possibilities for young men who didn't grow up envisioning many options for becoming publicly recognized.

For instance, one night I was hanging out with "Legacee" outside Project Blowed. He said someone from MTV was on the block to find people for a hip hop show. We approached the scout, who was talking to a group of rappers: "We're producing a show that would feature guys battling." The crowd got riled up. Someone said, "Let me get on there! People ain't seen a nigga like me spit!" This got everyone laughing. Someone else belted out, "They ain't ready for us! They ain't ready for us!" The scout seemed pleased and handed out her business cards.

Legacee and I waited until most of the guys had walked away before pressing her for more details. "It's going to be a rap game show," she explained. "Rappers will answer trivia questions and do challenges, like battle." She must have sensed that I was confused, because she added: "It's still really early, so I don't know what it will be about, but we've been talking with Eminem about possibly hosting the show." Legacee was impressed. "Oh really? Y'all are talking to Em?" "Yeah," she said, "and some other people, too."

When I asked about her own role in the production, she said that she was an intern scouting for this show and others. She also explained that she was a struggling actress. She was doing this work on the side while actively pursuing her own dreams of being on TV. "I'm really an actress and I've been trying to get into acting, but that is sorta slow, so I looked into media work, because that's what I studied when I was in college," she said. I nodded and asked, "What kinds of things have you acted in?" She smiled widely and told us about some of her recent auditions and breaks: "I just recently filmed an episode for *The Office.*"

Although this hip hop game show never got off the ground, for a few minutes, the prospect of getting on MTV felt real for the guys on the corner. The scout's visit provided glimmers of hope to a group of young men hungry for exposure.

Later that night, some of the guys talked about how this would be a turning point in their careers. "Rizin," a guy who was not around that much, said, "I don't care. I'm gonna go on there and shut it down. They ain't ready for me." Another guy chimed in that he was excited to check it out and felt like lots of other things were starting to come together. A few others called the scout and arranged to audition and do screen tests. The show never aired, but for this group of men, the prospect of getting on MTV and rapping—even on a game show—was an inroad that made blowin' up feel just a little more attainable.

Some of the young men were able to get onto shows that actually aired. MTV recruited Nocando and Sahtyre to appear on a short-lived show called *From G's to Gents*. Created by Jamie Foxx, it was developed as a makeover show hosted by Fonzworth Bentley, famously fashionable former personal valet to P. Diddy. Contestants entered the show under the premise that they would be transformed from "roughnecks into gentlemen."

Nocando and Sahtyre were originally slated to be rap coaches for contestants in a hip hop–inspired challenge. During a short break on the set, Nocando gave a candid cell phone camera interview to a friend who was there with him:

> Me and Sahtyre from the Swim Team [a hip hop group created at Project Blowed] ended up doing this, uh, because, we need money, and they're firing people at alarming rates in America. A'ight? So, usually a young underground rapper like myself wouldn't be fuckin' with them at all, but gotta keep the bills paid. But we're sitting down in the studio, and they're having us write rhymes to battle each other, and they start giving their input like, uh, "Maybe you should start saying something like this, maybe should start saying something like that." Then, sooner or later, they started saying, "You should say 'bling bling,' 'ice,'" so Hollywood is still evil. I don't want you to get that shit wrong![7]

Others got onto MTV reality shows that had nothing to do with hip hop or their rhyming talents. Scouts recruited CP for an episode of *I Have a Jealous Girlfriend*, a show in the network's larger True Life documentary series. MTV crews followed him, VerBS, and St. Nick (who later became Vann Clayton) as they hung out around Los Angeles. These three, who had been best friends since their days at Hamilton High School, had created a rap trio called the Citi. Although crews recorded them freestyling together and hanging out at Project Blowed, that footage never aired. Instead, the show focused on CP's explosive relationship with his girlfriend La Toya. The following synopsis is directly from MTV's archive:

> La Toya and Christian [CP] have been together for almost three years, but Christian cheated two years ago. At the mall, some girl tells La Toya that she kicked it with Christian at the beach long ago. Christian gets fed up with La Toya constantly accusing him of cheating when he's done nothing wrong for two years. To escape, Christian parties with his friends, but La Toya wants to tag along to spy on him. At work, La Toya's boss warns that being jealous means she hasn't forgiven Christian, and he may leave. After another argument over jealousy, Christian decides that he is tired of having to explain himself. Finally, Christian leaves. He and La Toya are no longer together.

VerBS was able to parlay this experience into his own reality TV appearance on a dating show called *Wanna Come In?* During their dates, contestants—presented as nerds—were coached by a more experienced dater. The coach would feed contestants like VerBS pickup lines through a hidden wire. At the end of the date, women had the option to ask men if they wanted to come into their homes. If they got invited in, contestants won cash prizes. VerBS was excited to get on TV, even if it meant being on a dating game. He eagerly volunteered to play the nerd role. VerBS leant me the videotape of his appearance on the show. "So did you actually go out with her again?" I asked. "Nah. I wanted to, but it was all part of the show. At the end, she asked me in or whatever, but it wasn't like that. It was just for the show."

* * *

Getting on MTV was exciting. Interactions with scouts, recording promos, and appearing on reality shows left these young men feeling hopeful about the future. These interactions felt momentous. Even though they weren't getting recognized for their talents, these minor roles represented possibilities for young men who had grown up in communities that do not sustain the image of limitless future possibilities. They represented brief openings in the larger opportunity structure from which working-class young Black men so often feel excluded. Brushes with network types rewarded and motivated their eagerness to meet more people in the entertainment industries. They felt that they were one momentous interaction away from possibly breaking their career wide open.

But many of these opportunities did not fulfill their expectations. Their appearances on MTV were often in roles that did not showcase their talents. Even when their talents were filmed, MTV did not air those segments. In more challenging moments, the men realized that they were subject to a larger industry, less interested in discovering unsigned hype and more set on reproducing the stereotypes of young Black men that the network's fan base wanted to watch. Far from being platforms from which artists could launch a career, the shows funneled young men into set roles created for mass consumption.

The ease with which these men could access MTV was its own source of momentum. Fleeting encounters with intern scouts and more significant involvement in pilots and reality shows were tantalizing experiences for young men from South Central and other working-class areas of LA. Those who got on TV enjoyed the added exposure and for brief moments became local celebrities among friends and family after their shows aired. While their appearances on TV did little to boost their credibility as aspiring artists, they fueled hope. The men who got on MTV (and others around them) felt that with a little more luck and persistence, one of the appearances might move them closer to realizing their rap dreams.

Connecting with Support Personnel

When most people think of Los Angeles, they think of celebrity culture: the Hollywood Walk of Fame, celebrity home tours, and international events like the Academy Awards. Visitors flock to movie stars' homes in Bel Air, swanky retail like Rodeo Drive in Beverly Hills, and red carpet premieres where stars greet fans and the press.

But Los Angeles is also home to a much larger and less visible population of people who work behind the scenes in entertainment. These are people Howard Becker calls "support personnel."[8] In his study of art worlds, Becker shows the constellation of people who come together to make art possible. Indeed, while we typically think of artists as lone wolves, Becker shows us that artists, musicians, and other creative types generally exist at the center of a web of people whose cooperation and varied expertise make art work possible.

As I described in the last chapter, young men with rap dreams eventually come to a point in their careers when they shift their energies away from performing at Project Blowed. Instead of trying to impress their peers, they focus on becoming polished recording artists. They want to be perceived as professionals with a professional product. This inspires them to reach out and work with studio engineers, who can help them record, mix, and master an album for distribution and sale. Relationships with studio engineers provide another source of momentum. The men hope that, with a polished product, they will be noticed and taken seriously by an A&R, record label intern, or someone who can discover their talent, put their CD in the right hands, and help them blow up.

These interactions also introduce rappers to a new division of labor in the creative process. They learn that studio engineers do much more than they imagined. During recording sessions, they see that engineers are much more than just technical aids who try to optimize the sound quality of recordings. Rather, studio engineers guide moment-to-moment creative decisions and use their expertise to determine what is and what is not possible, given technological constraints. Some instruct rappers on how to say things differently. Others offer feedback on choices that will and won't work in a recording. In many situations, the creative power lies in the hands of the studio engineer whose sonic and technological sensibilities shape finished songs.

Flawliss was able to get professional recording help from a recording engineer named "Corey." He met him after performing at Zen Sushi, a trendy restaurant and bar that doubled as an underground hip hop club in Silver Lake (a hip, diverse area for nightlife in LA). This felt like a big, even momentous, step in his career because he had never worked with a professional engineer before. In his mind, a professionally mixed and mastered album would only boost his chances of getting discovered and signed.

After Flawliss performed for a small crowd, some of whom had come to see hip hop and others who were only interested in maki and sake, we all met up at the venue's open-air lounge and patio. Corey was frank: "I think you are great, but the beats you got aren't so great." Flawliss agreed. "Yeah, I know. Most of the stuff I got, it's because people just give me beats. Like people I know and shit, just give me stuff that they don't want." Flawliss was tight on money (he was not currently working), so he was wary of spending too much on beats.

As the night wound down, Corey and Flawliss agreed on a working relationship. Corey would engineer music for Flawliss at $40 per hour. It was a fraction of what he typically charged musicians, voice-over artists, and others, who paid more than twice as much to record at his studio during normal business hours. Corey said, "You give me a product that you're willing to put your heart behind, and I'll mix the hell out of that thing!" The two shook on it.

* * *

For years, Flawliss had tried to put together a professional-sounding album that could be his professional "calling card." So far, though, he had trouble accomplishing this. He had only been able to record with self-taught, do-it-yourself producers who often operated out of a parent's garage or closet space in their bedroom. This wasn't ideal for acoustics or sound quality in his recordings. Much of his recorded music was filled with glaring technical issues that detracted from his skills as a songwriter and rapper. None was mixed and mastered professionally, and the vocals and instrumentals were usually badly balanced.

For instance, on one track, listeners could clearly hear Flawliss's voice at lower to midrange volume levels; on the next, it would be hard to hear him without the volume cranked up. Not only was this unpleasant to the listener; it made Flawliss uneasy. He wanted to be taken seriously by A&Rs and record industry scouts. He worried that an amateur demo could undermine his credibility in the eyes of A&Rs, fans, and other industry gatekeepers. He felt that this would make him come across as amateur to people who controlled access to the music industry.

Meeting Corey was an important step for Flawliss in moving toward his future goals. Although Flawliss was not yet signed to a label, he felt that his chances of being signed would drastically improve once he could present people with a professional-sounding product. His long-term goals seemed more doable to him once he started to record with professional help. Flawliss was energized and ready to seize opportunities; he saw Corey as one more rung up on his ladder.

Inheriting Creative Networks

In addition to collaborating with studio engineers, aspiring rappers became interested in making music videos. Much like the full-length album, they hoped a professionally shot and edited music video would help them broaden their fan base *and* signal that they were serious artists. These men grew up in an era of social media such as YouTube, Facebook, and SoundCloud. These outlets gave them free resources in their attempts to blow up. Artists could broadcast their music across the globe.

Still, they didn't want to put out something that looked and sounded amateur. YouTube and other online media outlets were full of low-quality videos. Instead, these young men wanted to increase their fan base and credibility with a music video shot and edited by professionals. With the right help and a little bit of luck, they imagined their clips becoming viral hits.

E.Crimsin reached out to an emerging video director named Hugo V. The two met at a local community college and instantly struck up a friendship. Both came from humble beginnings, loved hip hop, and dreamed of blowin' up. Although they were close friends, Hugo had much more experience working in the entertainment world and became an informal mentor in Crimsin's life. He had directed music videos for Cypress Hill, Psycho Realm, and other LA-based hip hop artists. After saving up some money, Crimsin paid Hugo to shoot a video in his apartment.

The video shoot was set up on a sunny Saturday afternoon. I arrived at close to four in the afternoon, noticing three stone-faced, buff-looking guys at the bottom of Crimsin's stairwell. Each wore a navy blue flak jacket with "Security" in bold yellow lettering across the back.

As I walked up, the oldest of the three guards stared me down. He seemed to be waiting for me to declare my intentions. I said, "I'm friends with Crimsin. Is there a video shoot?" "What's your name?" I replied, "Jooyoung," and he shot me a quizzical look before pulling out his walkie-talkie: "Somebody named Joo . . . is here." I recognized Hugo's voice from on other end, saying "Yeah, he's cool." The security guards stepped aside and allowed me up.

The living room was a tangled mess of wires, cameras, and electric cords. I spotted Hugo sitting in a cloth-bound director's chair. He had his hair wrapped beneath a slick fedora that partly covered one of his eyes. "Wassup, bro?" he said. "Not much, man. This is crazy. You got all this set up," I replied. Hugo nodded and introduced me to his two camera assistants, gangly White guys named "Kevin" and "Todd."

Later that night, the crew from *The Grimmie Wreck TV Show*, an urban lifestyle show in San Diego, showed up to cover the shoot. Hugo explained that he had invited the crew to generate buzz around Crimsin's song release. They interviewed E.Crimsin and Trenseta, who had just finished recording vocals for an unreleased song, "Fill Your Cup."

Crimsin was pumped up. He had never been interviewed for a television show. Although *Grimmie Wreck* was a local San Diego show, the lights, cameras, and microphones made the whole event feel momentous. Crimsin felt like a celebrity in his own home. The whole event left Crimsin feeling inspired. No longer was he just some artist recording a music video in his apartment—he was somebody getting interviewed on TV.

Later, Crimsin talked with E-Low, the host of the *Grimmie Wreck* show. E-Low told him stories about how he had been mentored by Jerry Heller, the longtime CEO of Ruthless Records. He also named a wide range of celebrities and other media types he knew in San Diego. Crimsin listened closely, growing more excited by the moment. At a break in E-Low's stories, Crimsin beamed: "I gotta come down and visit you out there." E-Low extended his hand: "F'sho, f'sho. You can come down anytime. Any friend of Hugo is a friend of mine. I'll introduce you to everybody!"

* * *

The men who had proved themselves at Project Blowed saw their goals shift as they got serious about trying to become signed recording artists. They focused on finding ways to signal their professionalism and commitment: recording with professional engineers, producing slick music videos, and shaking hands with anyone who could broaden their network. The process of working with professional help represented a big step in a longer process of becoming a recording artist.

On some occasions, rappers would inherit the creative networks of key people they met in the entertainment world. Their initial collaborations would become springboards for new contacts. E.Crimsin's ongoing relationship with Hugo helped him meet the production team from *Grimmie Wreck*, other artists, and people working behind the scenes. His relationship with both Hugo and E-Low brought him into contact with a constellation of others working in the entertainment world. One of the cameramen from that night was also a Grammy Award–winning producer and became one of Crimsin's new professional contacts and collaborators. Crimsin also got to meet set designers, models, makeup artists, sound and lighting people, video editors, and a string of others connected in the collective production of music making. Plugging into these networks felt momentous. Crimsin knew he was comparatively better off than before he met Hugo. He had glimmers of hope that he was on the right path.

Working with Celebrities

Some young men were also able to strike up long-term working relationships with celebrities who'd already achieved the dreams they were chasing. These were not the fleeting interactions that E.Crimsin proudly told me about at his late-night parties. Instead, these were actual working collaborations. Working, sharing ideas, and learning how celebrities worked and lived, created an entirely different kind of hope among aspiring rappers. This didn't happen often, but when it did, it was cause for great excitement and urgency.

Trenseta was one of the few men to strike up such a relationship. Midway through my fieldwork, he started collaborating with the Academy Award–winning actor and aspiring musician Jamie Foxx. Although Foxx had begun his career as a sketch comedian on the TV comedy and variety show *In Living Color*, he had transitioned into serious acting roles. In 2004, he won both an Oscar and a Golden Globe for his portrayal of Ray Charles in the biopic *Ray*. Although all of his performances in the film were dubbed from original recordings, Foxx took singing lessons and discovered a passion for music. From then on, he wasn't only starring in Hollywood movies; Foxx was busy recording R&B songs and the hooks for rap ballads such as Kanye West's "Gold Digger."[9]

One afternoon, while Trenseta and I were hanging out in the studio space he rented above Crenshaw Faders, he told me about his chance meeting with Foxx. Trenseta's close friend was Jamie Foxx's longtime barber. This friend was invited to Foxx's house for a Memorial Day party and brought Trenseta along. At one point during the night, Trenseta and others huddled around the star in Foxx's home studio, watching him make beats on the fly. Everyone was vibing out; people were excited to jump on the track. Rappers came out of the woodwork to spit their hottest verses over the beat. The impromptu session continued for about twenty minutes while Trenseta "hung back in the cut," cool as a cucumber. He wasn't scared or nervous. He was waiting for the right moment to jump on the mic and "shut it down."

A veteran of open mics, Trenseta let other rappers have their turn— for a while. Deep down, he knew he was going to outshine everyone. "I was just hanging back at first, lettin' these other niggas spit they little bars. Just waitin' for the right moment." When others had spit their best flows, Trenseta was prodded by a friend. He asked to get on, then he unleashed his lyrical skills. "After that, Jamie [Foxx] came up to me and told me that he was gonna build a studio in his place and that he wanted me to come and do songs with them."

In rapping, much like in b-boying, popping, and DJing, a performer who gets onstage and performs significantly better than everyone else around can effectively "shut down" a cipher. They set a bar that is just too high for the next person.[10] Anyone who follows looks weak or unskilled in comparison. In this case, Trenseta's turn on the mic led to a long-term creative collaboration with a star. The two not only started recording together but also performed together at venues across LA. They became collaborators and friends.[11]

* * *

In LA, someone like Trenseta—who was born and raised in the shadows of gangs—*can* befriend and collaborate with an A-list mega-celebrity like Jamie Foxx. It's not a typical story, but it represents possibilities to other young men. Others saw Trenseta's new situation and believed they, too, could work hard and get in with someone famous. Big Flossy felt inspired after seeing Trenseta's success, and he set out to start networking with different people who could help him blow up.

On different levels, hip hop artists believe in the core tenets of the Horatio Alger rags-to-riches stories. They point to well-known examples of how struggling artists got discovered or "put on" by someone already in the entertainment world. They know bits of these stories by heart, repeating them as if they can will themselves into similar situations. For example, many know how hip hop moguls Dr. Dre and Jimmy Iovine heard Eminem's *Slim Shady EP* and signed him to Aftermath/ Interscope Records. They know how Sean "P. Diddy" Combs heard Notorious B.I.G.'s demo and signed him to Bad Boy Records. These stories are part of a larger hip hop folklore. Even though they are exceptional cases, by all accounts, aspiring artists see them as confirmation that their hard work can pay off.

Their own interactions with popular media outlets, support personnel, and celebrities add hope. Together, the success stories and their own first steps combine into a sense of momentum and urgency. The men never know when the opportunity they bypass or the one they jump on will be their big break.

Conclusion

In LA, young Black men from the 'hood have unique opportunities to interact with people involved in entertainment. Their proximity to one of the world's largest entertainment industries provides them chances to get on TV, work with support personnel who can help them address practical problems in their careers, and rub shoulders with celebrities. All of these interactions fill them with excitement and hope for the future. They are momentous interactions that can charge and sustain the aspirants' existential urgency.

Outsiders might be tempted to think that these relationships are just the end result of enterprising and industrious young men. Others might think they're the result of dumb luck. Neither view is totally wrong. But just being in LA does not guarantee connections that will help advance one's creative aspirations. Social networking takes hard work, persistence, and a little luck. Young people who want to forge these ties have to make a concerted effort to put themselves into situations that increase their odds of making fruitful connections.

This brings into focus the paradox of pursuing these dreams in Los Angeles. On the one hand, there are very real advantages to pursuing rap dreams (or entertainment careers) in LA that young people don't freely enjoy in other cities that do not have a vibrant entertainment industry. Los Angeles, Hollywood, and other outlying Southern California cities afford these men chances to meet people who could be very important for them in realizing their career dreams. It is an ecology that is uniquely enabling. Young men who live and work in LA can leave their homes every day with the sense that they may meet someone who either is famous or knows somebody in the entertainment industry. This is tantalizing. Aspirants operate in a world in which they think the next interaction *could* be the one that completely changes their lives.

On the other hand, most momentous interactions never amount to much. Collaborations with studio engineers, music video producers, and others in the entertainment industries can lead to appreciable advances in their overall creative *output*, but it's not clear that the collaborations end up *moving* these men closer to their rap dreams. This is the paradox of momentous interactions; many foster hope, but it's difficult to anticipate exactly how these interactions will ultimately affect the future.

At a broader level, the stories here also pose important questions for how we think about racial and ethnic segregation. For years, sociologists have focused on the processes underlying racial and ethnic segregation in neighborhoods and institutions. William Julius Wilson pioneered work in this area and showed how discriminatory housing policies, concentrated poverty, neighborhood violence, and other inner-city ills trap urban working-class Black families into small, mostly insulated neighborhoods that diminish their life chances.[12]

Wilson's theories explain some of the underlying social and cultural mechanisms that prevent urban working-class Black men from creating meaningful relationships with individuals and groups outside of urban "ghettos." But in addition to public places that provide occasions—however brief—for diverse groups to interact, there are also activities that bring people together into collaborative relationships.[13] Hip hop is one of these shared cultural activities. Its emergence as a global music and art form brings together youth from diverse situations who all share a love of hip hop.

In more practical ways, rappers who try to blow up rely on the help of others. Young men who live in segregated neighborhoods actively branch out into new and diverse social worlds. They experience what I like to call creative integration and connect with people whose lives are far removed from their own. These interactions are sometimes fleeting and rarely lead to appreciable changes in their career prospects, but the young men I met would momentarily integrate themselves into diverse networks to get their music careers off the ground.

7

Ditching the Day Job

We were next to the World Stage, a jazz club around the corner from Project Blowed. In the background, a trumpet player was jamming with a pianist and a drummer. It was like they were playing a somber soundtrack for our conversation. Flawliss sighed and told me, "It's time for me to make some moves. I can't work at my job no more. I'm not made to sell cell phones and shit. I'm finna come into my prime."

Flawliss worked five or six days a week selling cell phones from a Verizon kiosk. Although it wasn't his dream job, it helped him make ends meet. And he had taken to it quickly. Years of writing rhymes, freestyling, battling, and performing on stage made him a natural salesman. Customers were like audience members. To make a sale, he had to grab their attention, hold it, and keep them entertained. This was second nature after years at the Blowed.

But Flawliss was feeling stuck. Like most aspiring artists, he couldn't imagine working at his day job for the rest of his life. It was depressing to think of working at that kiosk while his talents went unused. In the best-case scenario, he might get promoted to manager. But he doubted that would help him move out of the 'hood, buy a small house, and send his son to a private school. Keeping his day job felt like a dead end.

We talked for a few hours. Near the end of our conversation, he said he was going to quit his job—at least for the time being. He had some money saved up and thought he could survive for a few months without a job. If his money got tight, he could trade in his car for extra cash. It would allow him to put more time and energy into pursuing his rap dreams.

A few weeks later, Flawliss made good on his promise. He quit his job and sold his car, using some of the money to pay for rent and the rest on beats and renting studio time. It was now or never.

Existential Urgency and the Day Job

In the song "Things Done Changed," the late Brooklyn rapper Notorious B.I.G. rhymes:

> If I wasn't in the rap game
> I probably have a key knee-deep in the crack game
> because the streets are a short stop
> either you slangin' rock or you got a wicked jump shot.

Notorious B.I.G.'s rhymes reveal a central theme in the working lives of young Black men from working-class neighborhoods: many feel shut out of the American dream and turn to alternative careers that seem to offer better chances at upward mobility. In the past twenty years, sociologists of urban poverty have focused on the allure of drug dealing, stick-up robberies, and other illicit hustles.[1]

But it's important not to overstate the popularity of illicit paths. Street hustling is one of many paths young men take when they can't find—or even see—pathways to mobility in the local labor market. Others are drawn to what Robin Kelley calls play labor, a range of skills and talents that might lead to a payday and upward mobility.[2] Like hoop dreams, rap dreams are a popular form of play labor among young Black men. They believe that their rapping skills could propel them into a high-status labor market. What's more, young men see rapping as a meaningful pursuit. They invest time and energy into improving their skills and feel that rapping is a representation of their talents, a more authentic reflection of who they are.

If rapping represents future possibilities, the "day job" is a dead end. Low-wage menial jobs are not often held in high esteem among young men who have other hopes and aspirations. They figure anyone can get those jobs. And they don't foresee many opportunities for upward mobility or for validating their masculinity in dead-end jobs. Jobs in the service sector require an unflinching deference that challenges the image and swagger that these men have worked hard to create in the underground hip hop scene.

Even so, none of this is a sufficient explanation for why the men I studied eventually ditched their day jobs. To really understand how and why they did, we have to understand how aging in fleeting careers shapes a person's views of the future—and more pragmatically, how this loosens their commitments to "day jobs." As they entered their mid-twenties and approached their thirties, young men like Flawliss realized that their window of opportunity to blow up was rapidly closing.[3] Hip hop, like many careers in the entertainment world, is a young person's game. They feared that in short time they would no longer be competitive in the world of aspiring rappers.

Moreover, adding to this was another, more practical inspiration to ditch their day job. For years, they juggled the job they *needed* with the career they *wanted*. Over time and as they approached what felt like their creative prime, these men became more aware of mundane conflicts between juggling the two. A day job imposes limits on the time one can devote to rap dreams. There is little room for scheduling flexibility when you're punching a time clock. This poses challenges for rappers who want to capitalize on opportunities to perform and to collaborate with other artists. They feel out of sync with the rhythms of the creative world.

In this context, the day job becomes disposable. These men don't see many opportunities to achieve their life goals in these jobs, so they don't feel worried about losing them. For them, there is no great opportunity cost in temporarily ditching a day job to focus on something more meaningful that holds the promise—however fleeting—of launching them toward a desirable future.

The Disposable Day Job

Sociologists offer different explanations for why young Black men from working-class neighborhoods avoid low-wage jobs. Many write that young men don't foresee pathways to mobility in menial jobs. Others avoid service jobs because they are stigmatized within their peer groups. Young people who have a street orientation, in particular, feel that the jobs are a stain on their reputation.[4] Additionally, rappers do not feel any sense of urgency around their day jobs. Most are entry-level positions. They assume they could get similar work even after taking a hiatus. Unlike a prized career with high wages and benefits, day jobs seem disposable.

I first learned about this with Big Flossy, who was cycling in and out of formal work every few months. Over the time I knew him, Big Flossy would sell cell phones and shoes, work at a car wash, as event security, and as a sort of "utility hustler," someone known on the streets for being able to get things. Unlike the drug dealer, babysitter, or off-the-books mechanic, the utility hustler is not tied to any particular kind of good or service. The utility hustler is known more for his ingenuity and opportunistic approach to hustling. He can locate multiple items and services and has diffuse connections to people who can help him locate things people want. If you need something, the utility hustler will get it.

For instance, one summer Big Flossy called to ask if I wanted or knew anyone who wanted to buy firecrackers for the Fourth of July. I told him that I didn't but would let him know if I heard of anyone who did. Big Flossy also explained that he was selling DVDs, belts, and a wide array of other items. He added, "If you ever need anything, let me know. I know people and I can get stuff. You just let me know." I asked Flossy about his decision to quit his job at a local cell phone store. He explained:

> I was like, "I could quit this job today and it won't matter." It's not like it's taking me somewhere. If this rap shit don't work out, I can always slide into some other job or I can make money like I'm doing now—selling things. It's easy. I just slide in and out when the time is right.

Getting and losing a day job poses no great risk, but rap dreams are time sensitive. Big Flossy and other men understand a rap career as a long shot in which everything must be perfectly executed. They were not delusional. They knew that the window of opportunity to blow up was extremely small and that the day they would be "too old" to blow up was nearing. This looming expiration date on their dreams shaped how they interpreted time conflicts.

Time Conflicts

Aspiring rappers face multiple dilemmas in juggling the job they need and the career they dream of having. At the core, they face dilemmas about how to spend their time—and, by extension, how competing time commitments shape their identity. For one, work schedules impose a cap on how much time rappers can devote to writing rhymes and songs, practicing, listening to music, recording in studios, performing in venues, and social networking. Aspiring artists feel that the hours they spend at work are hours that they *could* be spending making moves to chase their dreams. As they become more invested in this vision, they imagine that they are forgoing any and all additional opportunities because of their day job. This leads them to construct a hypothetical image of how they *would* live if they weren't encumbered by a day job. Interestingly, few wholly devote themselves to the pursuit of rap dreams after quitting work. Still, this hypothetical image chips away at their commitments to the day job.

The day job also requires an orientation toward time and time management that aren't always in sync with the worldview of a creative person. Most day jobs require people to schedule their time several weeks (if not months) in advance. This creates a predictable schedule and routine that organizes where and how a person spends their time.[5] Creative work isn't always so predictable. Aspiring artists in all fields are occasionally hit by flashes of inspiration. Sometimes this occurs at the end of a long night of writing rhymes and recording songs that feel like duds. Other times, this happens in the middle of another activity, one not related to music. Whichever the circumstances, the arrival of an epiphany is difficult to predict. This creates additional dilemmas for young men who see a trade-off in their hours on the clock and the time they might spend wading through drafts of a song or pursuing flashes of inspiration.

And then there are scheduling conflicts. Most concerts and recording sessions happen at nights and on weekends. While this isn't a problem for everyone, it creates challenges for some young men whose day jobs are actually night shifts. When we first met, Nocando bused tables at a small Italian restaurant in Hollywood. The job gave him a way to make ends meet but also made it difficult to book shows. Once while hanging out, Nocando told me about his scheduling dilemmas:

> It's hard getting off days. At a restaurant, you can't really get, like, Tuesday, Wednesday, Thursday, Friday, and the weekend nights off. Those are off-limits at the job. Those also happened to be the times when I get booked for shows, so it isn't really working out. I really want to work on my music, and the job really doesn't give me a lot of extra time to do that.

Nocando eventually quit to focus on his music. An uninformed critique of this choice might suggest that this was another example of how hip hop encourages idleness and an adversarial attitude toward work among working-class Black men. But this view is problematic and it misses how much time, energy, and planning rappers put into pursuing rap dreams. Nocando treated hip hop like a job. He was disciplined with his time and poured his energy into doing the things he couldn't while holding a day job. He performed at venues around Los Angeles, wrote feverishly to different beats, and recorded full-length albums. And he did all of this methodically.

Just a week later, Nocando and I met up again. He explained his new routine:

> Right now, you know, I'm not working a nine-to-five, so I try to make sure I put in eight hours a day into hip hop. On Monday night, I'll get up with Handprints [his DJ] and we'll rehearse a set, dig for records, or me and him will go and pick up a beat from somebody. Tuesday, in the daytime, my girl goes to school and I'll watch my daughter and her cousin, 'cause I'm, like, the babysitter [laughs]. Later I'll have a show. Like lately, I've been having three shows a week. Wednesday, when my girl doesn't go to school, I'll take that day off and stay at home and write, and I'll write

until I can't write no more . . . and if I'm not writing, I'm planning out song structures, and arranging how I have the vocals on the song I just finished, ya know? On Thursdays, I'll head over to the Blowed, or lately, I've been having a lot of shows on Thursdays. Fridays, my girl will go to school and I'll babysit. On the weekends, I do shows, shows, shows—in stores, janky [lame] house parties. If there's some battles, I just try to be as much of a rapper as I possibly can. If I don't have a show, I try to devote as much time to getting something recorded, selling CD-Rs, winning a battle. It's pretty much sacrifice time for me right now; I just hope my girl understands.

When I lived in LA, I met many middle-class and well-to-do types who had moved there to pursue their creative interests. Some were friends from college, whose parents were paying their rent while they tried their hand at acting, screenwriting, or filmmaking. In these cases, parents and others often see young people's creative pursuits as something to get out of their system before they grow up, get married, and have a real job and responsibilities. This was and continues to be an accepted—even celebrated—part of the life course for more privileged youth. Before committing to a long-term career, they *should* go out and explore who they are, careers, and the world.

Society holds different kinds of views for working-class young Black men who embark on similar pursuits: since Black men are in a different situation, they should not waste time chasing faraway dreams. This perspective assumes that it is more "rational" for people from disadvantaged situations to pursue a path that offers more immediate and practical benefits.

These perspectives fail to look at how young Black men make sense of future opportunities. For many of these men, the standard, middle-class route to mobility—go to college, get a job, and move up in the world—was not a taken-for-granted pathway into adulthood. They had grown up in neighborhoods in which existing jobs for young people with only high school diplomas offered few, if any, foreseeable pathways to mobility and validation. And instead of tolerating artistic flights of fancy, these men's families rallied behind their efforts and shifted their lives around to support their dreams. Indeed, Nocando's girlfriend at the time understood his passion for making music and that this could be their best shot at achieving mobility as a family. And so she made sacrifices as well, taking up work during the week when Nocando went out to work toward realizing his dreams.

In Search of a Flexible Schedule

Rappers also experience scheduling conflicts between their jobs and last-second chances to perform. The day job routinizes time. It structures how and where young men will spend that precious resource. Sure, some young men can request time off for upcoming shows, but many shows come together haphazardly—often just hours before they start. This means that rappers with flexible schedules have the best shot at capitalizing on opportunities. During my fieldwork, numerous rappers received calls from friends and promoters. I saw how they had to jump quickly at a chance to perform or lose the opportunity all together.

For example, one summer, CP, his then girlfriend Morgan, his father, his manager, and I drove to one of his performances in Van Nuys—a suburban valley city north of Los Angeles. Earlier in the day, we had all been hanging out at CP's mother's house in South Central, when CP got a call from a promoter. CP didn't hesitate. He quickly got a song list ready, called some friends, and shuttled out to the show.

I went to the performance with Jason, CP's manager at the time. We made the hour-long trek across clogged freeways and parked in an alleyway, just around the corner from the venue. Emerging from Jason's car, we spotted CP's family and some close friends who had carpooled and were stretching. After milling about for a bit, we started walking as a group to the venue. We didn't get far. A block from the club, we saw "Nick," a promoter who doubled as lead singer for a struggling rock band. CP gave Nick an upward head nod.

From the get-go, I could sense that something wasn't right. Nick was walking away from the club with a young woman. He shook his head as we walked closer, "Sorry man, it's off. Nobody showed up tonight. None

Figure 9. CP relaxing outside of a park, thinking about his future

of the bands promoted or brought people. We were gonna do it with just you, me, and another group, but nobody promoted, so there's nobody there." Jason was pissed: "What!? C'mon!" CP sighed and rolled his eyes, "Ahhh, shit! Man, are you f'real?!" Jason nudged me and groaned, "I hate this shit. Amateur shit. That's why I been telling CP not to fuck with these small-time cats anymore. Sorry for making you come all the way out here." I shrugged. "It's all good. That sucks for CP, though." We hung out in the alleyway next to the caravan of cars for a half hour, then went our separate ways.

More accomplished musicians have the power to demand that every detail surrounding a performance be tailored to their needs. Some of these demands are extensive, if not unreasonably specific. In 2012, *Business Insider* published the article "Here Are the Ridiculous Things Celebrities Demand Backstage."[6] According to this article, rapper Kanye West requires a barber's chair, Carmex lip balm, shower shoes, a tub of plain yogurt, four small containers of Yoplait yogurt, one bowl of assorted nuts, one bowl of Sunkist salted pistachio nuts (no red coloring), two packs of Extra chewing gum, one bottle of hot sauce, one box of toothpicks, one 750-milliliter bottle of Hennessy cognac, one 750-milliliter bottle of Skyy or Absolut vodka, one bottle of Patrón Silver tequila, and four six-packs of Heineken beer. Kanye and other megastars have the clout to make others wait on them and meet a series of demands.

CP and other emerging rappers are, instead, at the mercy of promoters. If they want exposure, they have to jump at last-minute opportunities to get on a show's bill. They have to be ready and willing to mobilize for these shows, or they might miss out on an opportunity. There are always other artists ready to jump at the chance, and over time, promoters come to prefer working with artists who can come through when needed. They develop trust with certain artists and call on them in a pinch. Rappers who develop reputations for being punctual and easy to work with—and of course, for responding when called on—get the gigs.

Recording schedules are similarly unpredictable. Many occur late at night and stretch into the early morning hours. Some rappers can rent time at a professional studio, which gives them some control over when they record. But most underground rappers cannot afford such fees. Instead, they must work out discounted ways to record. This means that they are at the beck and call of collaborators and have less power to make scheduling demands.[7] The inflexibility of wage work can indirectly constrain stage time and studio time.

For example, after quitting his day job, Flawliss began scouting studios and engineers. One evening he called to ask me to meet him at a small studio near his apartment in the Antelope Valley, north of Los Angeles. Although he was supposed to work the opening shift at his job, he drove out to the studio hoping to record a song quickly.

Unfortunately, "Josh," the engineer, did not have the same time constraints and didn't seem to understand that Flawliss wanted to record quickly. He also wasn't privy to what I knew: Flawliss had to be up early the following morning for work. About ten minutes after I arrived, Flawliss motioned for me to speak privately. "How long you been here?"

I asked. He shook head, "Man, too long." We walked into the hallway, away from the music, and Flawliss said he had been there for two hours and still hadn't recorded. "Man, I can't be here all night and shit. I'm not in school. I got *real* shit to worry 'bout. Nigga, I'm grown!"

Several times that night, Flawliss tried to coax Josh into recording a song for him. But Josh—who had friends visiting in the studio—seemed more interested in playing host. Much of Flawliss's time was spent listening to Josh's beats along with his plans to improve the studio. After almost four hours, Flawliss left without recording a single line. In the parking lot outside, Flawliss was disappointed but admitted that this was not the first time he had run into such trouble:

> That's the thing, I'm a broke-ass rapper. If I was Jigga [Jay-Z], or some big-time rapper, then I could come in, do my thing, and have niggas take me seriously and shit. But I'm not. I'm some nigga from Palmdale. I gotta come to these niggas with my hands open, like, "Yo, can I get on the mic!?"

Later, when I talked with Josh, he seemed surprised about Flawliss's "early" exit from the studio. I asked him if he knew why Flawliss left. He paused, "Yeah, I guess he had to get up early or some shit. I mean, I wanted to get him in here and record, but that's just not how it happens all the time. We were just chillin', ya know? I wish he would have stayed, though. Because I could have helped him now."

Josh—an undergraduate at a local university—did not have the same kinds of time or economic constraints that Flawliss faced. As an undergraduate, Josh was responsible for his studies and making good grades, but he did not have to work to support himself and did not have dependents. His family, in fact, helped him buy the equipment he needed to build his studio, which was outfitted with professional software, microphones, and production equipment. His situation was vastly different from Flawliss's. Although he was working hard toward degrees and pursuing his own musical aspirations, being in college was in many ways a time for Josh to explore his interests, some of which didn't map neatly onto a future career. Flawliss, however, was working to pay for his rent and child support. He could not afford to waste time.

In addition to forgoing money lost at day jobs, men like Flawliss drove long distances and sacrificed time they could have spent finding different ways to record or perform. In fact, these experiences sometimes inspired young men to take matters into their own hands. After a string of failed collaborations, some started taking a DIY approach, teaching themselves how to use recording and production software, like DJ Quik and Kanye West had done before them. Of course, it wasn't ideal. Professional mixing and mastering aren't easy to just pick up on the fly; the skills take years to learn, practice, and perfect, and the men I knew certainly didn't have time. More often than not, then, rappers remained at the mercy of others who could help them record.

* * *

Time conflicts lead to much larger identity dilemmas. Charles Simpson describes this conflict among aspiring painters and visual artists who hold jobs that are only marginally related to their creative lives.[8] Over time, some feel that the job threatens their identities as artists. The more they immerse themselves into their jobs, the more they become attuned to the everyday rhythms and dilemmas of a workplace removed from the world of their art. Their role at work becomes their master identity, eroding their artistic self.

Flawliss and other young men also felt the strain of juggling a job they need to survive and a career they want to pursue full-time. But moments when they are unable to get work off to perform, or when they miss out on last-minute chances, take on amplified significance because of where these men are at in their lives. The window of opportunity for them to blow up is small, and they don't foresee many other options for them to achieve upward mobility. These competing pressures make the day job feel that much more disposable. Indeed, these men reasoned that ditching their day job was an investment in a more promising—if unlikely—future.

Stepping-Stones

As I described in the last chapter, the young men in this book had different opportunities to meet and collaborate with folks in the entertainment industries. These interactions felt momentous and provided them with glimmers of hope. While many had opportunities to work fleetingly but closely with people in entertainment, some, like VerBS, were invited to go on tour. This forced VerBS to choose between staying at his job and what felt like a major stepping-stone in his career. He chose the latter.

Here, I introduce stepping-stones as a forward-looking concept. People talk about stepping-stones as they try to imagine how their lives will turn out, to forecast how upcoming events and processes *could* alter their trajectory. As such, stepping-stones are a cousin concept to the turning point, which Andrew Abbott describes as a narrative concept people use to make sense of and organize events in their past.[9] Turning points provide people with ways of organizing events that have already happened; stepping-stones are a narrative concept people use when trying to predict their future.

When I first met VerBS, he was eighteen and living with his mom near the Mar Vista Gardens, a housing project in Culver City. He worked in the shipment room at American Apparel. Sometimes, I'd visit him on his lunch breaks along the Third Street Promenade in Santa Monica, a short bus ride from his mom's apartment. As we walked around, he told me about some of the friends he made working along this trendy strip. On some occasions, he'd groan about his job unloading, loading, and breaking down boxes of clothing. The job wasn't fun, but it paid well enough and was stable. At the very least, VerBS could practice his rhymes while he counted down his hours.

But the job became more of a drag as VerBS started making a name for himself across Los Angeles. Like other men who have their sights set on blowin' up, VerBS began branching out into new scenes. On the first Friday of every month, he hosted and performed at the Spliff Showcase, a monthly hip hop show at R.E.H.A.B. Records, a small record store in West LA. The gig was getting VerBS known all over the city. Fans would crowd into sweaty little venues to see VerBS rock the mic in his bright red, rolled-up beanie.

One summer night, VerBS performed "Journey to Fame" at the Spliff Showcase. He really rocked the mic, and the crowd loved his performance. As I scanned the cheering audience, I spotted Murs, an LA rapper who was once part of Living Legends, a California based hip hop supergroup. Back then, he had signed with Warner Music Group. Murs stood near the front of the stage, rocking out in a hooded sweatshirt and holding a skateboard. After the set, he approached VerBS to ask for a copy of his album. VerBS was delighted—getting props from Murs was an affirmation of his emerging talents. VerBS eagerly gave Murs two copies of the album (one for himself and one for his manager). Murs looked it over and said he would be in touch with VerBS in the near future. The two dapped it up and that was that.

A week later, Murs called. He asked VerBS to come by his personal studio. It was the start of a nice little run for VerBS. As the two got to know each other better, Murs would invite VerBS to come on tour with him and Little Brother—a rap group from North Carolina also signed to a major record label. VerBS faced a choice: continue working at American Apparel under a supervisor he didn't like, or go on the road with rappers whose careers he hoped to emulate. He quit his job just a few days later.

A few weeks before he was scheduled to go on tour, VerBS and I met up at a burrito stand in Culver City. We ordered some burritos and washed them down with Jarritos. The night air was cool, and VerBS seemed excited about his upcoming adventure. I was curious to know more about his preparations: "What are you guys doing?" He chomped away at his burrito and said, "He just had me over there, recording music, rehearsing for the tour." During their nightly sessions, Murs drilled VerBS, getting him ready to be on tour. He showed him some of his tricks acquired from years of performing: how to hype an audience, how to work a larger stage. They would practice some of the back-and-forth they might do together on stage. VerBS already knew many of these skills, but he picked up some new tricks from Murs along the way. He felt grateful to have this chance and was hopeful that the tour would lead to bigger and better things in his rap career. In the best-case scenario, Murs or Little Brother would recognize his talents and help him get a record deal with their label. And although he was dead broke and wouldn't get paid for the tour, the very prospect of going on tour felt like a major stepping-stone in VerBS's career.

* * *

Aspiring rappers juggle their day job with other emerging opportunities to further their rap dreams. While many have momentous interactions that inspire hope, some receive what feel like bigger, even once-in-a-lifetime opportunities. A young man's already-precarious attachments to a day job loosen even further when he encounters such a stepping-stone.

In addition to going on nationwide tours with signed recording artists, Lyraflip and Dumbfoundead (two of the only Asian regulars in the scene) had an opportunity to tour the United States and Canada with the annual Asian Hip Hop Summit. Even though they had steady day jobs, they jumped at the opportunity to go on tour.

The excitement wasn't only about a potential career payoff. It had larger, existential significance. Most of the men I followed had not traveled very far outside of California or even LA. For example, before touring with Murs and Little Brother, Southern California was as far as VerBS's geographic experience stretched. The chance to go on tour also represented an opportunity to travel, meet new people, and ultimately broaden one's horizons.

This, too, differentiates the experiences of working-class early adults and those from middle-class and more well-to-do backgrounds. Traveling and stepping outside of one's immediate context are taken-for-granted parts of how middle-class and well-to-do young adults grow up. For many young people, this begins in college, when they leave home and attend a school in another city, state, or country. Once in college, privileged young people might study abroad or backpack in foreign destinations, or simply go off to live independently. For the men in my book, the chance to travel, perform, and tour represented a way for them to access to this part of growing up.

Entertainment Hustles

Aspiring rappers face new dilemmas once they have ditched their day job. Although they are able to devote themselves to their rap dreams, they also feel financial strain. Some rush back to low-wage jobs, realizing they cannot sustain themselves while out of work. Others find ways to use their creative talents in the nearby entertainment industries. They take up "entertainment hustles," ways to get paid for short-term work in the entertainment industries.

These hustles are typically off the books or short-term contract work, but they are important for two reasons. First, they provide aspiring rappers with ways to make money, which allows them to remain out of work. Second, entertainment hustles help them to sustain the feeling that they are getting closer to—or at least actively pursuing—their rap dreams. Indeed, while many of these entertainment hustles are a far cry from a young man's dreams, they are nonetheless located within industries that are marginally *closer* to the music industry. These hustles are small affirmations that keep a sense of looming possibilities alive.

Los Angeles is a city full of entertainment hustles. Many are "passive"—positions for which artists don't utilize their talents. For instance, some men were extras on Hollywood movie and TV sets. The year-round production schedule provided a contingency plan for struggling artists looking for ways to get paid. Although they do not make a lot of money this way, they are able to strategically dip into these positions when times get tough, or when calls for extras emerge. For instance, "Murk" would occasionally work as an extra on TV shows. He'd receive a small fee—usually no more than $100—for anywhere between four and eight hours of work.

Other young men plied their talents more actively. A select group found jobs ghostwriting for more established artists, who would get authorial credit. Although it is not often mentioned in popular media (perhaps because it would challenge the public's perceptions of stars), many of the most visible rap artists do not write their own lyrics.[10] For example, the multiplatinum rapper and producer Dr. Dre has long relied on ghostwriters. In some cases, the ghostwriters are acknowledged in the liner notes of his work. In others, they are left unnamed. As Aftermath producer Mahogany told *Scratch*: "It's like a classroom in [Dr. Dre's booth]. He'll have three writers in there. They'll bring in something, he'll recite it, then he'll say, 'Change this line, change this word,' like he's grading papers."[11] Similarly, Jay-Z is credited with assistance in writing "Still D.R.E." on the album *The Chronic 2001*.

VerBS, too, got into ghostwriting. After completing a short tour with Murs, he returned to the corner outside of Project Blowed. He described how he supported himself by selling his CDs on tour, but Murs had helped him land a ghostwriting job for another well-known artist after the tour. "Yeah, it was crazy, so he calls me up the other day and asks if I wanna ghostwrite."

"How much you gonna get paid?" I asked.

"He told me like a hundred a song."

"Nice, how many songs you got?"

"He told me that they got like seven or so right now."

Verbs seemed excited about this opportunity, so I asked the obvious: "How do you feel about ghostwriting?" He shrugged his shoulders and smiled: "Man, I'm cool with it. As long as I get paid." I pushed further: "So you don't care that you won't be getting any props for it?" "Man, Pharoahe Monch wrote for Diddy. I can do this and make some money. That's fine with me."

Ghostwriting can be bittersweet for aspiring rappers. While it is far from an ideal job, some see it as a small validation of their creative talents. VerBS felt fortunate to get paid to write rap songs. In addition to giving him time to work on his own music, ghostwriting was more fulfilling and gratifying than the menial work he and others left behind. Plus, ghostwriting places many of these men in contact with artists, producers, management, and other personnel with ties to the music industry. These are important and momentous connections in their own right. They offer the possibility that a young man might meet someone who could propel him closer to his rap dreams.

Others found ways to use their rhyming talents in the adult industries. For example, a few weeks after he quit his job, Flawliss showed up to the corner outside Project Blowed and told everyone he had just returned from a porn shoot. He had written and recorded a music video for the song "Ms. Applebottom," featured in a porn movie series.[12] Numerous international studios distributed and marketed their wares out of studios scattered across the "Silicone Valley," or San Fernando Valley.

The following week, Flawliss motioned for me to come talk and grinned: "I did another video today . . ."

"A what?"

"Another video. A song for a porn video. This time, though, I was up in a Jacuzzi with just my boxers on, so it looked like I was naked."

He told me that the producer of the video, an ex-porn actor named TT Boy, had called the night before to ask if Flawliss wanted to do another video. Flawliss agreed, went out to a rented house in the valley, and wrote and cut (shot video for) the song. He pocketed $500 for the video and had plans to do another the following week.

Later that night, Flawliss explained, "See, here's how I see it. Everybody watches porn, right? I see this as free advertising!" Flawliss saw it as a unique type of guerrilla marketing. In his mind, people watching porn would come across his music. Some would listen, and others would tune out. But in his mind, the porn industry would become part of his promotional campaign. He joked, "I don't care how I get out there. But people are gonna recognize me! They gonna be jackin' off and hear my shit and think, 'Damn, that nigga got bars!'"

Entertainment hustles offer contingency plans for rappers who have ditched their day jobs. Although these are not long-term or stable arrangements, they give young men enough to get by on temporarily. Perhaps more important, these entertainment hustles validate a young man's talents. Even though they aren't using their talents to record their own music or go on tour, they are still being paid to write songs and record.

But there is a darker side to the glittering entertainment industry. Although it provides enterprising young men with ways to ply their skills for short-term money making opportunities, few of these connections blossom into significant career gains. And in some ways, entertainment hustles can threaten artists' reputation. While talking with "Jessie," an A&R assistant at a major label, I learned that ghostwriters occasionally transition to solo careers as recording artists, but it isn't common. Reputations are sticky and follow artists. Someone who gains the reputation of being a songwriter or ghostwriter is seen by A&Rs, producers, and others in that role. It can be difficult for songwriters and ghostwriters to transcend these roles and move into the lead artist roles.

Similar reputational pressures fix people in other careers. For example, academics looking for a faculty position in a top research university face hurdles if they have been working as an adjunct or in another profession before they apply. In both ways, people who want to break into an exclusive professional field risk losing legitimacy in the eyes of others if they take on too many roles *outside* of that field. Past professional roles can shape how gatekeepers see that person—and by extension, they can block a person's future prospects. This pressure is a big part of what aspiring rappers face trying to blow up.

In the end, it's impossible to know how or to what extent Flawliss's foray into porn soundtracks or VerBS's ghostwriting may have shaped their careers. It's possible these ventures helped increase their overall exposure to potential gatekeepers, but it's equally likely that these hustles curtailed their chances of becoming seen as serious recording artists.

Conclusion

Young men with rap dreams have to juggle a job they need and a career they dream about. Their day job is often an unglamorous service industry position that offers few, if any, pathways to upward mobility. Moreover, a day job imposes constraints on the time they can devote to recording songs, rehearsing, performing at shows, touring with more established artists, and doing other things that improve their chances of blowin' up. Just a few missed opportunities can inspire a voluntary exit from the labor market.

Day jobs become more even more dispensable as these men age, realizing that the window is closing on their chances to become competitive candidates in the exclusive music industry. They sense an expiration date for their rap dreams and as such become more motivated to pursue rapping. As they were entering their midtwenties, many felt that their window of opportunity was rapidly closing. This inspired strategic exits from their day jobs and a redoubled focus on blowin' up.

And although this book looks at young men from South Central and other working-class neighborhoods across Los Angeles, the stories here resemble other young people's trajectories: many young adults delay their transitions into long-term careers (whether or not they have graduated from college) to pursue what feel like more meaningful, if impractical, careers in the arts, music, and entertainment. In their twenties they explore their passions, in anticipation of a time when they will not be able to pursue their interests. So they double down, bracketing off other commitments for the time being.

But when middle-class and elite kids bounce around at jobs and try their hands at chasing different passions, we do not frame this as a waste of time or evidence that they have bad cultural beliefs and values. Instead, we talk about their pursuits—even their failures—as an important part of growing up. Some of this is shaped by their fallback options and social capital in the event that it turns out they don't have a viable future option. The rise in young adults returning to graduate and professional schools seems to attest to this.

Still, the different ways of talking about young Black men who pursue rap dreams is rooted in value-laden cultural debates about how working-class youth should organize their lives. Critics argue that, because of their disadvantages, young working-class Black men should not invest their time and energy in careers that are unlikely to pay off. These arguments are not only normative and problematic prescriptions for how people ought to live; they don't fully consider the processes that inspire career-related decisions in the first place.

The young men in this book pursued their dream careers under different circumstances. They weren't graduating from colleges, and they didn't have family who could put them up or support them. In many cases, they had children and were not chasing their rap dreams to pass the time before they "grew up" and got a real job. Instead, blowin' up as rappers was their best chance to achieve a life that more privileged young adults take for granted.

Still, there are some hidden, long-term consequences that come with periodically ditching the day job. Most did not consider the repercussions of taking multiple leaves from the formal labor market. In the short-term, they were merely giving up regular wages but gaining time and emotional energy they could channel toward rapping. At first blush, this doesn't seem like much of a trade-off. Unlike leaving plum jobs with health insurance and other benefits, ditching a low-wage job does not mean missing out on upward mobility or long-term stability. If anything, the men in this book felt that if their rap careers did not work out, they could always go back to their previous jobs.

But a checkered employment history can also affect some of the modest advances that someone might accrue if they stayed at their job and got promoted. While rising to management is hardly a pathway to upward mobility, steady employment could be a small bonus to people whose employment options are otherwise limited.[13] Thus, while the decision to leave their service jobs didn't pose any real immediate problems, the longer-term repercussions of cycling between work and rap dreams may have further dampened their prospects for modest gains toward a better life.

8

Gang Violence and Dreams Derailed

It was a little after midnight, and Flawliss wanted to get into a studio. He was brimming with ideas and was eager to record them. Unfortunately, he had no car and his cell phone was cut off. But he knew that flashes of inspiration didn't just happen. So he left his apartment and walked to a pay phone at the end of his block.

When he got there, Flawliss called "Quantum," a producer who would give him a ride to the studio. Flawliss called twice, but Quantum did not pick up. Instead, making peace with his situation, Flawliss started walking home—when the pay phone rang. "At this point, I think it's Quantum, and that he may be trying to call me back. So I run back and pick up the phone." He picked up the receiver but nobody was on the line. Hanging up, Flawliss made one more try.

This time, Quantum picked up and the two talked about recording. Flawliss almost missed two hooded figures walking across a large intersection near where he was standing. "They weren't looking at me. They were looking straight ahead and walking on the other side of the street. So at this point, I'm thinking 'They ain't trippin' on me.'"

And then the figures circled back. Two men were walking toward him, now on the same side of the street. Flawliss remembered, "My first thought is, 'Man, fuck that! I'm gonna whoop these niggas, if he fuck with me!' Cuz, they was like a little eses [slang for Latino gang members], and I'm pretty big, like, 'I'ma fuck these niggas up!'"

But as they got closer, Flawliss saw that one was reaching for his waistband—a dead giveaway that he was carrying a gun:

Now, my problem is I live *that* way, and they're *coming* from that way. So I can't run to my fuckin' house, 'cause I would have to run right past them. So I'm thinking, should I run to the fuckin' boulevard and shit? But it's late and there ain't any cars on the boulevard, so I'm fucked!

Flawliss didn't know what to do or where to run. Meanwhile, the gunmen closed the distance. One of them asked, "Where you from, homes?"[1] Flawliss knew the drill. Gang members asked each other this question to see if a stranger was a friend or foe, sometimes as a prelude to violence. He quickly denied having any gang connections: "I ain't from nowhere. I don't bang."

Flawliss remembers one of them grabbing his gun—a .44 caliber pistol—and saying, "Well, fuck that! We're some nigger killers!" Flawliss dropped the receiver and took off running. He felt a surge of adrenaline. "I'm big, but when I heard him say that, I broke! Like, I started running at the speed of light and shit!"

The gunman fired multiple rounds. One after another, bullets whizzed by, hitting parked cars and buildings. Two bullets hit Flawliss in the back. They shredded his skin, tearing through layers of fat and muscle, piercing his large intestine before exiting on the other side of his stomach.

Flawliss felt a sharp stinging sensation and his heartbeat quickened. Blood spurted out of his body.

Instinctively, he dove for cover between two parked cars. At first, he laid motionless on the concrete. "I thought he was gonna walk around the car and dome my ass out! But in that moment, something told me to scream. So, I just screamed."[2] Flawliss screamed again and again. He would either scare the shooters away or wake someone up and get help.

Time slowed down as he waited, preparing to die. But the shooter did not reappear. After waiting a little longer, Flawliss stood up and scanned the area. The shooter was gone. He rushed home, where he yelled into his housemate's room: "I got shot! I got shot! Wake up! You gotta take me to the hospital!"

Flawliss doesn't remember much after that. He has faint memories of a frantic drive to the hospital, and snippets of doctors, nurses, and family members standing around him:

> It's a trip being on life support, man. Nurses were telling me that I was trying to get outta bed and was like ripping all the cords outta my body. They had to sedate my ass 'cause I kept drifting in and out. I kept having the same dream. I thought I got shot and was laid out on a studio floor. I kept trying to get up so that I could go to the hospital.

* * *

I visited Flawliss while finishing this book. Although he had given me consent to write about his experiences, I felt torn about including this story and wanted to talk with him in person. That day, we sat in his truck listening to some of his new music. Years had passed since we hung out, but Flawliss was still a talented emcee. The added years of experience and practice had made his music more reflexive and political. Gun violence was on his mind. Some of his songs referenced the night he got shot and his struggles thereafter. Others alluded to the shooting deaths of unarmed Black men in America. At a break in the music, I said, "I'm thinking of taking the last chapter out."

Flawliss looked surprised, "Why?"

"I dunno. I couldn't live with myself if something else were to happen to you." Flawliss listened closely and joked, "Don't worry, gangstas don't read." We both laughed a little. He became more serious, "But f'reals. I want you to keep it. I want my kids to know my story. I want you to write about *everything*. I want everybody to know my story and what I been through."

We went back and forth for the next fifteen minutes. No matter what dilemma I posed, Flawliss was adamant. He wanted his story in the book. He felt empowered knowing that other people would read about his struggles: "Even if one person reads it, that will be a success, because that means my story is getting out there. Just knowing about that shit might help somebody else who is going through it like me."

We spent the rest of the day together and I got to reconnect with his family and hear about his ongoing pursuits. Ultimately, I decided that Flawliss deserved to choose how he would be written about. In ethnography, we often assume that giving people pseudonyms is the most ethical choice. But we often make this decision without consulting with the people we write about. While some are understandably hesitant about being identified, many others, if given the choice, might prefer being identified. It can be emotionally gratifying for some folks to see themselves in print.

Also, pseudonyms and creating composite characters do not necessarily guarantee anonymity. We live in an increasingly digital age, and people document and publicize their personal lives on social media. Flawliss has written about his shooting on multiple occasions, shared photos of his surgeries, and linked news stories of racialized shootings in Los Angeles and elsewhere. He also recorded and performed songs about getting shot in multiple public venues. This wasn't only cathartic; it was part of his process of trying to "blow up." Getting shot gave him street cred, and he was eager to tell people about his experiences. And in more general ways, his shooting was public knowledge among people at Project Blowed. In 2014, Nocando wrote a touching piece, "Steel Sharpens Steel: Flawliss, the Last Guy I Could Freestyle With," in the *LA Weekly*.[3] The article talked about his longtime rivalry and friendship with Flawliss at Project Blowed. It also talked about his own experiences growing up around gang violence and Flawliss's tragic shooting that slowed down his career. Together, these factors convinced me to keep this story. In the end, I hope that Flawliss's story contributes to a larger conversation about the different ways that gun violence constrains the lives of young Black men. Despite their efforts at getting away from gangs and shootings, young men like Flawliss continue to live in neighborhoods in which everyday life is filled with risks to their safety.

* * *

At a larger level, Flawliss's shooting was a tragic reminder of larger structural forces that constrain the lives of young Black men in the

United States. Across the country, the most frequent cause of death for Black males between the ages of eighteen and thirty-four is homicide.[4] In 2011, the National Violent Death Reporting System compiled data comparing deaths in seventeen US states. The findings revealed stark racial disparities. Black teenage males between the ages of fifteen and nineteen were killed by gunfire at a rate of 34.41 per 100,000, whereas their white counterparts were killed at a rate of 2.62 per 100,000. Black boys were thirteen times more likely to die in a shooting. These disparities widened by their twenties, when Black men died at a rate of 64.94 per 100,000, compared to white men at a rate of 3.77 per 100,000.[5] Black men in their twenties were seventeen times more likely to be killed by gunfire than White men.

And fatal shootings are only a small part of the overall gun violence story. Most people who are shot don't die. The Centers for Disease Control, for instance, reports that only one in five street shootings is fatal. Most young Black men survive shootings but suffer from lingering injuries, post-traumatic stress, and different health problems, like Flawliss did.[6] They struggle to adjust to the demands of their new bodies and are jolted out of the labor market (sometimes indefinitely). Gunshot victims who survive live with lingering physical and psychological scars. Life after the shooting is hell.[7]

Both fatal and nonfatal shootings send emotional waves through a victim's social network. Seeing a loved one's brush with death is an existential shock, reminding each person of her or his own vulnerability and life chances. But to understand the significance of Flawliss's shooting, we have to place it in a larger context of racialized gang violence in South Central and other parts of Southern California.

Fear and the Racial "Green Light"

Flawliss's shooting was part of a larger history of Black and Brown gang violence in LA. According to a report by the Southern Poverty Law Center, much of Black and Brown gang violence stems from rivalries between the prison gangs of the Mexican Mafia and the Black Guerrilla Family in California.[8] Intermittent shootings and violence feed rumors of OGs and "shot callers" issuing a "green light"—essentially, open season—on racial and ethnic others outside the prisons.[9] Of course, these reports focus on gang conflicts and neglect more routine, and civil, ways that Black and Brown residents coexist in South Central. Nevertheless, these reports—and news reporting more generally—have helped create a climate of fear and distrust in South Central neighborhoods.

This racial green light poses practical problems for people trying to avoid gang violence. It transforms bystanders into potential targets. Under other circumstances, unaffiliated men could "rank out" and disavow ties with gangs to avoid physical altercations (although there is always the possibility of getting caught up in the crossfire of a gang war). As Robert Garot shows us, young people have multiple options when asked "who they claim" or "where they're from" by gang members.[10] On the surface, these questions are quick interrogation tactics that gang members use to figure out if someone is a friend or foe. The questions also create the occasion for violence. The person "hitting up" or asking the other person about their affiliations is also sizing that person up, waiting for an opportunity to attack.

But these options disappear (or become harder to deploy) when gang violence becomes organized along racial and ethnic lines. Instead of seeing specific individuals or rival gangs as "enemies" and "targets," gangs begin to treat entire communities as their enemies and targets.[11] At least this is what many youth experience. Any person in another racial or ethnic group becomes fair game. This makes it harder for people to fully distance themselves from violence.

I first learned about local fears of this green light on May 5, or Cinco de Mayo, during my first year of fieldwork. It was a warm night, and I was hanging out with N.A. at his apartment in Mid-City. Much of the city—including some of my middle-class graduate school friends—was celebrating with happy hours at Mexican restaurants. They were gorging on fish tacos, cheesy nachos, and half-priced margaritas. But, N.A. was not interested in going out. He was holed up and had skipped work.

While playing *John Madden Football* on his PlayStation, I asked, "You gonna go to the Blowed tonight?" N.A. shook his head. "I'm not trying to go out tonight. I didn't even go to work. I mean, things are too crazy. You got all those freeway shootings, and I dunno. I gotta ride public transportation, so I wasn't trying to be out there and have some people mistake me for somebody."[12]

N.A. showed me an email that his boss at a local adoption agency had forwarded to staff. The email was supposedly written by a member of the Mexican Mafia, and it described a recent falling out with the Rollin' 60s Crip gang. It promised violent retribution on random Black men wearing white T-shirts. The email had stirred up controversy. Some thought it was fake—the stuff of urban legends. Others believed it. And some, like N.A., didn't know how to feel but didn't want to risk anything, particularly if his boss would let him miss work. N.A. showed me the email:

> Unfortunately, the word on the street (which has been confirmed by a probation officer) is that the 60s stole 160 kilo's [sic] of cocaine from the Mexican Mafia. In retaliation, the Mexican Mafia and other Mexican gangs have decided to target and kill 400–1000 black men of all ages who are wearing white t-shirts. This is not limited to the freeways. . . . I understand that this is very real and very serious. Please pass this on to EVERYONE that you know. I suggest you do not wear any white shirts at all if possible. Also, if you have on a dress shirt, consider wearing your jacket over it . . . PLEASE BE CAREFUL. WARN YOUR HUSBANDS & SONS.[13]

This wasn't the first time that the Mexican Mafia, affiliates, and other Latino gangs had made local news. As I searched news archives, I discovered multiple instances when the media and law enforcement had linked the Mexican Mafia to hate crimes against Black residents. In 2000, members of the Avenues gang entered the home of Anthony Proudhomme, a biracial twenty-one-year-old, and killed him execution-style. Police, gang experts, and the state attorney's office framed the murder as a hate crime. In 2002, three Latino members of the Pomona 12 gang (from just outside LA) attacked Kareem Williams, a Black youth. When his uncle, Roy Williams, went to help, one of the members shouted, "Niggers have no business living in Pomona because this is Twelfth Street territory!" Witnesses at the scene heard: "Pull out the gun! Shoot the niggers! Shoot the niggers!"[14]

These and other cases mobilized the Los Angeles Police Department to target Mexican and Latino gangs suspected of hate crimes. Many of these efforts came to a head in 2009, when the department launched Operation Knockout, a sweep on the Hawaiian Gardens barrio, home to a Latino street gang accused of systematically targeting Black men in violent crimes. According to the indictment against the Vario Hawaiian Gardens gang, "VHG gang members have expressed a desire to rid the city of Hawaiian Gardens of all African-Americans and have engaged in a systematic effort to achieve that result by perpetrating crimes against African-Americans."[15] Of course, news reporting, police accounts, and statements by district attorneys are often biased. They tell a particular version of social reality. I found few accounts implicating Black gangs in responding to or initiating violence. The dynamics underlying gang violence are often more complex than what's reported in the media.

Nevertheless, media depictions (however partial and sensational) and official police responses shape people's sense making. Many of the young men I write about heard of or witnessed similar events, which only reinforced their growing distrust and fear of Latino gang members. These moments made young men feel unsafe—as if they had little control over determining their futures. Racialized violence became a powerful omen of their vulnerability.

Making Sense of the Shooting

Unjust World

Shootings also affect friends, who take stock of their own lives after someone close to them gets shot. Tellingly, Flawliss's friends were saddened by the news but not surprised. Most knew family and friends who had been shot. Some had their own near brushes with violence. This latest shooting seemed to confirm their views of an "unjust world" that could be cruel and unpredictable. This existential view of the world is perhaps best captured in the saying "shit happens." Young men invoked this saying when talking about Flawliss's shooting and other episodes of violence that struck close to home.

Although he had never been in a gang, E.Crimsin had grown up around gang violence. He lived near a contested border between long-time rival sets the Harlem Rollin' 30s and the Neighborhood Rollin' 40s Crips. As a youth, he heard about and witnessed shootings in and around this border, which introduced him to the possibility of violent death from an early age:

> That's how shit goes down out here. Shit, I remember being young and hearing shootings out there on the boulevard. Niggas are active out here. You see people who get shot. You know people who been shot. That's how it goes down![16]

In addition to knowing other people who had been killed in gang shootings, Crimsin also had his own memories of scary situations. Once while hanging out at a park in high school, Crimsin was shot at in what he believes was a case of mistaken identity. That day, he was with friends in "the Jungles," an area where the Black P. Stones Bloods gang lived. At dusk, they spotted a car circling the park. Someone in the car fired multiple bullets in their direction. Crimsin and his friends escaped without any physical harm, but the memory haunted him. It was a reminder of how quickly his life could change—or end. In his matter-of-fact way, he explained:

> Shit, that's how it is out here in the 'hood. *Shit happens*, my nigga. Like you could be driving home with your girl or whatever and some drunk driver crashes into you and then that's it, you're dead. It's the same thing. You could be at the wrong place at the wrong time and then that's a wrap!

Big Flossy had similar views of violence. We hung out at his apartment a week after Flawliss's shooting. Even though he lived a few blocks from Project Blowed, he had grown up in the heart of the Rollin' 40s gang territory and had lost friends in gang shootings growing up. Flawliss's shooting was an all-too-familiar tragedy. Like E.Crimsin, Big Flossy remarked on how violence was a tragic—but not surprising— part of life in South Central and other neighborhoods with gangs. He too talked about how "shit happens" in the 'hood:

> Here's the situation. This is also part of growing up in the 'hood. First and foremost, *shit happens*. Shit happens all the time. Most of the time you cool if you ain't tryin' to bang on people and look for trouble. But, trouble can find you.

Big Flossy also asked if I had any updates on Flawliss's status. I told him I had been talking with Flawliss's brother and heard Flawliss had left the hospital and was with family. I didn't know much else. Big Flossy sighed, "Man, Jeeyoung, I'ma tell you right now. I thank the Lord every day, but that's how it is out here. I can't even count how many niggas I know who been shot or dead."

Big Flossy also reflected on his life after Flawliss got shot. He talked about his own brief stint in a local Crip set and leaving that life behind to focus on rapping. Even though he wasn't involved in gangs, Big Flossy did not feel totally shielded from the specter of gang violence. From time to time, he worked as a security guard for hip hop event promoters. He had a permit to carry a firearm and wore a Kevlar vest. Although most of his security jobs were uneventful, some would escalate into dangerous situations. Once, Flossy did not let a small group of Latino men into a club. While patting them down, he discovered that one of them was carrying a gun:

> I told him, "I can't let ya'll in with that." They had guns. Not on some disrespectful shit, but I'm there to make sure everything goes smooth and that there ain't no fighting and shooting and whoopty-whoop up in the club, ya feel? This nigga pulled out and I yanked my gun out. I told him, "I don't give a fuck, we can get off right now. I'm ready for war." And his boys, luckily were there to calm him down.

I asked Big Flossy if he was scared and he shrugged off my question. At first he seemed uncomfortable talking about his own fears. But as he explained his mind-set, I began to better understand the pressures he faced in these situations and many others in his daily life:

> Let me put it like this. When a pack of wolves come up on me, you can't show no fear. I let them know what it is. That shit ain't no different from how it goes down in the 'hood. Growing up in the 'hood, you gotta fight, you can't be no punk in front of your boys, when they say go beat that nigga ass, you gotta do it.[17]

A few weeks later, Big Flossy told me about a fellow security guard who got shot and critically wounded after the two of them worked an event. Big Flossy had visited this friend in the hospital, who had been shot in the mouth and neck:

> One of the guys at work, he gangbang, and the dude got shot through his mouth, and the bullet went through his neck. Some niggas rolled up on him and asked him, "Where you from!?" "What 'hood you bang?" and whoopty-whoop. And he told him where he was from and they shot his ass! I told him, "Why didn't you tell them you didn't bang? Did you know you could have lost your life for representing some shit that wouldn't give two shits about you if you was in jail?"

Big Flossy had seen a lot in his life, but was still saddened and bothered by Flawliss's shooting. In his mind, the shooting had violated an unspoken moral code that *should* protect unaffiliated people from violence. Big Flossy said, "Man, that's some cold shit. It's one thing to pop someone who active, but my nigga Flawliss don't get down like that. That's some cold shit."

I told him that some people were speculating that Flawliss *was* in a gang. Big Flossy shook his head, "Yeah, some people just be sayin' shit, and they don't know what the fuck they talkin' about. Lotsa people talkin' and shit, but that don't mean they know what Flawliss is up to."

* * *

When people think about gunshot victims in places like South Central or other neighborhoods with gangs, they think about people who must have been doing something to get shot. Seeing many of the same patients over time, doctors and nurses unconsciously blame victims for their plight. They assume that victims must be caught up with gangs and the street life.[18] These folk explanations are examples of social psychologist Melvin Lerner's just-world theory. According to Lerner, people believe in a morally just world in which individuals reap what they sow. To help sustain this image of "justice," they misattribute causes of violence to victims' choices instead of digging for more nuanced explanations for violence and other tragedies. Ultimately, Lerner's theory shows that people are more comfortable blaming victims for their plight instead of looking at what perpetrators did or how other factors might have led to violence.

But in telling their stories, E.Crimsin and Big Flossy had invoked the limits of these explanations. They had seen gang violence negatively affect people who had no direct links to gangs. Although things *should* be different, they knew that stray bullets from drive-bys, cases of mistaken identity, robberies, and other gunfights led to the deaths and injuries of bystanders, whom outsiders later assume to be gang affiliated.

Still, although they knew that random violence could happen anytime and anywhere, they were still upset to know that one of their friends had been critically injured in what seemed to be a gang-inspired hate crime.[19] At an existential level, Flawliss's shooting confirmed an "unjust world" in which innocent people—those with no ties to gang violence—can suffer life-altering and life-ending injuries. Regardless of whether and who they claim, where they're from, or how they identify on the streets, gang violence could and did abruptly derail the lives of young men.

A Career Boost?

I met up with some of Flawliss's friends a few weeks later at Project Blowed. I expected to find a somber crowd, but instead of openly mourning, they talked about how his shooting might also be a possible career boost. Getting shot solidified his street cred and gave him new identity and career options. He could now talk about getting shot in his music, which might help boost his mainstream marketability. In these moments, Flawliss's friends would reference a mainstream hip hop industry that normalizes violence as a mark of Black masculinity.[20]

But beneath the surface, these accounts were another coping strategy. Instead of fully meditating on Flawliss's shooting, friends were putting a positive spin on his situation. This helped them come to terms with the realities of an unjust world. In the aftermath of violence, redemptive and optimistic stories become a resource for family and friends of the deceased and injured. They provide an emotional buffer against the gravity of trauma. In this way, the mainstream hip hop industry provided Flawliss's friends with a narrative that helped them rally themselves and make sense of his injuries.

I first learned about this while talking with Psychosiz, one of the first people I talked to on the corner. Even though he and Flawliss rarely saw each other outside of Project Blowed, Psychosiz was distraught knowing that a fellow Blowedian was gravely injured. Years freestyling together on the corner had created a strong bond between the two. But Psychosiz also had another way of interpreting Flawliss's shooting. In another breath, he put a lighter, ironic spin on the situation:

> You see how the industry works. Look at 50 Cent. You could argue that he got even bigger after he'd been shot. Like, people wanted to sign him and hear him. Flawliss just passed that bar now. He has all kinds of new things he can talk about.

Psychosiz wasn't the only person who felt this way. Later that night, I hung out with VerBS, who had a similar interpretation of the shooting. On one hand, he was deeply saddened by the news and seemed distraught: "Shit is crazy, man. Lots of people out there are trippin'. That's why I keep to myself." VerBS had his own daily encounters with Latino gang members in the Mar Vista Gardens area of Culver City. Even though he was never mistaken for a gang member and was friends with local Latinos, VerBS was cautious while walking around his neighborhood. He knew that local Latino gangs sometimes had conflicts with Black gangs on the Westside of LA, and he always tried to be aware of his surroundings. He also expressed similar ideas about how the shooting might affect Flawliss's career prospects: "These days it seems like you gotta be shot to be taken seriously in that [mainstream] genre of hip hop. Like, how many niggas you think will come out now who been shot since 50 got shot?"

And even though he was still reeling from the news, E.Crimsin wanted me to videotape him leaving Flawliss a short message about his injuries:

> Yeah, man, I just got the news, man. Big ups to Flawliss. All the great rappers get popped, Pac [Tupac Shakur] got popped, ya know what I'm saying? Who else, who else got shot? Fuckin' all the real niggas get shot. Biggie [Notorious B.I.G.] got popped! You a big ass nigga, too. I guess your flesh is made of Teflon, though. Stay up, glad you alive, we gotta do a track together. Call it "Bulletproof Flesh" or some shit, my nigga. You gonna make it now because you got shot. So, uh, congratulations. Everybody wanna get shot, like, "Please shoot me! Please shoot me so that I can become rich and famous!" Stay up, my nigga. Good luck!

This was a common theme throughout the night. Although people were upset by the news, they also talked about his shooting as a career boost. Getting shot was not necessarily an event that would derail Flawliss's musical career. If managed the right way, his near-death experience could become a powerful part of his evolving musical identity.

In these moments, Flawliss's peers were drawing from a wider Hip Hop industry that romanticizes and normalizes violence as a defining feature in Black masculinity. They would compare him to famous rappers like Tupac and Notorious B.I.G. Fatal shootings only seemed to enhance both artist's commercial appeal.[21] Others would compare him to 50 Cent, who was shot nine times outside of his grandmother's house in Jamaica, Queens, New York.[22] When talking about 50 Cent, they'd mention how 50 Cent had *survived* a brutal shooting, solidifying his reputation as a "hard" rapper. One of the bullets pierced his left cheek, resulting in the loss of wisdom teeth and a permanent slur in his speech. Instead of ruining his career, his injuries and the story of his near-fatal shooting boosted his street cred in the eyes of the industry, fans, and his peers.

These experiences carry weight in the music industry. The young man who is shot but survives takes on a resilient identity. He is also shielded from the discrediting label of "studio gangster," or someone who makes false claims about being gang affiliated in his music. Flawliss now had access to these stories and an identity that made him potentially more marketable in the mainstream hip hop industry.

* * *

In South Central and other working-class Black communities in the United States, shootings and other daily violence elicit complex emotional and social reactions from a young man's family and friends. Young people who are confronted with their own and one another's mortality develop various ways to cope with the stress of almost losing a friend. In addition to accepting such events as a routine—if not inevitable—part of everyday life, others would put a positive spin on violent victimization. This was a pragmatic part of coping with tragedy. People can be overwhelmed if they stopped and really considered the gravity of recurrent violence and loss in their neighborhoods.

Hip hop, in these situations, provides people with a readymade script for how violent victimization can be reinterpreted as a good thing— as something that could help propel someone closer to blowin' up. In subtle ways, the stories of artists who turned their injuries into career boosts helps buffer young people against the stress and despair that can follow the near death experiences of a friend.

The Shame of a Colostomy Bag

While Flawliss's friends were reflecting on what the shooting might mean for them and Flawliss's career, Flawliss was busy adjusting to his new life. The bullet had wreaked all kinds of havoc on his body. After surgery, he had to wear a colostomy bag.[23] Not only was Flawliss reeling from the pain caused by wounds; he was also deeply ashamed of the bag.[24] He felt what I call ancillary trauma, which is the lingering trauma that someone experiences *after* an assault. In the wake of gun violence, victims suffer from lifestyle changes and subsequent health problems that continue to impact their quality of living. The gunshot victim who lives with a retained bullet feels the pain of the bullet lodged in his or her body; over time, the bullet can lead to arthritis and other health problems. Victims who lose the use of limbs, feel ashamed of lingering scars, or whose health worsens, all experience ancillary trauma.

Flawliss was traumatized by his colostomy bag. He saw it as a dirty and shameful object that represented his mortality and dependence on others. It threatened his masculinity and his sense of independence. These would become themes in his life and his music—he was a far cry from the confident, independent person I knew before the shooting.

I observed many of these changes on the first night he came back to Project Blowed. It had been three months and then, out of the blue, he showed up with his new girlfriend, "Shanice." At a glance, it seemed nothing had changed. Flawliss was back.

People flocked around him with questions about his shooting and recovery, and Flawliss enjoyed the attention. He told the story dramatically, reenacting the role of the shooter. With a cold and serious look, he mimed a gun in his right hand, bit his bottom lip, and squeezed an imaginary trigger. He also mimicked the moment he was shot, violently arching his back and cringing in pain. The audience ate it up.

People wanted to know whether it hurt to be shot. Flawliss replied, "Hell, yeah, I felt pain! I felt it right away. It stung!" As he told his story, the crowd became mesmerized. He told them: "I just kept thinking he was gonna come around the car and smoke my ass . . . so I just started praying, 'Dear Lord . . .'"

Flawliss was given a hero's welcome that night. His brush with death had transformed him into the most popular guy in the scene. I kept waiting for Flawliss to get tired of retelling the story or shy away from detailed questions, but he seemed to revel in the spotlight. With each retelling, his fervor and enthusiasm increased.

But the tone changed instantly when "Proliffick" asked, "Where did you get shot?" Flawliss paused awkwardly and touched his lower back. "I got shot back here." "So, is . . . everything in there OK?" Proliffick asked. Flawliss shook his head. The crowd fell silent. "Nah, man. I'm all fucked up. They fucked me up. I got a fuckin' colostomy and shit!" Some cringed and some gasped. In a matter of moments, the heroic survival story was shattered.

Erving Goffman wrote about the face-work that friends and family members extend to "their own," engaging in "protective" face-work and ignoring traits that are potentially discrediting or harmful to another's identity.[25] Proliffick's curiosity got the best of him, and the questions chipped away at Flawliss's confidence and presentation of self. I hoped we could change the subject, but Proliffick continued, "So, your *stuff* is just all right there." He pointed to a small bulge under the left side of Flawliss's T-shirt. I looked around as the crowd stared down at the colostomy bag. Previously invisible, now it was all they could see.

Flawliss's mood clouded. He stopped smiling and his voice became less animated. He seemed embarrassed and turned away slightly, as if he were trying to hide his bag. But with a sea of eyes monitoring his every move, he simply adjusted it and said, "Yeah."

Someone else asked, "Is it hard to change? How do you clean it?" Within moments, the crowd became fixated, intensely curious about the colostomy bag. Now it was all about the bag. Flawliss's answers became shorter, and sweat beaded on his brow. He looked uncomfortable, as if he were on display. Shanice interjected, "It's not that bad. It's not that hard to change." Flawliss seemed relieved and eager to lighten the mood. Shanice had given him an out. Flawliss joked, "I don't know how she does it. That shit is gross!" Both Flawliss and Shanice laughed, and she gently placed her hand on his shoulder. Flawliss continued to laugh, nervously, as people stared at his colostomy bag.

Around eleven, much earlier than usual, Flawliss told me he was leaving. Before, he was always one of the last to leave the block, usually around two in the morning. I gave him daps and realized that he wasn't just nervously sweaty like before. He was *dripping* sweat. He wiped his face with one sleeve and said, "I'm feeling pretty tired, so I'm gonna go home now. And she's driving." Shanice yawned, looking exhausted. "All right, homie," I said. "I'll see you real soon. Lemme know if there's anything you need." Flawliss smiled and gave me daps again. "F'sho. I appreciate it, Joo."

* * *

Flawliss's return revealed tensions between the public perception and private experience of gunshot injuries. At first, he was greeted with a hero's welcome. Everyone was excited to see him. He spent the first part of his night recounting his harrowing escape from death. He enacted his trauma and described, in careful detail, the immense pain he felt both during and especially after the shooting. He was in command of the situation and afforded a level of respect.

But this identity and his reception were fragile. One blunt question about the nature of his injuries transformed the situation. In a flash, Flawliss went from being an animated storyteller recounting his heroic survival story to someone ashamed of his newly disfigured body. After being asked to talk about his injuries, the focal point of the interaction shifted. The crowd became less interested in his bravery and resilience, and more interested in the clunky colostomy bag hanging off the side of his stomach.

Flawliss later told me that he did not yet feel comfortable talking about his bag in public. He felt bothered that he was asked to do so. Luckily, Shanice interrupted the situation. When she admitted to helping him, he made a joke. This gave him an out and allowed him to save face.

Publicly, Flawliss was embraced by his peers, who saw him as tough, streetwise, and "hard." Some even joked that his shooting would become a major stepping-stone in his path to stardom. But beneath the surface, Flawliss was grappling with life-altering changes to his body and health, with the effects of ancillary trauma. Life with the colostomy bag was shameful, frustrating, and at times emasculating. This part of the private experience of injury was usually not part of the public conversation of his shooting. But on this particular night, the guys at Project Blowed got a glimpse into the private hell he was experiencing every day.

Existential Urgency

The experience of being shot also seemed to energize Flawliss. He worried that he might not be alive in the near future and became increasingly focused on putting his energy into writing and recording new music. During this time, he worked closely with "DJ D," a White producer who ran an independent record label out of his parents' garage. To maximize his time, Flawliss slept on a futon in DJ D's garage. He would try to write music and record around the clock. Once, while hanging out after recording, Flawliss told me that writing new songs and recording was cathartic for him: "Right now, I just feel like I'm on a mission. Getting in the studio and putting it all down helps me get some of this shit off my chest. I just want to make sure I put everything out there, so people can hear what I got to say."

But although songwriting helped improve Flawliss's mental health, his physical health continued to decline. He started gaining weight and tipped the scales at nearly four hundred pounds. He also lumbered about as the result of his new, much more sedentary lifestyle. Surgery to remove the colostomy bag had to be repeatedly postponed because of his high blood pressure, weight problems, and cardiac arrhythmia. At his most vulnerable, he was hospitalized for a series of minor heart attacks. All this was weighing heavily on Flawliss, who told me he was thinking about death. If he was going to die, he wanted to leave behind music that would capture his struggle and his story.

One afternoon, he called and asked if I could bring my video camera to his old apartment. He told me: "I'm at a crazy crossroads now. I just want you to get everything. That way, when I'm gone, people will know my story." Alarmed, I replied, "Don't say those things, man. You're gonna be all right." But even then, I thought, "What if he's right and he doesn't have long to live?" Flawliss interjected: "Don't worry, man. I'm cool with it. I haven't been back [to the neighborhood where he got shot], but I want you to come with me and get some good footage."

I agreed to meet Flawliss near the crime scene. The sounds of an ice-cream truck and kids playing on their bicycles gave the neighborhood a friendly feel. It was hard to imagine Flawliss getting shot here. Flawliss led me up a staircase to a small roof overlooking the street. We sat there for the next several hours, talking about his life since the shooting. "Getting shot changed *everything*," he said. "After that shit happened, I realized that I could die, like, tomorrow."[26]

Flawliss dropped hints about these thoughts when we spoke on the phone, but hearing him say such things in person was different. He seemed cold and impersonal rather than sad or distraught. I couldn't really think of how to respond, so I just listened. Flawliss was more doubtful than ever about his future. "The craziest thing is that it's probably not going to happen," he said. "Not statistically, at least."

At the same time, Flawliss's will was not broken. In spite of his situation, Flawliss was channeling his pain into songwriting and recording. He felt that his experiences were only making him a better all-around artist. He communicated a sense of urgency that I had never heard from him:

> I'm at the bottom now. I've already lost everything. I don't have my car, my clothes, or my apartment. I can't work because of my injury, and I'm falling behind on my child support. Even though I'm at rock bottom now, I feel like this is all preparing me to make a big comeback. I feel like I'm way sicker now as an artist. Like that experience I went through just adds that much more to my music. I feel like people hear my shit now and can tell that I've been through something.

Later that afternoon, we returned to the actual crime scene. The nearby parking lot of a small convenience store was buzzing with *norteño* music coming from a car. When I asked how Shanice was doing, Flawliss paused and smiled:

We still together. But I don't know for how long. I dunno. I mean, I really appreciate everything she did for me. Like she was there for me when I got out the hospital. She changed my colostomy bag and cooked for me. I mean, I really love her. She's a true person. But I dunno if she's the right one for me.

I felt sad that he was having his doubts about Shanice. During his recovery, it had been nice knowing that Flawliss had someone willing to go through his darkest hours with him. A part of me had really hoped that they would work out. "Oh, that's too bad," I said, struggling to find the right words. Flawliss shrugged and smirked, "Yeah, she's coming over in a bit. We got into it earlier. You might not want to be around when she's here, because I think shit's gonna get real."

For the next thirty minutes we stood outside the convenience store, facing the sidewalk on which Flawliss was shot. He seemed on edge, but I couldn't tell if it was because he was anticipating a fight with Shanice or reliving the traumatic memories of getting shot. When I asked, he said, "Ever since I got shot, I just keep my eyes open. You never know when something might go down." When two young men walked by, Flawliss turned around and scanned their faces. He watched them closely as they disappeared down the block.

Conclusion

Before he got shot, Flawliss was a confident young man approaching the prime of his creative life. He felt like he was on the brink of something big, and his hopes weren't unfounded. For every fizzled lead, Flawliss had made inroads with people who were close to real decision makers in the music industry.

The shooting and its aftermath transformed him into a shell of his former self. He faced an entirely different set of choices and opportunities for his future. In addition to lingering health effects, the shooting left him with a colostomy bag that imposed constraints on his body and his sense of independence. He came to rely on his girlfriend at the time, Shanice, who helped him change the bags, attach new ones, and clean the wound site. These were ancillary traumas. As a young man, the colostomy bag threatened his tough exterior and sense of independence. It made him look and feel vulnerable and dependent on others.

Flawliss's shooting also had ripple effects on the people around him. His friends related to his shooting. For them, it was further confirmation of an "unjust world" where "shit happens." Some reflected on their own experiences with violence, and others framed it as an instant boost to his street cred. Both were ways to deal with the traumatic experience of losing a friend—or their own lives—to gun violence.

In the end, young Black men like Flawliss know these feelings all too well. In places like South Central, they grow up surrounded by people whose lives have been shaped by street gangs and violence. From family members to close childhood friends who have been wounded or are dead, gang violence casts a dark cloud over life. They know that even without connections to gang violence, anyone can get caught in the wrong place at the wrong time. Physical safety is not always a taken-for-granted part of everyday life in South Central and other neighborhoods with long histories of gang violence. Ironically, this very tension is something that animates their passion for making meaningful music. Ultimately, the frequency and anticipation of violence and tragedy inspires uncertainty and, by extension, a sense of existential urgency. If they don't know how much time they have, they'd better do all they can to blow up fast.

Conclusion

NURTURING THE CREATIVE LIVES
OF YOUNG BLACK MEN

In 2013, First Lady Michelle Obama gave the commencement address at Bowie State University, Maryland's oldest historically Black university. She started her twenty-two-minute speech congratulating the class of 2013, praising their hard work. She also encouraged graduates to thank their families, who had supported them. And throughout her speech, the first lady reminded graduates of the historical importance of their achievements. Recounting the struggles of Dr. Martin Luther King Jr. and other civil rights activists, she remarked, "For them and so many others, getting an education was literally a matter of life or death."[1]

The speech then took a turn toward the present. The first lady compared the past struggles of civil rights activists to the current generation of Black youth. "When it comes to getting an education, too many of our young people just can't be bothered," she said. "Instead of dreaming of being a teacher or a lawyer or a business leader, they're fantasizing about being a baller or a rapper."

The first lady's comments rehashed an old critique of hip hop. Critics still argue that hip hop negatively affects the life chances of working-class Black youth in America. They argue that it glorifies violence, misogyny, and materialism. And they claim that youth emulate the sometimes problematic images and themes in hip hop. These critiques rely on problematic assumptions about how images and lyrics translate into behaviors and worldviews. But to understand hip hop's effects on Black youth, we have to get close to the action and see how it shapes their lives on the ground.

This book has shown how hip hop positively shaped the lives of "at-

promise" young Black men in South Central LA. The stories in *Blowin'*
Up challenge simplistic caricatures of hip hop as a cultural problem. Instead of funneling youth into gangs and violence, hip hop had the opposite impact, shielding working-class Black men from peers caught up
in that world. Although they grew up in the shadows of the Crips and
Bloods, these men were drawn to alternative identities in hip hop. Some
hung out with peer groups immersed in conscious hip hop; others were
simply attracted to the poetic rhymes and storytelling in underground
hip hop. Some were given a pass from gangs and were left alone to pursue their creative interests. And some were drawn to hip hop after experiences that foreshadowed dead ends awaiting them in gangs. In different ways, hip hop provided these young men with a creative outlet
and identity away from gangs.[2]

As these men got older, hip hop became a shared activity that connected them to youth from different neighborhoods. This was especially
significant in places like South Central, where gang rivalries and gang
injunctions restrict young people's mobility and connections across
neighborhoods. Hip hop was a social glue that helped youth transcend
those local neighborhood forces.

But these friendships didn't emerge out of thin air. They were nurtured at Project Blowed. By immersing themselves in the scene, young
men participated in the vision of Ben Caldwell, who believed that the
arts could deter young people from gangs. Project Blowed achieved this
by creating a scene that encouraged collaboration among young men.
While the code of the street dictates that young men use violence to
gain status and respect, Project Blowed was organized under different
rules. Young men coming into the scene were socialized into a local culture that valued creativity and charisma.[3] Rappers weren't interested in
where people were *from*. They wanted to know if you had "bars," if you
could *rhyme*.

Similarly, at Project Blowed, rappers connected with mentors who
helped them learn how to rhyme and peers interested in the same
things. This approach was a marked departure from law enforcement's
own approach to the "youth problem." In an era of gang injunctions
and police surveillance, Project Blowed provided a safe space for young

people to connect with mentors and peers who supported them away from the daily stresses of their neighborhoods.

And later, as they gained more confidence, hip hop became a perceived way up in the world. Some developed larger career goals, setting their sights on branching out of the local scene. Instead of trying to impress their peers, they focused on recording full-length albums, networking with other creative professionals, and trying to build a larger fan base; all of this was done in the hopes of getting discovered by an A&R or record label intern. Hip hop represented future possibilities not immediately visible in their social world.

And at its core, hip hop was a fun and challenging creative outlet. Each time they tried to get better at performing, freestyling, battling, or even songwriting, they would pour their energy and focus into the creative process. They'd get lost in the simple joys of practicing their art and improving their skills. This, on its own, was rewarding—an avenue to achieve what the psychologist Mihaly Csikszentmihalyi calls flow.[4] Indeed, Csikszentmihalyi argues for the psychic benefits of having challenges that require one's total, devoted focus and attention. These activities are not only psychologically stimulating; they also give people a feeling of mastery, which can feel especially empowering to young people whose lives are marked by larger uncertainties.[5]

On Existential Urgency

Blowin' Up also examines the transition into adulthood. In some ways, the stories in this book resemble ones we commonly associate with "early adulthood."[6] Like other twentysomethings, the men in this book felt uncertain about the future. They wanted to become independent and financially secure while doing something meaningful with their lives. And they didn't want to get stuck doing menial work while their talents went unused. These concerns are part of the human condition; they transcend race, ethnicity, gender, and class.

But unlike their more privileged counterparts, the men in this book did not grow up seeing multiple fallback options or safety nets. They did not take for granted that they would go to college and experience upward mobility. Instead, their lives were marked by social forces that cast doubt over their futures. Perhaps more than anything, the specter of gang violence—both past and present—shaped how they envisioned their lives playing out. Many had grown up with friends who had been injured or killed in shootings. Others glimpsed the dead ends awaiting them in the gang life. And all of the men were living in a time of escalating Black-Brown gang violence in LA.

These experiences created a sense of *existential urgency*, a heightened time sensitivity around life and career goals.[7] Existential urgency inspires a feeling that one does not have time to waste. To be sure, it is a general experience that many people encounter at some point in their lives. Those who are aging out of a time-sensitive career, hitting a midlife crisis, or approaching the end of life experience similar urgency. In these and many other situations, the perception of diminishing time to achieve goals refocuses people's commitments and priorities. People pursue what is most meaningful and bracket other paths that feel less immediately important.

But urgency is not just caused by perceptions of time running out. It is also *sustained* by interactions that give a person cause for hope. Los Angeles is an environment in which hopefuls can feel close to fame through chance encounters with celebrities, fleeting appearances on reality TV, and collaborations with creative professionals. These momentous interactions create swells of excitement and make blowin' up feel more attainable. Aspirants feel encouraged on the heels of these experiences.[8] Even when distilled and fleeting, hope can be a powerful motivator. Some men imagined that their next interaction would open up their career and dramatically affect their chances of being discovered or signed. These momentous interactions seemed to signal promising leads right around the corner.

This lens helps us understand why these men were so committed to their rap dreams and so noncommital to day jobs. While critics often argue that hip hop repels working-class Black youth from the labor market, this perspective risks misrepresenting people's motivations. These men weren't committed to their day jobs, but it wasn't because they were lazy or because they had rejected the notion of work. Their day jobs placed practical constraints on the time they could devote to performing, writing, recording, networking, and promoting—key steps in trying to blow up. The day job became temporarily disposable during a specific time in their rap careers. These men knew that their time to blow up was limited and doubled down on their rap dreams while they still had the chance.

We often celebrate this same entrepreneurial spirit and risk-taking among more privileged young adults. The person who chases an impractical career dream is valorized for his or her enterprising spirit and industry. We talk about them as exemplars of the American dream. But the public conversation is very different when young Black men (or working-class youth of color more generally) embark on similar paths. These perspectives show a profound disconnect with the actual work and process of trying to blow up. And they show the persistence of narrow, stereotypical understandings of young Black men trying to make it in hip hop. At the core, the story of rap dreams is a story of young people trying to create something from nothing. It's a story of young people's resilience in the face of staggering odds and harsh circumstances.

Learning from KAOS

Blowin' Up shows how Project Blowed (and KAOS Network more broadly) became a creative intervention in the lives of at-promise youth.[9] This scene nurtured their creative talents and connected them to supportive mentors and peers. It also facilitated friendships, encouraged collaboration, and was for many a respite from the stresses of their neighborhood life.

In many ways, KAOS Network represents an alternative to punitive and reactionary approaches to reducing gang violence and activity. The city of Los Angeles continues to issue gang injunctions, which are court orders preventing suspected gang members from participating in public activities thought to abet local gang violence. These injunctions identify safe zones in different neighborhoods and criminalize a number of "risky" activities, some of which are already illegal (e.g., selling drugs) and others of which are more mundane (e.g., congregating in large groups, using a cell phone).

Although lawmakers and police celebrate injunctions and argue that they make communities safer, locals are often more critical of them. Some feel that they give police too much discretion over determining who is and who is not a gang member. Others complain that the injunctions create an additional rationale for racial profiling. Under the injunctions, police have even more reason to stop and question youth about their gang affiliations. Not only does this breed police distrust; it also discourages community life in neighborhoods identified as gang hot spots.

Injunctions are well intentioned, but they approach gang violence through a punitive and reactionary lens. Under this logic, communities with a history of local gang activity require intervention. The problem with this approach is that it intervenes at a point when youth are already at high-risk of different negative outcomes.

KAOS Network represents a more upstream, preventative approach to reducing gang violence. Instead of increasing the surveillance on suspected gang members, KAOS Network helped deter young people from joining gangs in the first place. It also supported alternative identities and careers outside of gangs and is an example of why community-led arts organizations deserve public support and funding.

In this climate, the arts and other preventative approaches to gang violence don't garner the same media attention as punitive approaches, which local political leaders rush to adopt since it makes them appear tough on crime. Organizations in LA that nurture the creative lives of Black youth face steep competition with funding for other, more punitive ways of responding to youth. And the picture isn't much better in public education. For example, in 2012 the Los Angeles Unified School District attempted to cut *all* funding for the arts in public education. This motion, though defeated, revealed the diminishing public support for the arts, music, and creative education in places like South Central. In the long run, creative mentoring programs and public arts education are two important parts of a much larger effort to enrich community life and deter youth from gangs. But their survival and continued success require the collective support of politicians, community leaders, and progressive foundations whose funding makes them possible.

KAOS Network stopped hosting Project Blowed near the end of 2009. Attendance had been waning and Ben Caldwell was leading other programs with similar aims. He still hosts weekly outreach programs at KAOS Network and continues to support the lives of local youth through the arts, music, and other multimedia.

Still, many Blowedians get together once a year for an anniversary concert. The show is a celebration of the Project Blowed's influence on underground hip hop in LA. Others remain connected through ongoing artistic collaborations. And a new generation of artists are coming together at "Bananas," a monthly music showcase hosted by VerBS at KAOS Network. Rappers are still allowed to get on stage and freestyle, but performers at "Bananas" are booked in advance and are expected to perform as part of a live showcase. Project Blowed was an open mic where artists would get together to practice, but Bananas is a scene where artists perform as if they were part of a festival lineup, or on tour.

Evolving Dreams

As you may have figured out already, none of these men became platinum-selling recording artists. No one was signed to a major record label. But this doesn't mean that they felt despair or that their stories are examples of failed careers. Such a perspective focuses too heavily on measuring success by specific outcomes. Sure, getting signed to a lucrative record deal, touring worldwide, and becoming famous are milestone accomplishments for any recording artist. But few ever achieve that kind of notoriety and fame. More problematically, viewing success this narrowly neglects the subtler ways that rappers' lives have changed while chasing their rap dreams.

Some of the most interesting biographical changes unfolded after I had already left Los Angeles. This was the dawn of a new era in underground hip hop. While previous generations relied on handing out their music and spreading the word about themselves at local concert venues, the new generation was capitalizing on emerging social media.

Event promoters played a big role in this transition, creating online rap battle leagues like Grindtime and King of the Dot. These were not the spontaneous street-corner battles outside Project Blowed among friends and collaborators. These were "written" battles, in which rappers knew who they would battle long in advance, writing specific disses tailored to their opponent.

As one of the most widely respected underground scenes in hip hop, promoters reached out to rappers at Project Blowed like Nocando, VerBS, Open Mike, and others. Not surprisingly, they thrived in this new online venue. Their training at Project Blowed had prepared them well. For years, they had sharpened their freestyling and battling on the corner. They had also developed the swagger that comes from performing and being evaluated by the often hostile crowd at Project Blowed's open mic workshop.

The online leagues were a big launching pad for Nocando, who was featured in a dozen or so different battles. He became one of the most recognizable names in the Grindtime and King of the Dot series, catapulting him into a new realm of hip hop visibility. During this time, Nocando continued to write songs and record, eventually landing a single album deal with Alpha Pup Records, an independent label that had signed other Project Blowed artists in the past. Although this deal was mostly for distribution, it gave Nocando a way to get his music out to fans in ways he previously could not have accomplished.

Meanwhile, Nocando continued establishing himself as a mainstay in the LA hip hop underground. In addition to performing at various venues, he started performing regularly at Low-End Theory, a weekly hip hop showcase. While on tour with artists and promoters from Low-End Theory, Nocando had an important epiphany: "I realized there's no one putting our records out, so fuck it, I'll do it!" Determined to promote his music and the music of other talented underground artists who weren't recognized by major or indie labels, Nocando started his own imprint label, Hellfyre Club. This gave him a chance to help promote other artists he knew from Project Blowed like Open Mike. At the time of this writing, he had released a second solo album on Hellfyre Club, developed an online following, and was writing short essays about hip hop for *LA Weekly* magazine.[10]

Nocando also branched out into songwriting. For years, he had written songs for other artists, selling them on the side. This got him a co-publishing deal with a record label as a songwriter. When I asked about this, he told me that his training at Project Blowed had prepared him for this next venture:

> Basically, there's an arms race for older guys who came up in that generation who could freestyle and just like go into the recording booth and freestyle a chorus or a cadence and build from that. Like, I can write a sappy love song that doesn't fit my brand, but it can go to [a] nine-, ten-year-old girl who is making R&B music for the first time.

Others would be signed to artist development deals, which can be precursors to more significant deals with record labels. Flawliss was signed to a development deal with TrackMartianz, a production company that has ties with different recording artists who have been signed to Atlantic Records. This deal would help him get a professionally produced, recorded, and mixed album. It would also help him promote and distribute his music. And perhaps most important, it would give him a foot in the door with producers who had connections at a major record label.

Flawliss also used hip hop as a form of creative therapy. Surviving a shooting had awakened in him new political sensibilities. This transformation continued over the years, as news stories of other young Black men dying in shootings captured public attention. He started posting on Facebook about high-profile cases like Trayvon Martin, Michael Brown, Freddie Gray, and other young Black men killed by vigilantes or police. On one of these posts, he announced to his Facebook friends that he was no longer making "negative music" and instead was focusing on making positive, uplifting music that would address police brutality, poverty, and other structural constraints felt by working-class Black men in America. Flawliss would record a song and music video for "I Am Trayvon." When I asked about the song, he laughed: "I retired the other me. Now, I'm just making conscious hip hop. I want to use my music to change the world."

Others did not get signed and slowly exited the rap career. Blowin' up became a distant goal to them as they transitioned into jobs, families, and other commitments that took precedence. Big Flossy transitioned into long-haul truck driving. He took great pride in his ability to focus for long periods of time and attributed this to his years as an emcee, when he developed a tireless work ethic and an ability to concentrate on one thing for long periods. In addition to enjoying the regular pay, Flossy liked driving big rigs because it gave him a chance to see more of the country. Every once in awhile, he would post videos of different places he was driving through on his hauls. One was of his first paycheck. Another was of him seeing snow for the first time. When I was putting the finishing touches on this book, Flossy told me:

> I'll always love hip hop. I'll still jump in the cipher and spit with people, but now it's just a hobby or pastime that I do to relieve stress." He added: "I'm about making that paper and truck driving gives me a way to live large. How many niggas you know who eating like me and my girl eat? We go out to nice places, spend money, and enjoy having a little more financial security.

Many others were like Big Flossy. They came to the realization that they weren't going to blow up and transitioned into different kinds of work. But even though they weren't actively trying to blow up, hip hop still played an important role in their lives. It was a creative outlet, a favorite pastime that still brought them joy.

* * *

Ethnographers often face a tough question: When is the work "done"? We spend years with people, learning about their lives, sharing our own lives with them, and then one day—it's all over. Many of us walk away feeling as if we could have spent more time in the field.[11] Professional time constraints force an unnatural end to our data collection. In many cases, we don't have the luxury to spend what we feel is a sufficient amount of time collecting data. Or we find ourselves in our own transitions, moving between jobs and stages in the life course. This creates a silent insecurity. We become haunted by whether we "got it right" or "got enough." "Not quite yet," we think, hoping that a little more of this or a little more of that will help us feel that we've reached the scope or depth of our work to call it complete.[12] Indeed, if the goal of extended fieldwork is to understand how people change over time, we might follow the same group of people for the rest of our careers. Documentary filmmakers have experimented with these methods and had amazing results in the process.

I spent nearly five uninterrupted years collecting the data for this book and enjoyed my time immensely. I have fond memories of my time at Project Blowed and I still keep in touch with some of the young men I met there. I'm proud to consider them my friends and I've tried my best to represent as fully and completely the lives and challenges of those who were gracious enough to let me hang around. I hope that the book I've written honors them and showcases their immense talent. I also hope that the book sheds light on the challenges that they faced and persevered through despite larger obstacles. And I hope that, in some small way, the findings here add to larger conversations about racial inequalities, hip hop, gang violence, and the creative lives of young Black men. Finding your way through—and out of—an adolescence marked by gang violence, poverty, and police surveillance is nothing short of a triumph. For the men I met at Project Blowed, their rap dreams evolved, but they didn't die. And in a world where violence and other kinds of uncertainty shape the lives of young people, I'd say that making meaningful music, connecting with friends from different parts of the city, and expressing yourself count as dreams fulfilled.

Shout Outs

I am deeply grateful to the rappers I met at Project Blowed. Without their support, this book would not be possible. You welcomed me
into your lives and taught me about underground hip hop. Flawliss,
E.Crimsin, Big Flossy, Nocando, N.A., E.M.S., Dibiase, Trenseta, CP,
VerBS, Open Mike, and many others contributed to this project. I am
grateful for your friendship and hope that in some small way this book
captures your love of hip hop and resiliency. I'm also grateful to Ben
Caldwell, who always welcomed me at Project Blowed. I hope that this
book is a testament to the important work you have done to support the
arts and youth in Leimert Park.

I was lucky to have wonderful mentors and colleagues in the Department of Sociology at UCLA. Stefan Timmermans, Bob Emerson,
Darnell Hunt, David Halle, Jeffrey Prager, Anthony Alvarez, Curtis
Jackson-Jacobs, Brandon Berry, Anthony Ocampo, Michael DeLand,
David Trouille, John O'Brien, Forrest Stuart, and Philippe Duhart read,
commented on, or helped me think about my work. Your feedback,
critiques, and support helped me tremendously. Amada Armenta and
Anup Sheth both read this book from cover to cover. And when he was
alive, Melvin Pollner would always welcome me in his office to bounce
around ideas. His warm smile and imagination are sorely missed. I am
deeply indebted to all of you.

I'm also grateful for H. Samy Alim, who organized UCLA's Hip Hop
Working Group. His passion for hip hop is rivaled only by his passion
for bringing hip hop "heads" together. This group connected me to an
interdisciplinary group of scholars who helped me think about how

my work contributed to a growing world of hip hop studies. Christina Zanfagna, Lauren Mason-Carris, Catherine Appert, Melanie Arias, and Mark Villegas read earlier drafts of my work and were the best community of hip hop scholars I could ask for.

I'm also grateful to Jean Shin and the Minority Fellows Program (MFP) in the American Sociological Association. I was fortunate to receive three years of fellowship support from the MFP as a graduate student. The fellowship enabled me to spend lots of time doing fieldwork. The MFP has also connected me with a wide community of inspiring minority scholars in sociology. I'm continuously amazed and inspired by the great work done by MFP scholars.

Jack Katz has been and continues to be a wonderful mentor. I was lucky to be one of your students at UCLA. You took me under your wing, pushed me to work hard, and gave me the best gift of all: a sociological imagination. In our meetings, you encouraged me to look for luminous data and taught me to how to think creatively. Your feedback, critiques, and encouragement helped me finish my degree in a timely manner. I am forever grateful. In small ways, I try to pass along these same lessons to my students.

After leaving UCLA, I benefited from time to expand my training in the Robert Wood Johnson Foundation's Health & Society Scholars at the University of Pennsylvania. David Asch, Robby Aronowitz, and Jason Schnittker were wonderful program directors who supported and helped me in different ways. I was lucky to be program colleagues with Alison Buttenheim, Amy Gonzales, Laura Tach, Eran Magen, Samir Soneji, and Sarah Gollust, who all provided feedback and general words of encouragement while I wrote earlier drafts of this book. Michael Bader and Andrew Deener read many drafts of my work and would often brainstorm with me in the office or in pubs across Philly. Melissa Kulynych was a key supporter who helped make my transition smoother and everyday life brighter. Philippe Bourgois, Randall Collins, David Grazian, Charles Branas, Douglas Wiebe, Therese Richmond, and David Gibson also helped support me when I was at the University of Pennsylvania. I am grateful to all of you.

During this time of my life, I was lucky to be in an ethnography writing group. Our group met just about every month and comprised of urban ethnographers in New York and Philadelphia. Colin Jerolmack, Iddo Tavory, Harel Shapira, Lucia Trimbur, Tyson Smith, and Erin O'Connor offered careful readings of my book and are an ongoing source of community and friendship. Over the years, I've also benefited from knowing and sharing ideas with a wide variety of sharp urban ethnographers like Jacob Avery, Robert Turner, Alice Goffman, Alex Murphy, Victor Rios, Scott Brooks, Waverly Duck, Robert Garot, Cid Martinez, Josh Pacewicz, and Ashley Rondini. Gary Alan Fine helped me think about this book and provided me with feedback on an earlier chapter.

I am also grateful for Elijah Anderson's support over the years. I still remember my first ASA meeting, when you invited me to hang out with you. Over the years, you have encouraged me to keep writing. You also invited me to present an early version of this work at the 2008 Urban Ethnography Conference. I was only a graduate student then, but that experience gave me wonderful feedback and introduced me to many lifelong colleagues.

As the book neared its completion, I received editorial help from Kay Alexander, Letta Page, and Katherine Faydash. Letta, in particular, helped nudge me to the finish line. Her careful eye and knowledge of hip hop helped me tie up loose ends. I'm also grateful for the support and editorial help of Doug Mitchell, who originally took an interest in this book and helped me see it through. Doug's creative vision, editorial guidance, and warm words of support were indispensable as I revised and rewrote chunks of this book. Tim McGovern and Kyle Wagner worked behind the scenes, helping make the whole process run smoother. And my new colleagues and students at the University of Toronto were warm and encouraging as I finished the book. Erik Schneiderhan, Hae Yeon Choo, Jennifer Carlson, Randol Contreras, Dan Silver, Phil Goodman, Pat Erickson, Julian Tanner, Scot Wortley, Bob Brym, Adam Green, Anna Korteweg, Markus Schafer, and Bob Anderson have helped make my time at the University of Toronto intellectually exciting. I could not think of a better set of colleagues to help me develop my ideas.

Over the years, different friends have shared ideas with me and helped keep me grounded. Evan Doheny, Carlos Soto, Osage Soto, Brian Stephens, Skye Girardin, Jason Sprague, Jarmin Yeh, Anthony Ervin, Donald Blanchard, Eric Hole, and all my jiu jitsu friends—I couldn't have done this without you. Thank you to Isa and Isidro—you have welcomed me into your home and I'm grateful for all your support. Thank you to Halmonee for always being there for me and for teaching me the value of hard work.

While writing this book, my partner, Vanessa Baptista, was a continued source of encouragement. You have filled my life with joy and laughter. I could not have done this without you. Last, I thank my mom. Your sacrifices have helped me pursue my dreams. I hope that this book is a small token of my immense gratitude for your love and support over the years.

* * *

Visit www.jooyoungkimlee.com to watch videos and hear music from artists in this book.

Methods Appendix

VIDEOS IN ETHNOGRAPHY

The rise of inexpensive and ubiquitous video cameras raise important questions for ethnographers: Should we use them? What insights can we glean from them? And what challenges come with using a video camera and video data? Although some ethnographers have started using videos, many have been reluctant to adopt them into their repertoire.[1] Some are hesitant for good reason. They worry that a video camera might disrupt the ordinary flow of social life in the community they're writing about. Others say (or think), "That's not what we do." Or worse, they worry that videos might diminish our place at the table. Who needs ethnographers if video cameras can capture everything?

In truth, I didn't start with a clear picture of how I would use my video camera, or of whether any of these videos would make it into my analysis. I started using a video camera to help rappers at Project Blowed. They wanted to post videos of their performances on You-Tube but didn't have someone to record them. I was eager to help and bought a 16x optical zoom JVC Mini-DV video camera from Best Buy. It cost $259 and wasn't anything fancy, but it got the job done. At the very least, I figured having a camera would give me a good reason to be around more. And in the best-case scenario, I imagined how posting videos might help someone get noticed by the industry.

Over the next several years, I recorded ninety hours of video. In the process, I became something of a "video guy" for rappers. In addition to recording performances at Project Blowed, I also recorded music videos, studio sessions, and other promotional footage. This process showed me how videos could enrich my understandings of interaction.

Although sociologists have long-standing interests in interaction, most focus on the verbal side of communication. Conversation analysts have pioneered research on talk, but their work does not show how people use their bodies and physical space in interaction.[2] Videos give us a more nuanced appreciation for the many ways people communicate with one another.[3] But first a word about some common challenges in fieldwork that videos helped me address.

The Chaos of Fieldwork

The street corner was already bustling when I showed up on my first night of fieldwork. There were a handful of ciphers already happening as I floated around the corner. Every once in a while, one of these ciphers would turn into a battle. There were also people performing inside the open mic workshop. I'd spend a few minutes observing one cipher and then I'd jump to the next cipher that seemed interesting. As I bounced around the scene, feeling more scattered by the moment, I wondered, "What should I focus on?"

Ethnographers face this question when they enter a fieldsite.[4] Even the most banal settings have many things going on at once. It is impossible for ethnographers to observe everything. Instead, we make decisions—conscious or otherwise—to focus on some things while neglecting others.

After bouncing around for much of the night, I forced myself to observe a single cipher. I figured that focusing on one specific cipher would give me more detailed insights into how they worked. I ran into a related problem. Despite my newfound focus, I still had trouble remembering "what happened." I would make a mental note of what someone rhymed in one moment, only to forget it once the next person said something else that caught my ear. There was simply too much stuff happening quickly for me to keep up. Here is an excerpt from my fieldnotes that demonstrates the challenges of re-creating even short bursts of interaction in fieldnotes. I tried my best to re-create this scene on the page:

At the tail end of his verse, another emcee enters the cipher. He is a slightly older looking black guy with tightly pressed "locks" spilling from a knitted black ski hat. He has a neatly cropped moustache and small goatee and is wearing a nice mustard colored turtleneck and dark pants. He gets into the circle and closes his eyes as he rhymes. His flow is a little more erratic than the previous guy's; at certain points his flow becomes quicker and more syncopated with the beat. Despite this, he is always able to "land" back onto the beat. While "flowing," he moves only his right hand. In fact, he holds his index finger outwards in a 'pointing' gesture and moves it in a "figure eight" motion next to the right side of his head.

This process continues for about 15 more minutes. Emcees take turns rhyming in the circle, and generally before entrance, use a statement like "Yo, listen" or "Check it" as a way to cut into another emcee's freestyle. Remarkably, nobody ever outwardly demonstrates any signs of offense when another emcee interjects into their freestyle. It is as if an emcee's first entrance words (the aforementioned) socially queue the performing emcee and others in the circle that he is about to flow. Likewise, to show approval or "give props" to someone's rhyme, crowd members will make a high pitched "Woo" sound usually accompanied by the previously mentioned "hand pat" in the air. At one point, a short and stocky emcee wearing a white LA Dodgers baseball hat and an Ecko T-shirt steps into the cipher and begins his rhyme. At several points during his rhyme, people in the circle make a high "Woo" and hand pat gestures.

Finally, emcees are also able to sometimes elicit laughter from people within the circle. During one emcee's flow (the slightly overweight black emcee with a Cleveland Cavaliers sweatband), he invokes several clever rhymes. One of the rhymes that I could remember said something to the effect of him "not being some 'hood rich cat" and actually "being a suburb nigga." There is a much larger context of words and sounds that these notions were used within—unfortunately, I cannot remember exactly how he set these ideas up. In any case, his reference to being from the suburbs made a few people within the circle and outside of the circle laugh. Their laughs were followed by the hand pat.

Although these notes give a basic picture of the cipher, they leave much to be desired. My notes captured a couple memorable lines or actions from rappers and audiences but lacked much else. They were a summary description of vastly more nuanced interactions. More than anything, much of what I was observing happened quickly, making it hard for me to remember—let alone process—it.

I tried using "jottings" to help improve my fieldnotes. On some nights, I would structure my observations, systematically taking a five minute break every half hour. During these brief asides, I'd scribble down notes away from the cipher, hoping to write notes that would help me re-create what I had just seen. On other nights, I would limit my observations to a few memorable passages in a cipher. Afterward, I would step away from the cipher and record what I had seen and heard. These methods marginally improved my notes. But no matter what I tried, I always felt like I was just scratching the surface. Reading my notes the following day, I was struck at how little I had captured.

The Riches of Video

Videos helped me overcome some of these challenges. Although they did not give me an omnipresent view of everything, they did give me a raw account of an unfolding interaction. By keeping the camera rolling on a single activity (e.g., cipher, battle), I could rewind and rewatch fleeting moments in clearer detail. This exercise was useful. In addition to adding depth and nuance into my understanding of interactions, these videos also gave me a way to compare the relative strengths and weaknesses of observational, interview, and video data.

Here is an excerpt from my fieldnotes. It captures a battle that escalates into an argument between Big Flossy and E.Crimsin. Recall that battling is *supposed* to be playful. Even though people diss each other, participants are always supposed to "keep it hip hop" and should avoid trying to escalate the situation into violence:

Mimicking Flossy (who is becoming more angry by the moment), E.Crimsin starts raising his voice, puffing his chest out, and cussing back at Flossy.

Flossy keeps yelling at E.Crimsin to "Hold on my nigga . . . let me spit . . ." E.Crimsin continues to interrupt Flossy, which only adds to his frustration. In previous weeks others have gotten annoyed with E.Crimsin and his failure to observe cipher/battle etiquette. Some people think he cuts people off mid-sentence.

At one point, E.Crimsin shouts over at Flossy, "Nigga, you bleed food!" Onlookers laugh heartily at this one. After E.Crimsin delivers this punch line, onlookers begin playfully "ooohing" and "aaahing" while pushing each other around. There are intermittent moments where Flossy and E.Crimsin try to organize their interaction into a legitimate battle. Flossy begins spitting and then becomes agitated when E.Crimsin comes back at him with punch lines about his weight.

Again, my fieldnotes provide a summary description of E.Crimsin mimicking Big Flossy, who was growing impatient. The notes also include descriptions of a back-and-forth that emerges between the two, with memorable lines that each said and how audience members responded to these lines. For instance, Big Flossy broke from the play frame of the battle and started yelling at E.Crimsin, "Hold on my nigga . . . let me spit." This marked a significant shift in his orientation to Crimsin and the battle more broadly. I also keyed into a memorable rebuttal, where E.Crimsin shouts at Big Flossy, "Nigga, you bleed food!" This was noticeable because it created a vivid emotional reaction among onlookers.

I also met up with Big Flossy later that week and interviewed him. We were at his apartment, talking about battling, when I asked him about his recent battle with E.Crimsin. I half-expected him to brush off the question, but Big Flossy seemed excited to share his experience. He said:

Ahh, man. That nigga! That nigga is always rappin' over me and shit. That time I think he just started getting too loud and couldn't handle that I was servin' him. I mean, I don't got beef with that nigga, but too many niggas talk all loud and shit!

Instead of saying what specifically had sparked this battle, Big Flossy talked about his growing frustration with E.Crimsin over the years. I later probed Big Flossy about what started the battle and he answered, "It was because he kept rappin' over me." Big Flossy paused, unsure of his response. "It might have been because he was rappin' all loud all the time. To be honest, I don't even remember, I just know that he [Crimsin] always tryin' to start something." Interestingly, Big Flossy's account did not include a description of the immediate catalysts for their battle. As it turned out, many rappers could not pinpoint the specific causes of battles. They could usually remember who they battled and whether they won or lost the battle, but many were mum on the processes leading to battles. Big Flossy's account situated the battle within a much longer history of strained relations with E.Crimsin. The interview account provided further context for making sense of this interaction.

And then I watched the video. The video uncovered new dimensions to this interaction. While rewatching the clip several times, I started seeing how both parties were using their bodies and spacing to shape the unfolding interaction. Although there are cultural variations in how people understand personal boundaries and "intimate space," bodily closeness is a necessary condition for violence. In confrontational moments, audience members look to separate people who are in each other's intimate space. The fear is that if people stay in each other's intimate space, they will eventually start pushing each other, ramping up the risks for a violent situation.[5]

Moments like these are ripe for escalation. Big Flossy and E.Crimsin become entangled at one point, so close that they were physically touching. Instead of standing firm or further inserting himself into Big Flossy's intimate space, E.Crimsin moved out of the way, a subtle sign of deference that helped defuse an already-tense situation:

FLOSSY: Somebody gonna feed you
I'ma have to sleep you

engage you

have to preach to you

you read you

you weak, dude!

E.CRIMSIN: Nigga you bleed food!

The fuck!

Nigga you [indecipherable]

[Crowd laughing at the back-and-forth between E.Crimsin and Flossy.]

FLOSSY: Straight boney

niggas, still talking about food

'cause he hungry

he won't stop it

he wants the 'wich [?]

stop stiff

and I'ma still fuck your bitch

[E.Crimsin makes a loud noise.]

FLOSSY: [directly speaking to E.Crimsin] Hold on let me rap my nigga! Why aren't you letting me rap, my nigga. Let me rap. I let you rap. Let me rap [both become entangled here].

E.CRIMSIN: All right, nigga [E.Crimsin walks off to the side].

The last exchange in this clip is important. Here, both Big Flossy and E.Crimsin have broken from the "play frame" of the rap battle (indicated by the change in transcription style). They stopped rhyming and were speaking to each other in a direct, confrontational tone. But in addition to what they were saying and how they were saying it, both parties were also inching closer together: they were entering into each others' intimate space—a potential danger zone. They walked into the center of the circle and their bodies came into contact for a moment. This was followed by light pushing. It looked just like the start of any street scuffle. But instead of escalating it into violence,

E.Crimsin helped defuse the situation by turning away and deferring to Big Flossy.

To start a fight, people have to move into striking or grappling distance. They have to be close to each other, eliminating physical distance from the other person. Of course, people might only be posturing and blustering, with no intentions of fighting.[6] And they can also disentangle from the other person by backing and turning away, or showing that they do not want to fight. But it becomes harder for one person or for both parties to walk away as they get closer and as their bodies are increasingly entangled. E.Crimsin seemed to sense that the interaction was ramping up toward a fight and helped defuse the situation by deferring to Big Flossy, giving him space. Beyond the words and the shared history of both participants, the video segment shows how bodily engagement and closeness can also steer interactions toward or away from violence.[7]

Of course, keen ethnographers can see this stuff firsthand and may be so lucky to have an interviewee who reflects on this in close detail. More often than not, though, our fieldwork is filled with many things that split our attention. And perhaps because we are in a written discipline, our work often privileges what people *say* over these more subtle interactional gestures. Videos give us a rare form of access into these sides of social interaction.

Some Challenges

Although videos helped me unpack previously hidden layers of nonverbal interaction, they also introduced new dilemmas in my relationships with people. I experienced some issues with my camera after word got around that I had one. Somewhere along the line, people started telling others that I was a "documentarian." I was flattered (since I greatly admire documentary work), but these moments reminded me of how my video camera was changing the ways people saw me in the field.

I first noticed this while hanging out with Flawliss in Long Beach. We were at an event and he was going around, hanging out with other rappers. At one point, he spotted people he knew and introduced me to his friends: "That's my boy, Joo. He makes documentaries and shit." The other rappers smiled and seemed interested: "Oh, word!? What kinds of stuff are you shooting?" I smiled, thinking carefully about my answer: "Everything, really. Ciphers, battles, events." I later told them that I was *not* in fact a documentarian but an ethnographer writing about hip hop. This seemed to burst their bubble. They didn't seem as interested in talking afterward.

As time went by, I learned to use this mistaken identity as a way to talk about—and clarify—my intentions and goals as an ethnographer. Instead of contrasting my work with documentary films, I told people that what I was doing was *like* a documentary, but in written form. This was a quick and easy way to clear up confusion. I would explain that I was aiming to do something similar to the documentary *Hoop Dreams*, but in a book.[8] Most of the young men had seen *Hoop Dreams* and knew the narrative arc of that project, so the comparison helped.

My video camera also posed some challenges around blending into the scene. Even though I worked hard not to change the natural flow of social interactions at Project Blowed, there were times when having my camera changed what was happening in the moment. Most often, rappers who didn't know me or my project would start rapping *at* me. They would see the camera and make a beeline for it, rapping directly at the lens.

This caught me off guard, but it shouldn't have. These rappers were interacting with the camera in ways that mirrored what they grew up seeing in many underground hip hop videos. Videos on YouTube often featured artists like Cassidy rapping directly to a virtual audience. These videos were very popular at Project Blowed, where young men studied the clips to dissect the style, cadence, and wordplay of artists from different regions of the country. For example, CP and SS had grown up watching the Crack DVD series and other underground hip hop videos featuring East Coast emcees.[9]

After a few false starts, I started encouraging people to just keep rapping as if I wasn't there. Sometimes this worked—rappers understood that I was trying to capture a "raw" picture and would quickly return to battling or freestyling. Others kept rapping at the camera, giving the lens their "hottest sixteen" (bars), followed by shout outs to friends, family, and associates. I would usually keep the camera rolling out of fear that I would offend someone by turning my camera off while they rhymed. On a few isolated occasions, I paused my camera to save the last few minutes of my battery life. The few times I did this, I had no reason to suspect that the person knew that the camera wasn't rolling. Nevertheless, it sometimes led to awkward follow-up interactions, when rappers asked me for the footage.

As time went by, a small and central cast of characters came to know about my research goals as an ethnographer. Wanting to help me get a "raw" picture of underground hip hop at Project Blowed, they discouraged their peers from rapping at the camera. Choppa—who had previously rapped at the camera on multiple occasions—once corrected others on the corner. He nudged a rapper I didn't recognize: "Don't rap at the camera! Just do your thing! He tryin' to get *that* on tape." As I became more familiar on the corner, others would intervene, too. Over time, the problem mostly became a nonissue, since regulars would quickly correct newcomers who rapped at my lens.

The camera raised all sorts of issues in my fieldwork. It helped me gain access into scenes and settings I might not have been able to observe without the camera. But it led to confusion about my identity and sometimes transformed situations. Ethnographers should try to minimize the extent to which they disrupt the natural order of a social world with their camera. Even in settings where people are accustomed to being videotaped, ethnographers who use video cameras have to figure out ways to record without fundamentally altering the social world under investigation.

The Future of Videos

Videos continue to evolve as a central and ubiquitous part of the social world. Many people now have smartphones equipped with high-resolution video cameras. Manufacturers like GoPro have also created cameras that are lightweight and discrete. In the coming years, this technology will only get better, leading to smaller, more portable, and more inventive ways of collecting videos.

At the same time, people have become increasingly used to being videotaped and broadcasting those videos to the world. Vine, Facebook, and other social media are virtual storehouses of videos that document people's everyday lives. Videos are becoming a routine part of social interactions. All signs seem to point toward videos becoming a wave of the future. The next generation of ethnographers will have grown up in a multimediated time. Who knows how long it will be until ethnographers have to justify why they are *not* using videos in their data collection?

Still, there are obviously situations in which ethnographers would not want to use videos. Videos are not present in every setting, and their use can transform how people interact with each other and the researcher. This situation should be avoided. But in settings where videos are common, videos are an added resource that aid in data collection and analysis.

In the end, videos cannot replace fieldnotes or interview transcripts. Although they give us powerful insights into "what happened" in interaction, our analysis of the interactions is shaped by larger context. The juicy backstories, life histories, and larger community inform our micro-observations and are accessible only through participant-observation fieldnotes and interview data.

As such, ethnographers can think of videos as an additional resource in gathering their data. Videos enrich our analyses of interactions. They allow us to document in close, raw detail "what happened." These data reveal the embodied and spatial layers to interaction that are difficult to observe and represent in fieldnotes or interview data. This shouldn't come as a surprise. Much of what we do with our bodies occurs below our *own* perceptual radars; we move, emote, and do things with our bodies often without noticing. Videos help us tap into that.

And even if ethnographers are not interested in adopting videos into their data collection, they might consider them as a pedagogical tool. Gary Alan Fine writes about the general problem of accuracy in ethnographic fieldnotes.[10] He describes an exercise in which he plays a recorded conversation for his students and asks them to try to re-create this conversation in their notes. The exercise is humbling and helps students realize that their fieldnotes are necessarily partial representations of "what happened."

While teaching ethnography, I've often adopted a similar test. I've played short videos for my students and asked them to try to re-create the interaction on the page. Students are always surprised at the varied ways people re-create these scenes. While some focus on dialogue, others pick up on facial tics, posture, eye contact, and other nonverbal aspects of interaction. This is a wonderful tool to show the interpretive work that goes into observing and representing some things over others. And if nothing else, these exercises help sensitize students to a broader range of phenomena that they can observe and write about when studying interaction up close.

Notes

1   Although South Central was officially renamed South Los Angeles in 2003, I use
    the name South Central because it's the term locals use when referring to the
    area. The city changed the name of the area because of its long association with
    gang violence, but residents were upset about the rebranding because they felt
    the city had ignored other aspects of community life in the area.

2   For more on the rich local history of Project Blowed, see Marcyliena Morgan's
    (2009) historical and ethnographic study of it.

3   For more on this, see Robert Garot's (2010) piercing ethnography of gang ritu-
    als among youth in LA. Garot writes extensively about the everyday negotiations
    that youth manage in schools and on the streets. In LA, youth from working-
    class neighborhoods are bombarded with questions about which gang they affili-
    ate with.

4   Everett Hughes (1997) defines a "career" as a moving perspective on people's
    lives. Contrary to the popular usage of the term, careers need not be linked to an
    occupational trajectory. Instead, careers key in sociologists to observing how and
    why people change over time.

5   No one exemplifies this better than Timothy Black (2010), whose ethnography
    of three Puerto Rican brothers chronicles nearly two decades in their lives. His
    study is an exemplar of long-term, immersed fieldwork that captures the many
    ways the lives of our informants change over time.

6   Both Mitchell Duneier (1999) and Colin Jerolmack (2013) identify participants
    in their studies. Both made available their fieldnotes, interview transcripts, and
    book drafts, giving their participants an active role in knowing how they were
    being represented. This is not only an important move for increasing research
    transparency; it also moves away from the assumption that concealing place or
    identities of people should be the default practice in ethnography.

7   For more about the history and role of "femcees," or female emcees in the scene,
    see Marcyliena Morgan's (2009) work on the experiences of women from an
    earlier generation of Project Blowed rappers. Morgan shows how these women
    collectively carved out a scene for themselves in the LA underground. She and
    other hip hop scholars, like Tricia Rose (1994) and Joan Morgan (1999), provide

rich insights into the experiences of young women in hip hop scenes. Although my book is not about women, I draw from the insights of these different authors to better understand the unique challenges young Black men face in trying to make it in hip hop.

Introduction

1   "Flipping the script" is a hip hop term for parrying another person's disses. Rappers at Project Blowed learn how to flip the script on someone who tries to unsettle them with disses.

2   Jay-Z's song "30 Something" is on the 2007 album *Kingdom Come*.

3   Eminem's *The Marshall Mathers LP* 2, Drake's *Nothing Was the Same,* and Jay-Z's *Magna Carta Holy Grail* album all sold more than one million albums. There were only three other albums that went gold that year. "2014/2015 Hiphop Album Sales Updated Weekly," *Kanye to The* (blog), http://www.kanyetothe.com/forum /index.php?topic=358972.0.

4   Derek Thompson, "How Musicians Really Make Money in One Long Graph," *Atlantic*, November 30, 2011, http://www.theatlantic.com/business/archive/2011 /11/how-musicians-really-make-money-in-one-long-graph/249267/.

5   Rose (2008).

6   McWhorter (2003).

7   In 1995, the late civil rights activist C. Delores Tucker launched a national campaign against the hip hop music industry over violent and misogynistic lyrics in some gangsta rap. She led the National Political Congress of Black Women's campaign against Time Warner Records that ultimately pressured the label into dropping Interscope and Death Row Records—two prominent gangsta rap labels. Tucker was famously dissed by Tupac Shakur in "How Do U Want It" (1996): "Delores Tucker yous a motherfucker, instead of trying to help a nigga you destroy a brother." More recently, Bill Cosby and Alvin Poussaint (2007) have argued that gangsta rap causes far-reaching damage to black youth: "Gangsta rap promotes the widespread use of the N-word to sell CDs among people of all ethnic groups. In fact, the audience for gangsta rap is made up predominantly of white youth, who get a vicarious thrill from participating in a black thug fantasy, including the degradation of women. Black youth, as well as some misguided adults, have defended the use of the N-word, suggesting they are somehow making it a positive term. Don't fall for that nonsense: the N-word is a vile symbol of our oppression by slave masters" (144).

8   H. Samy Alim (2006) argues that researchers should immerse themselves into the local scenes and sites of cultural consumption and production. In place of evaluating and analyzing cultures from an outsider's perspective, Alim makes a case for adopting a "hiphopagraphic" approach, which combines insights from ethnography as well as social and oral history.

9   James Scott (1992) developed the notion of hidden transcripts, which refers to everyday cultural practices that subaltern and dispossessed groups use when critiquing existing power structures. Tricia Rose (1994) borrows from Scott and writes about hip hop's historical legacy. She situates the emergence of hip hop

culture as a creative response to historical and structural transformations of the South Bronx during the late 1970s and early 1980s. During this period of rapid deindustrialization and institutional neglect, youth created a culture that was both cathartic and a creative way to represent one's lived experiences.

10   Sujatha Fernandes (2011) examines the rise of global hip hop and shows how politically marginalized youth in different contexts use and interpret hip hop in local political struggles.

11   Robin Kelley (1994) goes a step further, calling hip hop a "street ethnography." Songs that ostensibly appear to be about the glorification of gang culture, hustling, and violence must be decoded to understand their more subtle meanings and placed in a larger historical context that takes seriously racial, ethnic, and class inequality. When interpreted through this lens, "senseless" gangsta rap can be read as thick creative description from the streets.

12   Bakari Kitwana (2002) writes about how hip hop has become a rallying point for a generation of young people who grew up listening to and identifying with the music. In recent years, scholar-activists like Kitwana have been instrumental in using hip hop as a means to organize conventions and other local, grassroots political action among the hip hop generation.

13   Robin Kelley (1997) makes similar critiques of analyses that politicize hip hop: "By not acknowledging the deep visceral pleasures black youth derive from making and consuming culture, the stylistic and aesthetic conventions that render the form and performance more attractive than the message, these authors reduce expressive culture to a political text" (37). Joan Morgan (1999) and Edgar Tyson (2002) make compelling cases for how hip hop provides young men with a creative space to represent and reflect on their vulnerability.

14   Morgan (2009).

15   David Brooks writes about this in his article "The Odyssey Years," *New York Times*, October 9, 2007.

16   Katherine Newman (2012) describes this as a global phenomenon. She calls these young adults "boomerang kids" because they return home after going to school and working independently.

17   Al Young Jr. (2004) writes about similar themes in his ethnography of young Black men in a low-income Chicago community. Specifically, he describes how young people taper their expectations for the future after growing up amid poverty and violence.

18   Psychologists like Billieux and colleagues (2010) also write about urgency, but they write about it as poor impulse control or hasty decision making. While these ideas are informative, they focus on situated kinds of urgency. The person who can't delay immediate gratification experiences a different kind of urgency from that of the person who feels that his time to achieve meaningful goals is closing. More problematically, psychologists divorce these feelings from a person's social world, which is where they get ideas about their lives and futures. I frame urgency as an existential experience, caused by social experiences that send powerful signals about where a person is in his or her life, particularly the likelihood of realizing future hopes and dreams. Thus, instead of looking inward, I look outward at the social conditions that produce existential urgency in people's lives.

19   Al Young Jr. (2004) writes about this in his probing ethnography of young Black men in working-class neighborhoods of Chicago. Experiences with violence weigh heavily on the minds of young men, whose visions of the future are shaped by seeing and hearing about shootings and other gang violence around them.

20   Centers for Disease Control and Prevention, *Homicide Rates among Persons Ages 10–24 Years, by Race/Ethnicity and Sex, United States, 2010,* http://www.cdc.gov /violenceprevention/youthviolence/stats_at-a_glance/hr_age-race.html.

21   Ted Miller and Mark Cohen (1997) show that the costs of treating gunshot wounds are significantly higher than treatment for stab wounds.

22   EpiCenter, "Overall Injury Surveillance," http://epicenter.cdph.ca.gov/Report Menus/CustomTables.aspx.

23   John Hagan and Holly Foster (2001) have written about the life-changing implications of exposures to violence for youth. They describe how it leads to premature role exits from adolescence into adulthood. Young people who are exposed to violence have deflated expectations for the future and suffer lingering mental health issues as they age.

24   Anderson (1999).

25   Los Angeles Police Department, "Gangs," http://www.lapdonline.org/get _informed/content_basic_view/1396.

26   Contrary to public visions, gang violence in South Central isn't isolated to Crips versus Bloods. Sanyika Shakur (1994), a.k.a. "Monster" Kody Scott, for instance, writes about a long-standing Crip rivalry between the Neighborhood Rollin' 60s and the Eight Trey Gangster Crips and similar rivalries among many Crip sets and associated gangs.

27   Gang injunctions are restraining orders against gangs that prevent members from participating in certain activities thought to be linked to crime and violence. Los Angeles has a long history of using gang injunctions to crack down on gang activities in different neighborhoods. In 1987, the city attorney and the LA Police Department filed an injunction against the Playboy Gangster Crips. Today, many neighborhood gangs have injunctions against them. These injunctions criminalize various public activities and are measures that police have used to gradually escalate surveillance of neighborhoods with gangs.

28   Robert Garot (2010) takes a penetrating look at how young people selectively identify with gangs in heated moments when they're asked, "Who you claim?" In moments when they sense danger, Garot shows that young people have the option to disavow gang ties. It doesn't always help them escape violence (and it may have violent repercussions), but it is an in-the-moment option to escape an encounter unscathed.

29   Kathy Charmaz (1991) shows how chronically ill patients also channel their energies into meaningful identities and roles. The men in this book went through similar kinds of refocusing as they aged and became more aware of the constant, very real threat of death.

30   Collins (2004).

31   When I first moved to LA, I had run-ins with Hall of Fame basketball player James Worthy. I occasionally swam with actor Owen Wilson, and I saw actress Alyssa Milano in a coffee shop. I ate dinner next to comedians Andy Dick and

Bob Saget, and I voted next to actress Marcia Cross. Famous people were every-where.

32   Howard Becker (1982) writes about the networks of cooperation underlying artis-tic production. The artist, in effect, is often at the center of an interlocking web of others whose collective expertise helps bring art to fruition. Creative indus-try data also support these ideas. In 2011, the entertainment industry employed an estimated 247,000 workers in Los Angeles alone; 162,000 of those were wage and salaried, and 85,000 were freelancers and independent contractors. Together these workers accounted for nearly 80 percent of California's estimated 307,000 entertainment industry jobs. New York State—another US center of entertainment—employed 160,087 people in the entertainment industry in the same year. "Top Employment by Industry Sector," CareerOneStop, http://www .careerinfonet.org/industry/Ind_Employment_Data.aspx?id=&nodeid=50&stfips =06&from=Employment.

33   Morgan (2009) writes about how rappers judge one another at the open mic on the basis of their "lyrical fitness." She emphasizes the high lyrical bar that rap-pers created and held one another to at Project Blowed.

34   Lucie Cheng and Yen Espiritu (1989) have written about the racial, social-psychological, and materialist explanations for intergroup conflict between Korean immigrants and local Black communities in Los Angeles.

35   As Mitchell Duneier (2000) explains in his study of homeless Black men, researchers who presume "insider" status are often overstating the extent to which they are accepted. They are often guilty of ignoring the taken-for-granted privileges that they bring with them into many ethnographic settings.

36   Scratching is a technique that turntablists use when moving a "sample" or sound back-and-forth rapidly. There are various techniques within scratching, but all of them create a rhythmic syncopation layered on top of an instrumental beat.

37   A video of Tron practicing at a gym is available on YouTube: "tron robotic anima-tion 3," YouTube video, 2:30, posted by "regularolpoet," January 5, 2007, https:// www.youtube.com/watch?v=y9f7s3Qak5w.

38   Joseph Schloss (2009) writes about this in the world of b-boys and b-girls (break-dancers). Dancers take pride in representing their mentors, who are often asso-ciated with a particular historical lineage in the evolution of b-boying and b-girling.

39   Krumping is a fast-paced style of hip hop dance pioneered by youth in South Central. For more about it, see the 2005 documentary film *Rize*, directed by David LaChapelle (Santa Monica, CA: Lionsgate Films).

40   The 808 is a special drum sample that many producers use when making a bass-heavy instrumental track. It is a popular sample among many of hip hop's most noted producers, like Dr. Dre and DJ Mustard.

41   Victor Rios (2011) makes a compelling case for avoiding the label "at risk" in talk-ing and writing about Black and Brown youth from disadvantaged situations. Drawing on insights from labeling theory, Rios shows that the labels we attach are internalized by youth and powerfully affect how institutions see them. Key institutional actors—teachers, administrators, police officers, and others—tacitly use these labels to justify the unequal treatment and profiling of youth who they suspect to be "criminals" or "delinquents."

Chapter 1

1   Sanyika Shakur's (1994) gang memoir includes getting "courted in" to the Eight Trey Gangster Crips. In addition to enduring a physical beating, he and other youth had to commit crimes on behalf of the gang to prove their mettle. Victor Rios (2011) also writes about this in his ethnography of Black and Brown youth from Oakland and other low-income Bay Area communities. He describes how young people are "jumped in" by taking a beating, thus proving their manhood in the eyes of their peers.

2   For more on the Good Life, see director Ava DuVernay's 2008 award-winning documentary *This Is the Life* (Los Angeles: Ava DuVernay Company), DVD. Marcyliena Morgan (2002, 2009) also writes about the histories and linguistic practices at the Good Life Café and Project Blowed. Both provide important context for my work.

3   Anderson (1999).

4   *Riding* has many definitions, each of which is shaped by local culture. Alice Goffman (2014) describes riding in her work on everyday life in a hypersurveilled Black neighborhood of Philadelphia. Residents there understand "riding" as a more general kind of loyalty to a person. When someone shows commitment to another person over time, he or she is said to be a "rider." When a person betrays another or fails to come through, he or she is said to not be "riding right."

5   Kelley (1997).

6   Loïc Wacquant (2004) describes boxing similarly: his fieldwork shows how young Black men from working-class neighborhoods in Chicago are shielded from the perils of gang violence and street life through boxing. Their monastic devotion to practice and their future aspirations keep them away from their peers' drug trade and from gangs.

7   Victor Rios (2011) provides an in-depth, first-person account of why he and his peers were drawn to street gangs while growing up. He describes seeking protection in the gang. Sudhir Venkatesh (2006), in contrast, shows some of the economic motivations for joining gangs. Even though many gang members never make the kind of money they envision, they are still drawn to the hustling and moneymaking opportunities that elude them in the formal labor market. Rios (2011) reflects on his own path to show how teachers and other adults can have a big impact on young people by investing in their lives and well-being. He describes how a particular schoolteacher's empathy helped him leave behind the gang life. His work offers important insights into the more general ways that institutions can better support the aspirations of at-promise youths.

8   This is a part of Afrika Bambaataa's legacy in the South Bronx. Bambaataa famously united local gangs under the Universal Zulu Nation, a hip hop collective. For more, see Jeff Chang's (2005) history of hip hop culture.

9   Although my book zooms in on the lives of rappers, hip hop has similar kinds of protective functions in the lives of b-boys, b-girls, and others who are involved in hip hop cultural production (see Schloss 2009).

10   Spike Lee, dir., *Do the Right Thing* (Brooklyn, NY: Universal Pictures, 1989).

11   McWhorter (2000, 2003) makes this and similar claims in much of his writing

about hip hop. He does so, however, without a solid empirical foundation for his claims.

12   Hip hop's defenders will quickly point to conscious hip hop music when rebutting critics, citing artists like the Coup or Dead Prez as examples of how hip hop can politically energize young Black men. Defenders argue that critics have it all wrong and have focused their critiques on a narrow cross section of artists with violent and misogynistic lyrics. While some of this is true, it still misses the larger ways that hip hop shields young Black men from gangs and street activities. Playful songs, party anthems, and even mainstream jams that many of us love to problematize are positive influences, too.

13   For more on linguistic creativity in hip hop, see H. Samy Alim's (2006) work on Hip Hop Nation Language.

14   Robert Garot (2010) and Victor Rios (2011) have both written ethnographies showing how administrators create punitive school environments that marginalize young people most in need of support and help. This sometimes emerges around dress codes, which are often mistakenly linked to gang culture.

15   Robin Kelley (1997) makes similar arguments in his work. He describes the tendency of academics to theorize the joy and pleasure out of hip hop.

16   The term OG literally stands for "original gangster." It is an honorific term that gang members give to people who have long and storied histories in gangs. It is a sign of respect and a designation that denotes status within the gang.

17   This is a common story among young Black men who grow up around gang members but show a special knack for skills that are respected in their 'hood. For example, Compton-born rapper the Game grew up in Blood neighborhoods and had a short-lived career in basketball; gang members from Santana Blocc left him alone.

18   Sudhir Venkatesh (2000, 2006) writes about this in his work on street gangs in Chicago's Robert Taylor Homes. His work challenges simplistic representations of gangs as public menaces responsible for community problems by revealing how gangs also fund community centers and provide protection to residents when police aren't around or aren't trusted.

19   Alice Goffman (2014) writes about the ways young men value both loyalty and someone who will "ride" for them. This perceived loyalty is a currency in social relations.

20   Victor Rios (2011) provides an exception, showing us how teachers, community members, police officers, and others help youth transition out of gangs by providing a "youth support complex" that facilitates and supports their exit. Also, in their study of crime over the life course, Robert Sampson and John Laub (2003) found that most people exit a life of crime when they get married, get a stable job, or have children. These are important life course transitions that redirect the interests of young men toward their families and away from their peers.

21   To be sure, getting cold feet happens to people in varying social worlds: the bride who calls off her wedding and the law school aspirant who defers admission both feel unsure about their next steps. In these and many other examples people get "cold feet" and change their course of action.

22   Sanyika Shakur (1994) describes riding in this way, too. His account highlights

"riding" as a person mobilizing for battle against a rival gang. This is consistent with Tupac Shakur's song "Ambitionz az a Ridah," from the 1996 album *All Eyez on Me*.

23   Clifford Shaw (1966) shows us this mentoring in his classic study of Stanley, a youth who meets and learns from more accomplished inmates in halfway houses and youth detention centers. Through Stanley, we see how older boys in these institutions introduce younger boys to various tricks of their trade.

24   Sampson and Laub (2003).

25   See Elijah Anderson's (1999) work on the challenges of the "decent daddy" in inner-city neighborhoods.

26   Snoop Lion, formerly known as Snoop Doggy Dogg, talks about this process in the 2012 documentary *Reincarnated*, directed by Andy Capper (Vice Films), about his transformation into Snoop Lion. Specifically, he talks about how OGs in the Eastside Rollin' 20s supported his rap dreams. He got a pass because of his clear talents as an emcee.

27   Rose (2008).

28   I return to this theme later, when I describe how young men interact with LA's entertainment industries.

29   Wacquant's (2004) "carnal sociology" provides a framework that allows sociologists to develop comparative analyses of how and under which conditions people acquire new embodied habits and practices.

Chapter 2

1   Much like gang culture, younger rappers look up to OGs and treat them with respect. In many ways, OGs embody what they hope to become one day.

2   Marcyliena Morgan (2009) describes how locals at Project Blowed emphasize a rapper's lyrical abilities and expect one another to "come correct," or to perform at a high level.

3   As an ethnographer, I am committed to representing people in close, authentic detail. As such, I quote and write about people using the word *nigga*. I do this because young men routinely addressed me and one another this way in this context. It is a term of endearment, a way for someone to signal closeness and familiarity with another person. In other situations, people used it as a synonym for other nouns like *man*, *guy*, *friend*, and *dude*, or simply as a part of everyday speech. I did not use this term in interactions with others.

4   "DJ Premier—Boom (instrumental)," YouTube video, 2:02, posted by "Wild-Style32," February 11, 2009, http://www.youtube.com/watch?v=CiQ-DNpsZ18.

5   Morgan (2009).

6   Morgan (2009, 97).

7   Collins (2004).

8   Randall Collins (2004) writes about the power of group rituals, which draw people together for bursts of time. People coming into these rituals become entrained with one another and leave the situations feeling "charged up," full of what he calls emotional energy.

9   Pierre Bourdieu (1977) developed a sociological theory of the habitus (the durable kinds of dispositions that derive from a person's social position). Others, like Matt Desmond (2007) and Loïc Wacquant (2004), use this theory to make sense of various kinds of social learning that occur in different social worlds.

10   For more on the history of Black arts and activism in Leimert Park, see Duersten (2006); Pollard-Terry (2005).

11   Marcyliena Morgan (2009, 37) writes about this. She describes how rappers would see the no-cussing rule as an added challenge that allowed skilled rappers to showcase their talents.

12   These stories figure prominently in documentaries and studies of underground hip hop culture in South Central. Ava DuVernay's 2008 documentary *This Is the Life* features interviews with key figures who helped start the Good Life's open mic workshop. Eventually, the Good Life became a cultural and tourist destination for hip hop fans, artists, and celebrities from all over the country. Signed rappers such as Ice Cube and Snoop Dogg and musicians such as Lenny Kravitz all visited the Good Life at one time or another. Even the cast of *Beverly Hills 90210* was also spotted at the Good Life during its heyday.

13   Morgan (2009, 36).

14   This was accurate as of May 16, 2015, according to the Los Angeles Police Department: "About Gang Injunctions," http://www.lapdonline.org/gang_injunctions /content_basic_view/23424.

15   Grogger (2002) notes that injunctions lead to modest reductions in violent assaults in neighborhoods, but he also questions which civil rights are compromised when routine social activities are criminalized in neighborhoods. Ultimately, gang injunctions have been a contentious policy issue in LA and other cities. While proponents suggest that injunctions lead to drops in criminal activity, opponents claim that they disrupt community life and exacerbate already-tense community relations with the police.

16   Elijah Anderson (1999) writes at length about the code of the street, an informal culture that shapes public interactions among young people living in working-class urban neighborhoods. He shows that young people become socialized into acting tough or hard on the streets for self-defense and for pragmatic reasons; the youth who comes across as weak runs the risk of being targeted by others on the streets.

17   Collins (2008) writes about the "confrontational tension" and fear that precede violence, arguing that these emotions—not hatred, animosity, or other emotions more conventionally linked to violence—are the heart of what parties feel as they inch toward a violent encounter.

18   *Cuz* is a Crip term of endearment. Crip gang members refer to one another as *cuz*, which is short for *cousin* but also a more general greeting that Crips use with one another. The Blood term of endearment is *blood*.

19   Erving Goffman (1963) wrote that people in public settings avoid entanglements by feigning what he calls civil inattention. In broad strokes, civil inattention is the process by which people tacitly agree to ignore one another in public settings. Although they are aware of each other's presence, the social order of public life is made easier if people do not attend closely to each other.

20   Elijah Anderson (1999) describes the code of the street as a local cultural adapta-
       tion in working-class Black communities to deindustrialization and institutional
       neglect. It is a culture of self-reliance and one that prizes toughness and violence.

21   Elijah Anderson (1999) writes extensively about the social pressures that young
       Black men face in navigating the streets. In addition to being on guard against
       potential threats to their safety, they have to protect themselves from potential
       threats to their reputation and status. Those who abide by the code of the street
       have to show that they have nerve, or the willingness to become violent if tested.

22   Polanyi (1958).

23   Joseph Schloss (2009) reveals similar findings in his ethnography of b-boys and
       b-girls in New York City. In this scene, young men and women gain status and
       reputation among their peers for having unique dance styles.

24   Harold Garfinkel (1967) describes the various ways people account for situations
       that defy locally held expectations. They come to rely on various stock accounts
       for such aberrations. Similarly, the way rappers explain their past failures
       deflects responsibility from their own shortcomings as performers.

25   William H. Whyte (1993) shows us that working-class Italian American men used
       bowling as an activity to reproduce social roles within their group. He noted that
       some men would purposely throw games when playing against higher-ranking
       members of the group in order to preserve the group's social order.

26   In his study of violent crime, Jack Katz (1988) describes how ritual shame and
       humiliation are often precursors of rage and anger; that is, the person who feels
       suddenly "outside" a sacred community can become enraged as a way of recap-
       turing face.

27   Max Weber (1968) famously wrote about charisma as an innate attribute of
       specially endowed individuals. In his writings on authority, Weber noted that
       charismatic leaders were given power by their constituencies because of their
       perceived personal qualities. More recently, Patricia Wasielewski (1985) has
       written about the emotional basis of charisma. Using data from speeches deliv-
       ered by Martin Luther King Jr. and Malcolm X, Wasielewski shows that charis-
       matic leaders are especially attuned to the emotions of their audiences. They also
       invoke strong emotions in others, which gives crowds the feeling of solidarity.

Chapter 3

1   Joseph Schloss (2009) writes about the problems with the term *breakdancing*,
      which within the world of b-boys and b-girls is considered a media construction.
      Instead, people in this scene prefer the term *b-boying*.

2   Otherwise known as Baldwin Village, the Jungles is a notorious South Central
      neighborhood, located at the base of the Baldwin Hills. Behind the Magic John-
      son Theatre and the Walmart on Crenshaw Boulevard, the Jungles are home to
      the Black P. Stones, Los Angeles's largest Blood set. Infamously boxed in by the
      Baldwin Hills, the neighborhood feels like there's only one way in and out (a
      theme revisited in the cop movie *Training Day*, starring Denzel Washington).

3   Open Mike told me that he and Psychosiz named their group Parts Unknown in

honor of the Ultimate Warrior—a 1990s World Wrestling Federation superstar whose listed his birthplace as "Unknown Parts."

4   As far back as Aretha Franklin, *propers* or *props* has referred to hard-earned proper respect.

5   Freestyle Fellowship has a song called "Hot Potato." In it, members jump in after each other, like in a cipher, picking up where the emcee left off, responsible for keeping the energy level up. The idea is to prevent a stall in the energy that could kill the collective fun. Freestyle Fellowship, "Hot Potato," YouTube video, 4:09, posted by "VintageHipHopSeattle," November 9, 2009, http://www.youtube.com /watch?v=rOTapJYlawU.

6   Csikszentmihalyi (2008).

7   Sudnow (1993, 28).

8   For a video of what scratching looks and sounds like, see the video of DJ Qbert in a showcase at the 1998 DMC DJ championships: "Dj-Qbert @ The Summit [1998]," YouTube video, 4:22, posted by "FabiGER," September 6, 2006, https://www.you tube.com/watch?v=cSl0xQp5xJM.

9   As Joseph Schloss (2009) shows in his study of b-boys and b-girls, hip hop is a gendered culture in which most practices are referred to in masculine terms. This is changing, though, as women continue to carve out niches within the four elements of hip hop culture: b-boying and b-girling, DJing, emceeing, and graffiti art.

10   John Singleton, dir., *Boyz n the Hood* (Culver City, CA: Columbia Pictures, 1991).

11   Lowriding enthusiasts held "car jumping" competitions in parking lots while other youth watched or socialized with each other. For years, the LA Police Department tried to crack down on the scene because of its alleged links to gang violence. The city effectively criminalized cruising in 1994, but it continued informally for many years along the commercial thoroughfare on Crenshaw Boulevard. Michael Krikorian, "A Summary of Selected City Hall Actions Last Week That Affect the Westside," *LA Times*, June 19, 1994, http://articles.latimes .com/1994-06-19/news/we-5995_1_city-limits.

12   Loïc Wacquant's (2004) study of boxing sheds light on how people learn techniques through repetition. Through repetition, a boxer learns a move, develops a sensory awareness of it, and eventually begins reacting automatically to situations with the right moves. Repetition and drilling create embodied habits. Learning how to freestyle is similar. At first, the skill is foreign and difficult. Aspiring rappers stumble, unable to imagine a time when they will be able to freestyle without hesitation, much less gracefully or with confidence. But with regular—even obsessive—practice, they begin to train their bodies and minds to freestyle. They become habituated, and the skill ceases being something apart from their minds or bodies. They learn to think in rhyme.

13   Beatboxing is another time-honored skill in hip hop. Popularized by Rahzel, a former member of the Roots, beatboxing has become a global phenomenon. Although beatboxers often replace a DJ or drum machine at events, they also compete against each other. Scribble Jam, the national rap battle, also hosted beatboxing battles at their events.

14   Howard Becker (2000) writes about similar forces in his work on jazz sessions,

where people rely on shared conventions that are part of a local "etiquette" that guides group improvisation.

15   I write about how rappers escape embarrassing moments in ciphers in a previous article (Lee 2009b).

16   For more on the ways rappers frown upon other rappers who try to pass off written rhymes as spontaneous, see Pihel (1996).

17   Goffman (1967).

18   Schloss (2009).

19   Eminem, "I Just Don't Give a Fuck," on *Slim Shady LP* (Aftermath, 1997).

20   Faulkner and Becker (2009).

Chapter 4

1   These face-offs are not organized battles in which contestants compete against other rappers in a bracket or face off in a scheduled event. Instead, the informal battles are creative ways to resolve perceived disrespect in ciphers (Lee 2009a).

2   Anderson (1999).

3   Feeling "cut off" is a more general experience. Jack Katz (1999) foregrounds this in his work on Los Angeles drivers' emotional transformations when they have been cut off in traffic.

4   I had a variety of nicknames in my fieldwork, including those mentioned in the introduction. Additionally, some guys called me "Jeeyoung" or "G-young," and others called me "Joo" or "Dru-Young."

5   The interpretive work rappers do in these moments is similar to the interpretive challenges Clifford Geertz (1973) wrote about in his classic essay on "thick description." Geertz notes the inherent challenges in differentiating a blink from a wink: an observer will have difficulty understanding what a person is doing—winking or blinking—if he or she does not immerse into the local culture and know the person doing the action.

6   For more on this, see Emanuel Schegloff's (1992) work on the structure and dynamics of conversational repair.

7   In many ways, rap battles are similar to the dozens (also known as "yo' mama"), a form of verbal one-upmanship that has a long history in urban Black communities. The dozens let young men perform, besting each other with linguistic and improvisational skills rather than fists or weapons. In her pioneering work on verbal dueling, Claudia Mitchell-Kernan (1972) explores how inner-city Black youth gain status in the dozens and demonstrates the poetic dimensions of these performances. People who can "signify" with subtle and clever insults earn the most respect. "Flat-faced" disses do just that: fall flat.

8   Others recognize the similarities between different kinds of combat. Rza, the longtime producer and rapper from Wu-Tang Clan, is part of a collective that stages events that teach youth hip hop, chess, and Brazilian jiujitsu.

9   Schloss (2009).

10   Elijah Anderson (1999) and Jack Katz (1988) both write about how young men present themselves in public interactions. In different ways, young men put on identities that show they are "hard," "street," not to be messed with, or in Katz's

terms, "beyond reason" and a "badass." These fronts can shield young people from other youth looking to start something.

11   Chopped and screwed is a slow style of hip hop popular in Houston and other Southern cities, where famous rappers and their fans have been known to drink various mixtures of cough syrup, alcohol, and other downers. The effect of these concoctions is reflected in the slow and often distorted music. See pioneering deejay and producer Paul Wall here: "Chopped and Screwed—Paul Wall—Break'em Off," YouTube video, 6:17, posted by "SuaDuaBoy," November 27, 2009. http://www.youtube.com/watch?v=T4JH5DJ4Hvk.

12   Mike Jones became known as an emerging rapper in Houston's "chopped and screwed" scene in the mid-2000s.

13   Elijah Anderson's (1999) writes about the many strategies youth use while navigating public places. Even those who do not embody "street" values still have to be aware or their surroundings and abide by the code of the street.

14   Robert Garot (2010) writes about how youth selectively claim gang membership on the streets and at school.

15   James "Nocando" McCall, "Battle Rap: I'm Just Not That into You," *LA Weekly*, August 6, 2014, http://www.laweekly.com/westcoastsound/2014/08/06/battle-rap-im-just-not-that-into-you.

16   "Cassidy: It's Hard for Battle Rappers to Make Songs," YouTube video, posted by "djvlad," November 22, 2012, https://www.youtube.com/watch?v=WqCat99xSs4.

17   For more on this, see Scott Brooks's (2009) ethnography of aspiring basketball players in Philadelphia. He writes about a similar tension between street and organized basketball. Young men with "hoop dreams" sometimes have to change their style of play and expectations to transition from playground basketball to organized leagues, collegiate play, and the NBA.

Chapter 5

1   *OG* is an honorific title borrowed from gang culture. In street gangs, younger members refer to older gang members as "OGs," which means "original gangsters," and OG are people who command respect in a gang. Rappers at Project Blowed appropriated the term and used it to refer to older, more seasoned rappers in the scene. They also used it as a sign of respect.

2   Anselm Strauss (1997) writes about the changing nature of the mentor-mentee relationship. He describes how mentees outgrow their mentors after surpassing them in an "upward departure." Not surprisingly, this causes an identity transformation for both parties. In the aftermath, mentors and mentees experience uncertainty over how they will interact with each other going forward. The mentor might wonder whether she is still a useful guide for the mentee, who has surpassed her. Likewise, the mentee might also realize that she has reached the limits of her learning under her current mentor. These same transformations unfold among children visiting their families after "leaving the nest" and in many other life course transitions. Among the rappers I studied, though, the changing relationships with OGs aren't caused by upward departure. Instead, the changes are caused by a young man's changing goals, from trying to earn respect

at Project Blowed to faint dreams of blowin' up, all the way to a sincere and even attainable effort to hit the big time outside Project Blowed.

3   "Changing the game" is a popular saying that loosely means "blowin' up," but more closely describes how individuals hope to innovate and revolutionize the organization of the music industry.

4   Anderson (2012).

5   The recent tragic deaths of Trayvon Martin and Michael Brown attest to the enduring racial stigma that young Black men experience in public (see Anderson's [1990, 1999] work on Black men being confronted by strangers who assume they are criminals and threats to public safety). In both cases, unarmed Black men were accosted in public by an armed vigilante and a police officer, respectively, who were suspicious of them. These and many other tragic cases of the profiling, apprehending, and killing of Black men are a testament to the public's generalized fear of Black men.

6   These changes mirror those by many aspiring artists who begin to see their art or music as a long-term professional career (see Lee 2009c).

7   Rose (2008).

8   Gotti, "Unsigned Hype," *The Source*, July 2003.

9   "Chingy—Rught Thurr," YouTube video, 3:45, posted by "emimusic," February 24, 2009, http://www.youtube.com/watch?v=iO476kD-k0g.

10   Grazian (2003).

11   This view is not unique to hip hop culture. Indeed, Robert Faulkner (2013) shows how aspiring orchestra musicians—particularly those in the most elite orchestras—frown on music played for Hollywood movies because it does not have the same degree of difficulty or creativity involved in production. Howard Becker (1963) examines similar themes in his study of jazz musicians. Charles Simpson (1981) studies painters in New York City's SoHo neighborhood who view commercial art as less creative than avant-garde work.

Chapter 6

1   Howard Becker (1982) writes extensively about the diverse "support personnel" whose cooperation makes artistic production possible.

2   Collins (2004).

3   Rose (2008).

4   Hay (2001).

5   Hay (2001).

6   "The dozens," "ranking," "signifying," and other linguistic games have a long history in urban Black communities across the United States. Youth use these games as ways to negotiate a local pecking order, with most creative and witty players gaining status and respect within their peer group. For more on these games, see Abrahams (2006); Labov (1972); Mitchell-Kernan (1972).

7   "NoCanDo @ The From Gs to Gents Shoot MTV," YouTube video, 1:03, posted by "NonstopLAB," November 21, 2008, http://www.youtube.com/watch?v=f_1hQQ1CTvg.

8   Becker (1982).

9   "Kanye West—Gold Digger ft. Jamie Foxx," YouTube video, 3:41, posted by
     "KanyeWestVEVO," June 16, 2009, http://www.youtube.com/watch?v=6vw
     NcNOTVzY.

10   This is similar to what can also happen in academic settings. Public conversations
     develop their own rhythm. People feel unsure about sharing their ideas if they
     aren't refined after a string of ideas that the crowd deems "good."

11   For a video of Trenseta recording with Jamie Foxx in his personal studio, see
     "Trenseta—Jamie Foxx 'The Best Night of My Life' Session 10—Let Me Get You
     on Your Toes," YouTube video, 1:26, posted by "kashley077," November 10, 2010,
     http://www.youtube.com/watch?v=k3UWEdzYPz4. For Trenseta and Jamie Foxx
     at Foxxhole Live at the Conga Room: "Trenseta and Jamie Foxx at the Foxxhole,"
     YouTube video, 2:10, posted by "Chamoru InCali," November 10, 2010, http://
     www.youtube.com/watch?v=YgdMIL5Esk8.

12   Wilson (1997).

13   Elijah Anderson (2012) writes about "cosmopolitan canopies," which are racially
     and ethnically integrated public places in cities with segregated neighborhoods
     and institutions.

Chapter 7

1   Timothy Black (2010), Philippe Bourgois (2003), Randol Contreras (2013), Sud-
     hir Venkatesh (2006), and Loïc Wacquant (1998) offer complementary looks at
     the underground economy in urban working-class communities. Each shows in
     different ways that young Black and Brown men gravitate to street hustles in the
     face of limited legitimate opportunities, given changing economic infrastruc-
     ture, mass incarceration, and other social forces that limit their life chances.

2   Kelley (1997).

3   Elliott Liebow (2003, 41–42) writes about future projections in his study of Black
     "streetcorner men": "As for the future, the young streetcorner man has a fairly
     good picture of it. . . . It is a future in which everything is uncertain except the
     ultimate destruction of his hopes and eventual realization of his fears. The most
     he can reasonably look forward to is that these things do not come too soon."

4   Katherine Newman (1999) writes about the working lives of urban working-class
     youth. Although many avoid low-wage service work, many also take up jobs
     and work hard at them. Those who end up working at these jobs, develop moral
     shields against peer judgment they face for holding a "McJob."

5   William Julius Wilson (1997) writes about the social repercussions of deindustri-
     alization. Wilson notes that unlike past generations, working-class Black youth
     since the 1990s have grown up in neighborhoods where the majority of fami-
     lies were jobless and not seeking employment in the formal economy. This had a
     significant impact on the collective temporal rhythms of entire neighborhoods
     where adults were not working routine jobs.

6   See Ashley Lutz and Kirsten Acuna, "Here Are the Ridiculous Things Celebrities
     Demand Backstage," *Business Insider*, April 14, 2012, http://www.businessinsider
     .com/here-are-15-ridiculous-celebrity-backstage-demands-2012-4. Managers
     in the music industry often make extensive demands on behalf of artists as a lit-

mus test. The logic is that if promoters or concert venues do not honor or come through on an artist's demands, they are unlikely to follow through on more important items such as lighting, security, and other aspects of a performance.

7   The experience of having to wait and conversely making demands of others' time are reflections of power. Javier Auyero (2012) writes about the political meanings of waiting for administrative services in Buenos Aires, showing how the state exerts its domination over working-class people through a bureaucratic system that makes them wait for extensive periods of time.

8   Simpson (1981).

9   Abbott (2001).

10   Sarah Thompson wrote a piece dispelling ideas about artists who are thought to be sole authors of their work, but also describing some of the pressures that make artists reach out for help. Sarah Thompson, "The Secret Ghostwriters of Hip Hop," BBC, August 6, 2014, http://www.bbc.co.uk/news/magazine-28551924.

11   Edwards (2009).

12   "Apple bottom clear version icandi styles," YouTube video, 3:26, posted by "flaw-liss," June 14, 2007, http://www.youtube.com/watch?v=bPH8O4de_cw.

13   Katherine Newman (1999) dispels popular conceptions of low-wage service-sector work, showing that young people from working-class neighborhoods experience small improvements in their economic situation through long-term employment in these jobs.

Chapter 8

1   Robert Garot (2010) provides an in-depth explanation for how young men in Los Angeles use questions like "Where you from?" or "What set you claim?" to initi-ate street violence with possible rivals as well as strangers.

2   *Dome* is street slang for "head." Here, Flawliss believed the shooters would pur-sue him, shooting him in the head to make sure he was dead.

3   James "Nocando" McCall, "Steel Sharpens Steel: Flawliss, the Last Guy I Could Freestyle With," October 14, 2014, http://www.laweekly.com/music/steel -sharpens-steel-flawliss-the-last-guy-i-could-freestyle-with-5144476.

4   Data from the Centers for Disease Control, the National Vital Statistics System (Mortality), and the U.S. Census Bureau are reported by sociologists Lauren J. Krivo and Julie A. Phillips at "Social Fact: The Homicide Divide," *The Society Pages* (blog), August 2, 2013, http://thesocietypages.org/specials/sf-homicide-divide/.

5   See the website Injury Prevention & Control: Data and Statistics (WISQARS), at http://www.cdc.gov/injury/wisqars/.

6   For more on how being shot transforms the lives of young men, see Lee (2012, 2013); Rich (2009).

7   Some of my newer work examines the everyday lives and health of wounded young men. For more about identity transformations and how health-care inse-curity drives people to risky pain management strategies, see Lee (2012, 2013).

8   "Latino Gang Members in Southern California Are Terrorizing and Killing Blacks," Southern Poverty Law Center, 2006, http://www.splcenter.org/get -informed/intelligence-report/browse-all-issues/2006/winter/la-blackout.

9   Karen Umemoto (2006) provides a detailed account of how the Venice gang war erupted and how the media shaped the ways that gang members, local residents, and outsiders viewed the war in racialized terms. In some ways, it didn't matter if both gangs were originally motivated by racial antipathy. As the story began to take on a life of its own, all parties became consumed by the larger narrative of a "race war."

10   Robert Garot (2010) writes about the interactional strategies that young people use when confronting questions about their gang and neighborhood affiliation. His analysis shows that gang membership is a fluid, interactional phenomenon. Youth selectively claim membership when it is favorable to do so but downplay affiliations when unfavorable.

11   As both Randall Collins (2008) and Jack Katz (1988) have shown, violence unfolds within specific emotional situations.

12   A spree of freeway shootings occurred in Los Angeles and other Southern Californian cities that year. In addition to speculation that a serial killer was responsible, media also claimed that the shootings were attributable to the Mexican Mafia.

13   In 2005 and 2006, Jefferson High School (located in the Crenshaw corridor of South Central) was the site of race riots between Black and Latino students. In response to overcrowding and racial tensions at Jefferson, a new charter school, Santee Education Complex, opened. Racial tensions continued at this high school, however: two race riots occurred during its first year.

14   "Latino Gang Members in Southern California Are Terrorizing and Killing Blacks," Southern Poverty Law Center, http://www.splcenter.org/get-informed /intelligence-report/browse-all-issues/2006/winter/la-blackout.

15   "Latino Gang Members Indicted in Racial Attacks," Southern Poverty Law Center, 2009, http://www.splcenter.org/get-informed/intelligence-report/browse -all-issues/2009/fall/racist-street-gangs.

16   Being "active" can mean many things on the streets and in the hip hop underground. In this context, E. Crimsin meant those busy "putting in work" or actively committing violence on the streets.

17   Elijah Anderson (1999) writes about similar things in his work on the "code of the street." According to the code, young men cannot show fear or vulnerability when challenged on the streets. Showing any hesitation can be seen as a sign that a person lacks "nerve," or the willingness to become violent if challenged. Not only is this socially stigmatizing, it can also invite future unwanted challenges and provocations.

18   John Rich (2009) writes about how such stereotypes shape the kind of care provided to young Black men who have been injured.

19   Sanyika Shakur (a.k.a. "Monster" Kody Scott) (1994) wrote about these codes in his chilling memoir about his life as an Eight Tray Gangster Crip in South Central, describing how gang members go to great lengths to target other active gang members and to avoid targeting women and children, who are sometimes caught in the crossfire.

20   Tricia Rose (2013) writes about how the recording industry creates and reproduces narrow depictions of Black masculinity in hip hop.

21   In 1994, Tupac Shakur was shot during an armed robbery in the lobby of Quad

Recording Studios in Manhattan. Tupac survived and would later tell *Vibe* magazine that he believed Sean Combs (then known as Puff Daddy, now P. Diddy) and Notorious B.I.G. had ordered the shooting as part of a West Coast–East Coast hip hop rivalry. The day after he was shot, Tupac appeared in court for his arraignment in a sexual assault case. Nearly two years later, Tupac was killed in a drive-by shooting in Las Vegas while cruising Las Vegas Boulevard with Death Row Records CEO Suge Knight (who survived and has been attacked a number of times since). Journalist Ethan Brown (2005) has extensively researched Tupac's shooting, describing the web of different involved players in his book *Queens Reigns Supreme: Fat Cat, 50 Cent, and the Rise of the Hip Hop Hustler*.

22   50 cent has spoken publicly several times about being shot. He writes in his memoir: "The shooter was on me, emptying bullets. I jumped. I felt my legs on fire and fell back down. The shooter stuck his hand deeper in the window, still bucking. I reached for the jacket in my lap. I pointed the pistol at the shooter, but the gun wasn't cocked. There was nothing in the chamber. A bullet tore into my face and my mouth exploded. Another slug blew up my hand before the driver finally pulled off" (50 Cent 2005, 187).

23   Manderson (2005) has written about how colostomy bags shape the body image and self-esteem of patients who have to negotiate their sexual lives around new limitations.

24   I examine these themes more fully in articles that describe the everyday lives, identity transformations, and health of gunshot victims in Philadelphia (Lee 2012, 2013).

25   Goffman (1967).

26   Kathy Charmaz (1991) writes about these very moments in her study of chronically ill men adjusting to their new limitations and creating new identities.

Conclusion

1   Michelle Obama, "Remarks by the First Lady at Bowie State University Commencement Ceremony," College Park, MD, May 17, 2013, https://www.white house.gov/the-press-office/2013/05/17/remarks-first-lady-bowie-state -university-commencement-ceremony.

2   Andrew Papachristos (2009) shows that the vast majority of shootings in Chicago and Boston happen among young people connected to street gangs.

3   Others, like Joseph Schloss (2009), have shown youth who find alternative ways to gain status in the world of b-boying and b-girling. Loïc Wacquant (2004) makes a similar point in his study of boxers in Chicago and the "monastic" lifestyle they adopt when training and preparing for upcoming fights, becoming attuned and socialized to the rules of the gym, and how the boxing ring replaces the streets as their main socializing institution.

4   Csikszentmihalyi (2008).

5   What's more, critics rarely get upset with the music industry that promotes and reproduces narrowly defined images of Black masculinity and femininity. Indeed, critics often go after individual artists, who themselves are just one part of a much larger industry with an active interest in marketing and selling what

Tricia Rose (2008) describes as hip hop's "tragic trinity" of gangstas, pimps, and hos to mostly White male consumers. Likewise, these critiques rarely engage with the rich and vibrant world of underground hip hop, which is itself critical of much of the same music and problematic themes in mainstream hip hop that the scholars look down upon. As Marcyliena Morgan (2009) and H. Samy Alim (2006) have shown, the underground is a rich site of cultural production that is vastly different from the stereotypical images of mainstream hip hop.

6   Robbins and Wilner (2001) write about the personal and professional challenges young people confront in their twenties, informing public ideas about the nature of early adulthood.

7   Arnett (2006) and others have written about early adulthood as a time for identity and career experimentation. According to these accounts (typically from college graduates), young people enter the labor market and spend years bouncing around to different jobs, trying to determine whether one will stick.

8   Randall Collins (2004) writes about the power of interaction rituals. In his theory of social life, he argues that people seek out interactions that leave them full of "emotional energy." I borrow from Collins to help explain the appeal of rubbing shoulders with people who appear to have an "in" in the entertainment world. These interactions are enticing on their own but also leave young men feeling charged up and ready to continue pursuing their rap dreams.

9   Victor Rios (2011) writes passionately about the problems in labeling youth "at-risk." More than just a political move, Rios shows that such labels can trap youth into stigmatized identities in the eyes of institutions. Instead, Rios argues that we should adopt an approach to seeing young men and women from disadvantaged neighborhoods as "at-promise."

10 James McCall, "Battle Rap: I'm Just Not That Into You," *LA Weekly*, August 6, 2014, http://www.laweekly.com/music/battle-rap-im-just-not-that-into-you-4989098.

11 Few have achieved the kind of extensive, longitudinal studies of Timothy Black (2010), whose work is a testament to long-term ethnography. His work follows young men across various stages in the life course.

12 Howard Becker (2014) writes eloquently about these tensions in fieldwork and research more generally. Professional obligations that force us to stop (or complete) our work raise interesting dilemmas about following the same people over time.

Methods Appendix

1   Nikki Jones and Geoff Raymond (2012) have incorporated videos into a long-term study of police interactions with Black residents of a San Francisco neighborhood. The data point to interesting questions around the potential uses of other people's videos in our data analysis.

2   Sacks, Shegloff, and Jefferson (1974) outline the social organization of turn taking in conversation. In addition to promoting conversation analysis as a scientific project, they also make a strong methodological argument for using taped conversations as primary data.

3   Charles Goodwin (1994) is a shining example of how interactionists use videos to understand how people use their bodies and the social sense making around videos more generally.

4   Robert Emerson (2001) writes about this at length in his edited volume on ethnographic methods. Emerson sympathizes with inexperienced ethnographers who enter new fieldsites and discover that there is simply too much happening simultaneously and that it is impossible to observe everything. Fieldnotes are thus representations of the social world, which are shaped by a person's biography and the theoretical constructs that inform what they observe and find interesting in the first place.

5   The anthropologist Edward Hall (1990, 17) writes about cultural variations in how people understand personal boundaries around space. Although there are social differences in the length of this space, Hall notes that there are shared understandings of "intimate space," which he calls "the distance of love-making and wrestling, comforting and protecting."

6   Randall Collins (2008) writes extensively about the interactional and emotional pathways into violence. Contrary to what most people think, Collins shows us that only a select few are good—let alone competent—at violence. Many perform as if they want to become violent because it helps them save face when challenged. Others might also bluster, without any real intention of engaging in violence.

7   Collins (2008) writes about the many challenges that people face in overcoming "confrontational tension." In different violent situations, actors have to find emotional pathways around confrontational tension, which makes most people reluctant or scared to get into violent situations.

8   Steve James, dir., *Hoop Dreams*, 1994 (Chicago: Kartemquin Films), DVD.

9   "Meek Mill Finally Battles Cassidy for the 1st Time Ever and Loses!" YouTube video, 7:39, posted by "ESMSERIES," December 23, 2012, http://www.youtube.com/watch?v=m0ZgyFLG-wE.

10   Fine (1993).

References

Abbott, Andrew. 2001. *Time Matters: On Theory and Method*. Chicago: University of Chicago Press.

Abrahams, Roger. 2006. *Deep Down in the Jungle: Black American Folklore from the Streets of Philadelphia*. Chicago: Aldine.

Alim, H. Samy. 2006. *Roc the Mic Right: The Language of Hip Hop Culture*. New York: Routledge Taylor & Francis.

Anderson, Elijah. 1990. *Streetwise: Race, Class, and Change in an Urban Community*. Chicago: University of Chicago Press.

———. 1999. *Code of the Street: Decency, Violence, and the Moral Life of the Inner City*. New York: Norton.

———. 2012. *The Cosmopolitan Canopy: Race and Civility in Everyday Life*. New York: Norton.

Arnett, Jeffery Jenson. 2006. *Emerging Adulthood: The Winding Road from Late Teens through the Twenties*. New York: Oxford University Press.

Auyero, Javier. 2012. *Patients of the State: The Politics of Waiting in Argentina*. Durham, NC: Duke University Press.

Becker, Howard. 1963. *Outsiders: Studies in the Sociology of Deviance*. New York: Free Press.

———. 1982. *Art Worlds*. Berkeley: University of California Press.

———. 2000. "The Etiquette of Improvisation." *Mind, Culture, and Activity* 7(3): 171–176.

———. 2014. *What about Mozart? What about Murder? Reasoning from Cases*. Chicago: University of Chicago Press.

Billieux, Joel, Philippe Gay, Lucien Rochat, and Martial Van der Linden. 2010. "The Role of Urgency and Its Underlying Psychological Mechanisms in Problematic Behaviours." *Behaviour Research and Therapy* 48(11): 1085–1096.

Black, Timothy. 2010. *When a Heart Turns Rock Solid: The Lives of Three Puerto Rican Brothers on and off the Streets*. New York: Vintage.

Bourdieu, Pierre. 1977. *Outline of a Theory of Practice*. Cambridge: Cambridge University Press.

Bourgois, Phillipe. 2003. *In Search of Respect: Selling Crack in El Barrio*. 1996. Cambridge: Cambridge University Press.

Brooks, Scott. 2009. *Black Men Can't Shoot*. Chicago: University of Chicago Press.

Brown, Ethan. 2005. *Queens Reigns Supreme: Fat Cat, 50 Cent, and the Rise of the Hip Hop Hustler*. New York: Anchor Books.

Chang, Jeff. 2005. *Can't Stop Won't Stop: A History of the Hip-Hop Generation*. New York: St. Martin's Press.

Charmaz, Kathy. 1991. *Good Days, Bad Days: The Self in Chronic Illness and Time*. New Brunswick, NJ: Rutgers University Press.

Cheng, Lucie, and Yen Espiritu. 1989. "Korean Businesses in Black and Hispanic Neighborhoods: A Study of Intergroup Relations." *Sociological Perspectives* 32(4): 521–534.

Collins, Randall. 2004. *Interaction Ritual Chains*. Princeton, NJ: Princeton University Press.

———. 2008. *Violence: A Microsociological Theory*. Princeton, NJ: Princeton University Press.

Contreras, Randol. 2013. *The Stickup Kids: Race, Drugs, Violence and the American Dream*. Berkeley: University of California Press.

Cosby, Bill, and Alvin Poussaint. 2007. *Come On, People: On the Path from Victims to Victors*. Nashville, TN: Thomas Nelson.

Csikszentmihalyi, Mihaly. 2008. *Flow: The Psychology of Optimal Experience*. New York: Harper Perennial.

Desmond, Matthew. 2007. *On the Fireline: Living and Dying with Wildland Firefighters*. Chicago: University of Chicago Press.

Duersten, Matthew. 2006. "Leimert Park: The Story of a Village in South-Central." *LA Weekly*, June 7. http://www.laweekly.com/film/leimert-park-the-story-of-a-village-in-south-central-2143788.

Duneier, Mitchell. 2000. *Sidewalk*. New York: Farrar, Straus & Giroux.

Edwards, Paul. 2009. *How to Rap: The Art & Science of the Hip-Hop MC*. Chicago: Chicago Review Press.

Emerson, Robert, ed. 2001. *Contemporary Field Research*. Prospect Heights, IL: Waveland Press.

Emerson, Robert, Rachel Fretz, and Linda Shaw. 1995. *Writing Ethnographic Fieldnotes*. Chicago: University of Chicago Press.

Farrell, Michael P. 2003. *Collaborative Circles: Friendship Dynamics and Creative Work*. Chicago: University of Chicago Press.

Faulkner, Robert. 2013. *Hollywood Studio Musicians: Their Work and Careers in the Recording Industry*. 1971. Chicago: Aldine.

Faulkner, Robert, and Howard Becker. 2009. *"Do You Know ... ?": The Jazz Repertoire in Action*. Chicago: University of Chicago Press.

Fernandes, Sujatha. 2011. *Close to the Edge: In Search of the Global Hip Hop Generation*. New York: Verso.

50 Cent [Curtis Jackson]. 2005. *From Pieces to Weight: Once upon a Time in Southside Queens*. New York: Simon & Schuster.

Fine, Gary Alan. 1993. "Ten Lies of Ethnography: Moral Dilemmas of Field Research." *Journal of Contemporary Ethnography* 22: 267–294.

Garfinkel, Harold. 1967. *Studies in Ethnomethodology*. Malden, MA: Blackwell.

Garot, Robert. 2010. *Who You Claim: Performing Gang Identity in School and on the Streets*. New York: New York University Press.

Geertz, Clifford. 1973. *The Interpretation of Cultures*. New York: Basic Books.

Goffman, Alice. 2014. *On the Run: Fugitive Life in an American City*. Chicago: University of Chicago Press.

Goffman, Erving. 1963. *Stigma: Notes on the Management of Spoiled Identity*. New York: Simon & Schuster.

———. 1967. *Interaction Ritual: Essays in Face to Face Behavior*. Garden City, NJ: Anchor Books.

———. 1989. "On Fieldwork." *Journal of Contemporary Ethnography* 18:123–132.

Goodwin, Charles. 1994. "Professional Vision." *American Anthropologist* 96(3): 606–633.

Grazian, David. 2003. *Blue Chicago: The Search for Authenticity in Urban Blues Clubs*. Chicago: University of Chicago Press.

Grogger, Jeffrey. 2002. "The Effects of Civil Gang Injunctions on Reported Violent Crime: Evidence from Los Angeles County." *Journal of Law and Economics* 45(1): 69–90.

Hagan, John, and Holly Foster. 2001. "Youth Violence and the End of Adolescence." *American Sociological Review* 66(6): 874–899.

Hall, Edward. 1990. *The Hidden Dimension*. New York: Anchor.

Harkness, Geoff. 2014. *Chicago Hustle and Flow: Gangs, Gangsta Rap, and Social Class*. Minneapolis: University of Minnesota Press.

Hay, Carla. 2001. "Proper Role of Music TV Debated in US." *Billboard*, February 17, 2–17.

Hughes, Everett C. 1997. "Careers" *Qualitative Sociology* 20(3): 389–397.

Jerolmack, Colin, and Shamus Khan. 2014. "Talk Is Cheap: Ethnography and the Attitudinal Fallacy." *Sociological Methods & Research* 43(2): 178–209.

Jones, Nikki, and Geoff Raymond. 2012. "'The Camera Rolls': Using Third-

Party Video in Field Research." *Annals of the American Academy of Political and Social Science* 642(1): 109–123.

Katz, Jack. 1988. *Seductions of Crime: Moral and Sensual Attractions in Doing Evil*. New York: Basic Books.

———. 1999. *How Emotions Work*. Chicago: University of Chicago Press.

Kelley, Robin. 1994. *Race Rebels: Culture, Politics, and the Black Working Class*. New York: Free Press.

———. 1997. *Yo' Mama's Disfunktional! Fighting the Culture Wars in Urban America*. Boston: Beacon Press.

Kitwana, Bakari. 2002. *The Hip-Hop Generation: Young Blacks and the Crisis in African-American Culture*. New York: Basic Books.

Labov, William. 1972. *Language in the Inner City: Studies in the Black English Vernacular*. Philadelphia: University of Pennsylvania Press.

Lee, Jooyoung. 2009a. "Battlin' on the Corner: Techniques for Sustaining Play." *Social Problems* 56(3): 578–598.

———. 2009b. "Escaping Embarrassment: Face-Work in the Cipher." *Social Psychology Quarterly* 72(4): 306–324.

———. 2009c. "Open Mic: Professionalizing the Rap Career." *Ethnography* 10(4): 475–495.

———. 2012. "Wounded: Life after the Shooting." *Annals of the American Academy of Political and Social Science* 642(1): 244–257.

———. 2013. "The Pill Hustle: Risky Pain Management for a Gunshot Victim." *Social Science & Medicine* 99:162–168.

Liebow, Elliot. 2003. *Tally's Corner: A Study of Negro Streetcorner Men*. 1967. Boston: Little, Brown.

Manderson, Lenore. 2005. "Boundary Breaches: The Body, Sex and Sexuality after Stoma Surgery." *Social Science & Medicine* 61(2): 405–415.

McWhorter, John. 2000. *Losing the Race: Self-Sabotage in Black America*. New York: Free Press.

———. 2003. "How Hip-Hop Holds Blacks Back." *City Journal*, Summer, 1–8.

Miller, Ted, and Mark Cohen. 1997. "Costs of Gunshot and Cut/Stab Wounds in the United States, with Some Canadian Comparisons." *Accident Analysis & Prevention* 29(3): 329–341.

Mitchell-Kernan, Claudia. 1972. "Signifying and Marking: Two Afro-American Speech Acts." In *Directions in Sociolinguistics: The Ethnography of Communication*, edited by John J. Gumperz and Dell Hymes, 161–169. New York: Basil Blackwell.

Morgan, Joan. 1999. *When Chickenheads Come Home to Roost: A Hip Hop Feminist Breaks it Down*. New York: Touchstone.

Morgan, Marcyliena. 2002. *Language, Discourse and Power in African American Culture*. Cambridge: Cambridge University Press.

———. 2009. *The Real Hiphop: Battling for Knowledge, Power, and Respect in the LA Underground*. Durham, NC: Duke University Press.

Newman, Katherine. 1999. *No Shame in My Game: The Working Poor in the Inner City*. New York: Russell Sage Foundation.

———. 2012. *The Accordion Family: Boomerang Kids, Anxious Parents, and the Private Toll of Global Competition*. Boston: Beacon Press.

Papachristos, Andrew. 2009. "Murder by Structure: Dominance Relations and the Social Structure of Gang Homicide." *American Journal of Sociology* 115(1): 74–128.

Pihel, Erik. 1996. "A Furified Freestyle: Homer and Hip Hop." *Oral Tradition* 11(2): 249–269.

Polanyi, Michael. 1958. *Personal Knowledge: Towards a Post-Critical Philosophy*. Chicago: University of Chicago Press.

Pollard-Terry, Gayle. 2005. "Activism, Music Intersect in Leimert Park." *Los Angeles Times*, December 25.

Rich, John. 2009. *Wrong Place, Wrong Time: Trauma and Violence in the Lives of Young Black Men*. Baltimore: John Hopkins University Press.

Rios, Victor. 2011. *Punished: Policing the Lives of Black and Latino Boys*. New York: New York University Press.

Robbins, Alexandra, and Abby Wilner. 2001. *Quarterlife Crisis: The Unique Challenges of Life in Your Twenties*. New York: Tarcher/Putnam.

Rose, Tricia. 1994. *Black Noise: Rap Music and Black Culture in Contemporary America*. Middletown, CT: Wesleyan University Press.

———. 2008. *The Hip Hop Wars: What We Talk about When We Talk about Hip Hop—and Why It Matters*. New York: Basic Books.

Rosenberg, Bruce. 1988. *Can These Bones Live? The Art of the American Folk Preacher*. 1970. Urbana: University of Illinois Press.

Sacks, Harvey, Emanuel Schegloff, and Gail Jefferson. 1974. "A Simplest Systematics for the Organization of Turn-Taking for Conversation." *Language* 50(4): 696–735.

Sampson, Robert, and John Laub. 2003. *Shared Beginnings, Divergent Lives: Delinquent Boys to Age 70*. Cambridge, MA: Harvard University Press.

Schegloff, Emanuel. 1992. "Repair after Next Turn: The Last Structurally Provided Defense of Intersubjectivity in Conversation." *American Journal of Sociology* 97(5): 1295–1345.

Scheper-Hughes, Nancy. 1992. *Death without Weeping: The Violence of Everyday Life in Brazil*. Berkeley: University of California Press.

Schloss, Joseph G. 2009. *Foundation: B-boys, B-girls and Hip-Hop Culture in New York*. New York: Oxford University Press.

Scott, James. 1992. *Domination and the Arts of Resistance: Hidden Transcripts*. New Haven, CT: Yale University Press.

Shakur, Sanyika. 1994. *Monster: The Autobiography of an L.A. Gang Member*. New York: Grove Press.

Shaw, Clifford. 1966. *The Jack-Roller: A Delinquent Boy's Own Story*. Chicago: University of Chicago Press.

Simpson, Charles R. 1981. *SoHo: The Artist in the City*. Chicago: University of Chicago Press.

Spady, James, H. Samy Alim, and Samir Meghelli. 2006. *Tha Global Cipha: Hip Hop Culture and Consciousness*. Philadelphia: Black History Museum Press.

Strauss, Anselm. 1997. *Mirrors and Masks: The Search for Identity*. Piscataway, NJ: Transaction Books.

Sudnow, David. 1993. *Ways of the Hand: The Organization of Improvised Conduct*. Cambridge, MA: MIT Press.

Tyson, Edgar. 2002. "Hip Hop Therapy: An Exploratory Study of a Rap Music Intervention with At-Risk and Delinquent Youth." *Journal of Poetry Therapy* 15(3): 131–144.

Umemoto, Karen. 2006. *The Truce: Lessons from an L.A. Gang War*. Ithaca, NY: Cornell University Press.

Venkatesh, Sudhir. 2000. *American Project: The Rise and Fall of a Modern Ghetto*. Cambridge, MA: Harvard University Press.

———. 2006. *Off the Books: The Underground Economy of the Urban Poor*. Cambridge, MA: Harvard University Press.

Wacquant, Loïc. 1998. "Inside the Zone: The Social Art of the Hustler in the Black American Ghetto." *Theory, Culture & Society* 2: 1–36.

———. 2004. *Body and Soul: Ethnographic Notebooks of an Apprentice-Boxer*. New York: Oxford University Press.

Wasielewski, Patricia. 1985. "The Emotional Basis of Charisma." *Symbolic Interaction* 8(2): 207–222.

Weber, Max. 1968. *On Charisma and Institution Building*. Chicago: University of Chicago Press.

Whyte, William. 1993. *Street Corner Society: The Social Structure of an Italian Slum*. Chicago: University of Chicago Press.

Wilson, William Julius. 1997. *When Work Disappears: The World of the New Urban Poor*. New York: Vintage.

Young, Alford A., Jr. 2004. *The Minds of Marginalized Black Men: Making Sense of Mobility, Opportunity and Future Life Chances*. Princeton, NJ: Princeton University Press.

Index